Redney

REDNEY

A Life of
Sara Jeannette Duncan

Marian Fowler

Anansi

 Toronto　　Buffalo　　London　　Sydney

Cover design: Laurel Angeloff
Author photograph: Marie-Noëlle Chatelain
Front cover illustration: Sara Jeannette Cotes, circa 1890. Courtesy Metropolitan Toronto Library Board.

This book has been published with the help of a grant from the Canadian Federation for the Humanities, using funds provided by the Social Sciences and Humanities Research Council of Canada.

Manufactured in Canada, by

House of Anansi Press Limited
35 Britain Street
Toronto, Ontario M5A 1R7

Canadian Cataloguing in Publication Data

Fowler, Marian, 1929-
    Redney : the Life of Sara Jeannette Duncan

Bibliography: p.
Includes index.
ISBN 0-88784-099-X

1. Duncan, Sara Jeannette, 1861-1922.   2. Novelists, Canadian (English) — 19th century — Biography.*   3. Journalists — Canada — Biography.   I. Title.

PS8457.U52Z7   C813'.4   C83-098667-7
PR9199.2.D86Z7

Printed and bound in Canada by John Deyell Company

For Tim and Caroline

Contents

A human being isn't an orchid, he must draw something from the soil he grows in.

—Sara Jeannette Duncan, *The Pool in the Desert*.

Acknowledgements

I am grateful to all the librarians who helped me so patiently with my research, particularly Mary Hudecki and others at the Scott Library, York University, Edith Firth and others at the Metropolitan Toronto Library, Dr Michael Halls of King's College Library, Cambridge, Florence M. Jumonville of the Historic New Orleans Collection, Margery Trenholme of the Fraser-Hickson Institute in Montreal, Judith Roberts-Moore of the Public Archives of Canada, and to the staffs of the Province of Ontario Archives, the Brantford Public Library, the India Office Library, the British Museum Reading Room and Manuscript Room, the Guildhall Library and the Public Records Office, St Catherine's House, London.

For permission to quote from archival material, I am grateful to Dalhousie University Library; Humanities Research Centre, The University of Texas at Austin; King's College Library, Cambridge University; Herrick Memorial Library, Alfred University; Public Archives of Canada; the Lilly Library, Indiana University; Harriet Irving Library, University of New Brunswick; D.B. Weldon Library, University of Western Ontario; Baldwin Room Collection, Metropolitan Toronto Library; Chatto and Windus, Publishers, and Lee and Pemberton, Solicitors.

I am grateful for help received from Professors Clara Thomas, Lorraine McMullen, Van Derck Fréchette and Leon Edel; to E. J. Zinkhan, Rae Goodwin Storey, Alreta Turner, Byron Bellows, Gwyneth Lewis, Margaret Graham, Wilma Duncan, Mr and Mrs Edward Blake Duncan, Mrs Jane Turner of Chatto and Windus, and R.W. Noble. Brantford residents who helped me include Alice Clarke of the Brant Historical Society, Margaret Dowden, Mabel Wyatt, Barbara Woffindin, Catherine Duncan, Florence Bingle and Thomas Davy, Archivist with the Brant County Board of Education. I am particularly grateful for their hospitality, courtesy and help to Mrs Everard Cotes, Mrs Alison Payne and Dr Phoebe Mary Cotes. I owe a very special thank-you to Dr John Everard Cotes who was an indefatigable researcher into Cotes family history, and to Professor Thomas Tausky who was so generous in sharing his expertise with me, in lending me material and finally in reading the manuscript. Without his excellent critical study of Sara Jeannette Duncan my task would have been much more formidable. I am also grateful to my friend, novelist Norma Harrs, who read the manuscript and offered fine insights into Redney's character. Finally, I am very grateful to James Polk for his usual brilliant editorial advice.

I am grateful to the Association for Canadian Studies for a Biography Award in the fall of 1979 which launched me on this project, to the Canada Council for an Explorations grant, and to the Ontario Arts Council. I am also grateful to the Writers' Development Trust, for part of this manuscript was written at the Writer's Retreats of 1981 and 1982 in very pleasant surroundings.

One final note: since the majority of Sara Jeannette Duncan's letters—a slim collection—have never appeared in print before, I have, for the most part, quoted them in full, even though doing so tends to interrupt the narrative flow of her life story.

1
BRANTFORD
"A Margin and a Mystery"

> Whatever the place represented to
> their parents, it was pure joy to
> the young Murchisons. It offered a
> margin and a mystery to life.
>
> Sara Jeannette Duncan,
> *The Imperialist.*

Redney walked slowly down the stairs, across the wide hall, and into the drawing-room. She stood very still, very straight, just inside the door, assessing every detail of the room which she had created. It was the spring of 1912; she had been living in India off and on for twenty-odd years, and the climate had permanently smudged the skin beneath her eyes with violet, given a light-brown cast to her fair complexion. She had passed her fiftieth birthday. Her waist had thickened slightly, her aquiline nose had thinned, but, with her grey hair brushed back becomingly from her face, she was still an attractive woman, and the tilt of her chin showed that she knew it.

Yes, the room was finished now, exactly as she had pictured it in her mind for so many months. She loved the French doors and large windows through which she could see her cheerful garden flowers. Ever since the West Street house in Brantford where she had grown up, she had needed large windows and green vistas.

For these new windows she had chosen curtains of soft green velvet to link indoors to the greenery outside. On the chairs and sofa were slipcovers of ivory linen printed in moss rose-buds. She had brought the fabric back from her last trip to England. It was impossible to find that kind of thing in India where choice was so limited. She liked the linen's regal associations: it had originally been designed, so the polite young man in Liberty's had told her, for Queen Victoria's yacht.

"Dormers" had charming rooms; it was a charming house, but the dormer windows which had suggested its name spoiled the bedrooms. Recently, when doing her day's writing stint in bed, Redney could feel the sloping ceilings above her pressing down, flattening her ideas into clichés.

She had moved into Dormers a year ago, in the spring. Spring was always her most restless time, when she itched for a new challenge, a new setting, a trip to England, a different house. There had been so many houses since she had moved from India's hot plains to the hill-town of Simla fifteen years ago: Holcombe, Red Roof, Westonbert, and now Dormers. She had bought each one for its potential. All of them had needed repairs, structural changes, re-decorating. As soon as the final papers were signed which made a house hers, she would walk through its empty rooms and feel the old excitement and energy slanting through her like strong sunlight, wiping out the house's real darkness and dampness. She would go from room to room mentally enlarging a window here, knocking down a wall there. Her ideal house would bloom suddenly in her head, a glossy full-colour spread from *Country Life*.

Then would come the sketching, the consulting with carpenters, the daily supervising of the work. She would become obsessed with making the perfect setting for herself. And this time it *would* be perfect. For the first year or so after moving in, she would be content, or as content as she ever was. Then the house's defects would get beneath her skin and give her no peace: her bedroom was impossibly cramped, the chimneys smoked . . . more and more annoying prickles would frustrate her. Her energy would drain away, boredom would spread like fungus between the floor-boards after the rains, the tick of her old restlessness would burrow and she would start her search for yet another house, yet another setting.

The spring of 1912 found her even more dissatisfied and discouraged than usual. Her novel *The Consort* had just appeared — its middle-aged, defeatist hero reflecting Redney's own mood — and had been totally ignored by the critics. It was six years now since a novel of hers had been well received. Redney plumped a pillow, right-angled an ash-tray, stopped to look at the large canvas in oils above the sofa, one of her own creations. She had painted it just after the move to Simla, a watershed time in her life. Most of the canvas showed an empty cornfield, the horizon a thin, taut line stretched between earth and heaven. She had placed a young boy in the cornfield, painted him with his legs stretched out in front, stiffly, unnaturally, as if he were paralyzed, unable to move, his eyes fixed forever on that distant blue.

She turned her back on the painting and walked out to the terrace, to soothe her inner distress with roses, as she had been doing all her life. That was partly why she had insisted on moving from hot, dusty Calcutta up to the cool, Himalayan snows of Simla. Simla was the only place in India where one could grow roses, and roses were her heart's ease. This rose-garden was in fact a copy — of necessity an inferior one — of her mother's, that archetypal pattern of rose gardens, as perfect as everything else about the Brantford home of Redney's early years. As soon as her family had moved from rented quarters on Cedar Street into the big West Street house in 1875 when Redney was twelve, her mother had set herself a goal: to have the most beautiful rose garden in Brantford. She bought only the best varieties, cajoled the gardener, and worked long hours herself. By the time Redney was graduating from high school four years later, her mother had achieved her ambition. There was a full acre of garden and orchard at West Street, all of it her mother's kingdom. Her father's drive centered on more material, less aesthetic goals; he was much too busy running his business to pay attention to the roses.

Redney bent to sniff a coral rose in her Simla facsimile. Its scent immediately took her back to those happy days in June, 1879, when, just about to graduate from high school, she had dreamed and schemed away the late afternoons in the West Street rose garden. She always sat in the gazebo where she could see all the creamy-white and yellow and crimson buds promising a full flood-time of fragrance and bloom. She would sit in the gazebo planning her future, confident of achieving her goals, knowing that both her parents, in their different ways, had successfully planted in her the seeds of their own single-minded ambition. Fame and fortune would be hers for the picking.

Sara "Redney" Duncan was seventeen in 1879: tall, freckled, clever, and sure of herself. She was still something of a tomboy. Her mother, full of energy herself, knew that girls, as well as boys, needed lots of physical activity, as Redney was later to record. Her mother realized that

> romping and fresh air were important factors in your devel-
> opment, and while you may have learned your alphabet
> under the old system, you were not compelled to sit in the
> house and sew samplers and keep your petticoats clean, your
> slippers in shape, and your hair in curl, because you were a
> little girl. You climbed apple trees and fences and tore your
> clothes and raced and rioted and had as generally good and
> uproarious a time as your brothers had. Perhaps you even
> played hockey with them—I did, with crooked sticks and
> wrinkled horse-chestnuts, in intervals of taffy-making, over a
> big kitchen floor (*Globe*, Nov. 17, 1886).

Redney was the eldest child in the Duncan family, the first-born, Annie Isabel, born April 22, 1860, having died at nine months of age, two weeks after Redney's birth. Redney had arrived on December 22, 1861, and been christened "Sarah Janet" in Brantford's Zion Presbyterian Church the following May. In that June of 1879, as she sat in the gazebo, high-school days behind her, Henry was sixteen, Charles thirteen, Grace, as sweet and placid as her name, eleven, Gordon eight, Blake six. Leslie would celebrate his fifth birthday on June 23rd; Bessie was seventeen months, Ruby six months. Redney was the ring-leader of this large clan, planning wild escapades, bossing her young brothers, besting

them at athletics. (Henry, only a year her junior, was held
back by delicate health.) Redney was also her father's
favourite. Thrilled with the novelty of fatherhood, he had
spent more time with Redney than with the others, treating
her like a son. The attachment between them, as Redney was
later to describe it, was "very strong".[1] Charles Duncan
imbued her with masculine ideals, and made her ambitious,
aggressive, even a trifle hard-edged. Redney adored her
father. For the rest of her life, she would seek out strong
father figures in her chosen field of endeavour: men who
could inspire and encourage her, who could offer her role
models.

During her growing-up years in Brantford, she was
imprinted with her father's Calvinist pattern. Charles Duncan
had a driving ambition for material success, and a consum-
mate belief in his own abilities to achieve it. By 1879, his dry
goods and furniture store was already one of the biggest in
southwestern Ontario. Three years before, he had made a
bold move, his "sense of opportunity leaping sharp and
conscious out of early years in the grey 'wynds' of a northern
Scottish town" (*The Imperialist*, p. 30). He expanded his
dry goods business to include house furnishings, and had
moved, for the third time, to larger premises on Colborne
Street. Brantford folk shook their heads and prophesied that
the huge Masonic and Lawyer's Hall would prove too large
for him, but Charles ignored them, confidently running a
large advertisement in every issue of the Brantford *Expositor*.
One such trumpets "the daily arrival of new goods" including "one case raven black lustres and Brilliantines, wonderfully cheap", and announces that the dress-making service is
in full swing. This double-duty ad is designed to net not
only customers, but "apprentices to learn cloak-making" as
well (*Expositor*, Aug. 31, 1877). Charles Duncan had a canny
business sense and a fine eye for colour and line, both of
which Redney inherited, so that his customers got good
value, and good advice on how to dress and decorate.

He had been born in Cupar, Fifeshire, Scotland, in
February, 1832. His grandfather was a magistrate, and a
portrait of Bailie Henry Duncan suggests, in his long, dour

face and cold blue eye, that the justice he stingily portioned out was hard as Highland granite. Charles at nineteen, in company with his friend William Grant, had left Scotland's grey stones and cold winds for the rich green of St John, New Brunswick, where they had stayed several years. There Charles had fallen in love with Jane Bell of Shediac, born March 7, 1837, an Ulster Irish lass of light-hearted whimsy. She was tiny, only five feet tall, with delicate, almost sharp features, cameo-chiselled. They were married, and moved to Brantford in 1855, where Charles clerked first in John Taylor's dry goods firm, then became a partner in John Montgomery's. By 1862, he was in business for himself, competing with twelve other dry goods merchants for the town's trade, and gradually besting most of them, all except Ignatius Cockshutt, who was destined to become even richer than Charles.[2]

Charles Duncan had bought the imposing brick house at 96 West Street partly as a sign of his status in the community; to look prosperous, one of God's elect, was, eventually, to be so. But he also needed a bigger house. In addition to his nine children, there seems to have been a maiden aunt who lived with the Duncan family. It may have been the "Miss Duncan" who is listed in the old Central School registers as having taught the senior class from 1875 to 1888. Redney cherished fond memories of this aunt, who, in so many small ways, continually plumped up her niece's self-esteem and provided a handy mirror for her growing ego:

> At an early age she braided my hair in two small and excruciating tails, and tied them, crossed, with shiny brown ribbons behind each of my ears . . . She was a potent interceder and the spared rod that spoiled one child owed her much of its merciful inactivity. And how she helped us over the hard places in the geography lesson and enunciated the spelling column so that the veriest dunce might stumble through it! And how grateful she was for any little attention like a bunch of pinks for her belt (*Globe*, Nov. 1, 1886).

Apart from church activities, Mr and Mrs Duncan didn't take an active part in the town's social life. She concentrated on her children and garden, he on his business and books. The children, too, as often happens in large families, formed a close, self-sufficient unit. They were united in their Calvinist respect for hard-earned cash and cooperated in various wild ventures, with Redney leading the way. Once they sold all the cherries from the family tree to pay for a month's holiday in a cottage at Port Dover, a nearby summer resort. Once, without parental permission, they sold the family's old clothes, including their mother's only pair of comfortable shoes. Later, when Ruby was in her teens, she organized a weekly dancing-class for younger girls.[3]

The children expressed their fondness for each other in nick-names. Charles was "Chuck", Gordon was "Sock" or "Gid", Blake was "Book", and Sarah Janet, the origin of her nick-name forever lost, was "Redney".[4] It was the only name that would always be hers. For the rest of her life, everyone who knew her, friends and family and casual acquaintances, called her Redney. It suited her perfectly. "Sarah Janet" conjured up a very feminine image of someone content to embroider pillow-cases and embody the old-fashioned virtues. "Redney", on the other hand, with its faint echo of "Rodney", was suitably androgynous, neither markedly male nor female, leaving room for movement beyond the usual gender stereotyping.

The final member of the Duncan family, baby Archie, would arrive, much to Redney's dismay, early on New Year's Day of 1880. She had sent out invitations for a New Year's Eve dance at West Street, but of course with the baby's arrival so imminent, it had to be cancelled. The Duncans had chosen "Archibald Dufferin" should it be a boy. The second name showed the Duncan loyalty to Britain, for Lord Dufferin had, the previous year, completed his term as Canada's Governor-General. Redney told her friends that the party was off because "Archie" was about to be born, and "Archie" he was ever after. His father, to be sure, having had eleven children to name, had absent-mindedly registered him in Toronto as "Alexander Dufferin", but the family were more precise.[5] Archie was to prove very like Redney and Blake in temperament; these three were the lively ones, the charmers, as full of high spirits as their Irish mother.

Redney resented the fact that, being the eldest girl, she was often called upon to mind her baby brother. This annoyed her, not only because it interfered with her own absorbing pursuits, but also because it constrained her within the traditional female role—one which, for the rest of her life, she would consistently reject. Twice, when asked to mind Archie, she bundled him into a dresser drawer, open just enough to let in some air. Another time, after he had learned to crawl, she set him down in the middle of the wide upstairs hall, then tacked his skirts down in a complete circle, within which he could wiggle at will, without actually going anywhere.[6] Redney, on the other hand, knew at seventeen exactly where she was going, and nothing was allowed to impede her, certainly not a brother still in skirts.

From the distance of many years and thousands of miles, Sarah "Redney" Duncan was later to portray, vividly and accurately, her family, her home and her town, in her novel *The Imperialist*. "Elgin" is in fact Brantford; the Murchisons are the Duncans, and Advena Murchison is, in essence, Redney herself. *The Imperialist* not only fills in for us the foreground of Redney's formative years, but gives us, as well, her own point of view, the precise angle of her perspective. Much of the succeeding brush-work in this chapter is, therefore, her own, in the form of direct quotations from *The Imperialist*. There are also personal reminiscences of her early years which help round out the picture sprinkled throughout her Toronto *Globe* and Montreal *Star* columns.

The Duncan children were a clever, lively clan, and the house on West Street encouraged them to spread their wings. It was a grand house, standing in the midst of shady grounds, orchard and garden behind, wide lawn in front. A circular drive, marked by two lamp standards, gas-lit day and night, led ceremoniously to the front door. There was a verandah at the front, with ornamental iron palings above.[7] The house had a fine expansiveness in its design—even the bedrooms had eleven-foot ceilings and six-foot arched windows—it rose to a majestic height, it stretched out, it rambled. The Georgian windows and verandah joined

indoors to outdoors, the smaller to the larger world beyond.
The house had been built by Dr Peter Marter, a Brantford
physician, who had sold it, sometime in the 1850's, to
Alexander Bunnell, owner of a Brantford flour mill. It was
the Duncan family, however, who really stamped it theirs.
They were drawn to the house, because its character suited,
and in turn the house shaped them, made them its own.
Parents and children formed a strong emotional bond to it.
Its dignity of demeanour suited Mr. Duncan; "its personality sustained him, very privately but none the less effectively
through the worry and expense of it for years" (*The Imperialist*, p. 30). For the children, particularly for Redney, it was
"pure joy";

> It offered a margin and a mystery to life. They saw it far
> larger than it was; they invested it, arguing purely by its
> difference from other habitations, with a romantic past . . . the
> house revealed so much that was interesting, it was apparent
> to the meanest understanding that it must hide even more. It
> was never half lighted, and there was a passage in which fear
> dwelt—wild were the gallopades from attic to cellar in the
> early nightfall, when every young Murchison tore after every
> other, possessed, like cats, by a demoniac ecstasy of the
> gloaming. And the garden, with the autumn moon coming
> over the apple trees and the neglected asparagus thick for
> ambush, . . . these were joys of the very fibre, things to push
> ideas and envisage life with an attraction that made it worth
> while to grow up (*The Imperialist*, p. 31).

For young Redney, creative, ambitious, single-minded,
it was the perfect setting. She spent her adult life searching
for just such another, subconsciously wanting those sunlit
spaces in which her confident spirit had played more freely
than it ever would again. It did indeed seem "worth while to
grow up" in West Street's commodious and comfortable rooms.
To the left of the large front hall was a library, with a pink
Italian marble fireplace. The drawing-room was on the
right. While the young Duncans were growing up, this room
remained unfurnished, so that it was a splendid free space in
which to play games, or hold dances for their friends. At
these parties, shafts of light from golden windows lit up the
dark lawn, and all the garden trees glowed with Chinese

lanterns. The dining-room of the house was where the family most often congregated. Mr and Mrs Duncan often sat there in the evening, he with his newspapers and meerschaum pipe, she with her sewing. The large windows there, as elsewhere, had louvred inside shutters which could be closed, but which seldom were, so that summer's green shade or winter's naked radiance shone in. There was a fireplace in the dining-room, as in all the main rooms, and a very large sideboard, with a dumb waiter beside it to bring up cool bottles from the wine cellar. At mealtimes, Charles and Jane Duncan sat at opposite ends of the long, mahogany table. When chicken was served, she carved, neatly and efficiently. When there was a roast of beef, Charles carved, looking dignified and well-groomed—he was always that—in a black alpaca coat.[8] He was a reserved man, with none of his wife's easy ebullience, but with a quiet, self-conscious dignity. His "intelligent head appeared with the isolated significance of a strong individuality". "People looked twice" at him "in a crowd; so did his own children at home" (*The Imperialist*, p. 21). If his children were awed, their young friends who came to the house were positively fearful of this tall, tight-lipped man, with some of the flinty edges of Bailie Henry Duncan, whose portrait sternly dominated one end of the dining-room. Charles Duncan was a stickler for manners, and never allowed any of his children to leave the dinner table until the meal was, by his decree, over. Social forms were important in the general scheme of things, "not necessary to your existence", perhaps, as Redney was later to realize, "but necessary to the gratification of the esthetic sense in the broad meaning of the term—the sense of the beauty of propriety and consistency and deference" (*Globe*, March 18, 1887). In later life, Redney would take on much of her father's autocratic manner, and his rigid attitude to social conventions.

Redney's mother, too, stressed social forms, particularly those which etched the fine lines of class distinctions. The prosperous merchants and factory-owners of Brantford formed its aristocracy just as surely as British peers did England's, and Jane Duncan saw to it that her children never played with lower-class ones, nor were they allowed to play in the streets, though they longed to, on those "big, light, empty spring evenings after tea" (*Cousin Cinderella*, p. 2). Mrs Duncan's strictness, however, was only surface, for underneath bubbled an irrepressible energy and verve. She had the "most spirit of them all" and "on her husband's arm, stepped along with the spring of an impetus undisclosed" (*The Imperialist*, p. 202). She also had an Irish sense of humour, a wayward wit which Redney inherited and which, later, along with a tinge of her mother's Celtic romantic wistfulness would give a special texture to Redney's writing.

If Bailie Henry and Charles Duncan rather stiffened the dining-room with sobriety, the large kitchen, looking out on the rose garden, Jane Duncan's preserve, was all sunshine. There Mrs. Duncan's tiny figure bustled back and forth, glancing with annoyance at a set of useless bells on the wall, one for each room; none of them worked, yet they silently taunted, presumed the existence of many servants, when all she had was one slow-footed country girl. Redney was a complete dunce when it came to domestic matters. Whereas Grace was well on her way to neatness and efficiency, Redney couldn't even make her own bed properly. She simply wasn't interested, and her mother was always sighing to anyone who would listen that her eldest daughter would never be fit to manage her own home, "for ever and for ever, no matter what there was to do, with a book in her hand . . . . And if, at the end of your patience, you told her for any sake to put it down and attend to matters, obeying in a kind of dream that generally drove you to take the thing out of her hands and do it yourself, rather than jump out of your skin watching her" (*The Imperialist*, p. 32).

Domesticity was not for Redney. She wanted a career and had made up her mind what it was to be: she would become a writer. She had decided this at an early age:

> I remember once entertaining, and unguardedly expressing, at the age of nine, a wild desire to write a novel. "Put it out of your mind, my dear", nodded a placid old lady of the last century, over her knitting. "Novel-making women always come to some bad end" (*Globe*, Nov. 12, 1886).

Redney, however, didn't put it out of her mind, not for a moment. During those growing-up years while her mother despaired of her domestic skills and her sisters were perfectly content to devote their artistic energies to embroidered sachets and hand-painted tambourines, Redney nursed the secret of her strong ambition. She recalls that "she lived largely in a corner attic of her father's home in the society of three spiders, two mice, the family medicine chest, her grandfather's hat-box and a Secret Purpose".[9] She was determined to "distinguish herself in literature." If the females in the family looked askance at this, her father "wisely encouraged her wish to be independent, and to make herself a career in a line which proved more and more congenial".[10] Certainly her single-minded dedication to success leapt as "sharp and conscious" as his own. Redney told herself

> with a great show of candor, that she knew she was not a genius, but she had privately picked out two or three names of modest fame in the lighter arts of the pen, whose achievements she thought she might reasonably hope to parallel in the course of time . . . . At school her essays had a clever facility which interested her teachers . . . . Besides which, she absorbed the spirit of every artistic thing she read so thoroughly that for the moment she was almost ready to exhale something very like it with all the pride of conscious originality.[11]

She wrote poems, most of them "lugubrious", as well as essays on the seasons and stories which "chiefly concerned young women who wore straight skirts and girdles, and masses of dark hair, and were in doubt as to the true meaning of existence". Redney hopefully sent these efforts off to various publications, "accompanied by a stamp", only to have them rejected, every one. They "usually came back to her with a polite little printed form which read 'The editor regrets', etc. Sometimes the editor did not even regret, he embezzled the stamp, and took no notice". Redney, nonetheless, kept on writing, nourishing her Secret Purpose "upon the historic rejections of 'Sketches by Boz', and a large number of 'snow' apples daily — snow-white inside, rosy outside".[12]

During those adolescent years, "the margin and the mystery" called to Redney through West Street's windows.

She once wrote in her commonplace book, "the doors of Cranford opened on the street; the windows opened on infinity".[13] So it was with the West Street windows. Snug in her attic or bedroom in winter, away from the chatter and bustle of the family, what Redney saw through those windows, in fancy or in fact, kept her pen racing. As soon as the snow had gone, in March, her creativity pushed up like peony-shoots: "Their red-green beginning" sprouting beneath the windows "before a sign had come upon the apple-trees, before anything else stirred or spoke at all . . . the first happy vibration of the spring!" (*On the Other Side of the Latch*, pp. 46-47). In summer she could look down the hazy vista of the tree-lined street and lose herself in the mystery of blue hills. There was "a plank side-walk that half-heartedly wandered" out towards the woods, with a small grocery store half-way along where one could buy hickory nuts. "You got the meat out with infinite difficulty and a pin, and if it was obstinate you sucked it" (*On the Other Side of the Latch*, pp. 138-9). "The bronze and purple of the untrimmed woods", wrote Redney later in her life, "had always been for me the margin of the thought of home" (*On the Other Side of the Latch*, p. 153). Beyond the margin a whole world waited, and she would astound it with words both wonderful and witty. Within the margin, her young imagination roamed happily, in a Words-worthian seed-time for the creative soul, drawing sustenance from house, garden, woods. It was, as she later came to realize, the richest soil she would ever know.

There was another margin to Redney's world, this one internal: the line which memory draws across the mind, so that there is a "funny cloud that hangs like a drop-scene of life just in front of the time when you couldn't read" (*Cousin Cinderella*, p. 2). Near the margin cluster her earliest memories, later recorded in print—revealing ones, for two of them show the first twinges of Calvinist guilt. She remembers "the scratched paint on the back of a Presbyterian pew in Canada, and my own small boot", and feels "the emotions of a culprit" (*A Social Departure*, p. 372). She also recalls "days of juvenile pilferings" from the large round tin full of spices in the store-room, "and the awful results of being found out" (*A Social Departure*, p. 235). She remembers her seventh Christmas, hanging up her stocking on the chimney-piece, envying her brother "whose legs were that much longer", with hopes

> that Santa Claus would observe the palpable injustice and govern himself accordingly! And you fall to wondering whether any of the toys of later years have given you half the unalloyed bliss that Noah and his featureless wife did, and all his shaky legged quadrupeds, with their fascinating odor of paint and glue. I wonder what sum most of us would account too dear for a single hour of the simple enchantment of, say, one's seventh Christmas (*Montreal Star*, Dec. 24, 1887).

It seems fitting that for Redney the drop-scene of memory hung "just in front of the time when you couldn't read", for reading shaped her imagination. She had begun her adventures in the world of books just as Canada began its own saga as a nation. In 1867, Sarah Janet Duncan, a wiry little girl with tight pigtails, had been enrolled at Central School, built ten years before, the largest of Brantford's four public schools. Her father had that year been named chairman of the Public School board, a canny move towards closer control of his favourite daughter's education.[14] It was Charles Duncan who fuelled Redney's passion for reading, once she had learned her alphabet. He bought books "between long periods of abstinence, during which he would scout the expenditure of an unnecessary dollar, coming home with a parcel under his arm, for which he vouchsafed no explanation, and which would disclose itself to be Lockhart, or Sterne, or Borrow, or Defoe" (*The Imperialist*, p. 30).

Charles Duncan subscribed to a Toronto paper, probably the *Globe*, since he was a staunch Liberal, to *Blackwood's* and to the *Cornhill Magazine*. There were years of back numbers packed away in the attic, where Redney, in those growing-up years, stretched out to read them, along with *Good Words for the Young*, and the romantic novels of Mary Cecil Hay and Mary Jane Holmes, "whom every girl I ever knew adored with all her heart between fourteen and seventeen" (*Globe*, Nov. 10, 1886). When she ran short of books at home there were other fields to forage in. In 1853, Brantford had installed a library in the Mechanic's Institute and when that building was destroyed by fire in 1879 the books were moved to the second floor of an office block.[15] Redney read the classics, trash, anything, trying to absorb the secrets of how to marshal words on a page.

Redney's years at Central School were unmarked by any academic distinction. She was too preoccupied with her Secret Purpose to pay attention to any but her literature classes. She was particularly bad at mathematics, and had trouble with compound fractions. When the annual public school closing came, usually in the second week in July, an important social event in Brantford, Redney knew that her father was disappointed never to hear her name on the merit roll. She could see his fine head among the other fathers, none as handsome, at the back of the class-room, decorated for the great day with evergreen swags and inspiring verses. Sometimes she was chosen for a song or recitation, but when prizes were handed out to the deserving, she never got to walk proudly to the front, nor did her name ever appear in the long lists of prize-winners which duly appeared every July in the Brantford *Expositor*. Some of her siblings fared better. Her brother Charles, so delicate that he didn't enter Central School until he was eight, earned a second prize in General Efficiency, a $20 scholarship for the highest standing in the senior class, not to mention a prize for punctuality. Grace stood highest in the junior class in 1875, second highest in 1876, and highest again in 1877.

Redney was too caught up in her own special ambitions to be Generally Efficient or Perpetually Punctual. She did, however, pass the entrance examination to the Collegiate Institute, a two-day grilling which only half the aspirants to higher education succeeded in passing. The Collegiate was a dignified building on George Street, with about two hundred students, and seven teachers.[16] Redney studied languages and Latin, avoided mathematics and learned enough science to ruin three aprons, nearly deprive herself of her right thumb, and "burst twenty-seven glass tubes in learning how to make a certain acid with a most inexpressible smell" (*Globe*, Nov. 17, 1886). There is an apocryphal story suggesting that Sarah Duncan was once threatened with expulsion for "saucing" a teacher.[17] It may have been at this juncture that her parents enrolled her instead at the Brantford Ladies College, where, it is known, she received some of her secondary education. Perhaps her mother hoped a little feminine meekness would rub off on Redney, who was growing into a rambunctious and rather alarming rebel.

The Brantford Ladies College, for which Lady Dufferin had laid the cornerstone in August of 1874, was linked to the Presbyterian Church as a means of ensuring the correct moral training of its pupils.[18] There were about eighty young ladies attending, boarders and day-pupils, learning to keep their reputations and petticoats unspotted, their backs and moral principles rigidly unbending. The general tone of the school shows clearly in the two prize-winning essays read by pupils at the closing exercises of 1876. One was entitled "Knowledge" and the other "Progress and Perseverance". Redney herself won a composition prize of ten dollars, which she promptly spent, rebellious as ever, on the questionable fare of dime novels[19] which her pastor, Rev William Cochrane, the school's president, had referred to as

> the greatest social evils of our age [which] have their origin in the immaterial and morbid excitement of the imagination, caused by fictitious representatives of human nature. The appetite grows as it is fed by sensational novels, until body and mind are weakened, and the reason totters on the brink of a hopeless insanity" (*Expositor*, June 24, 1878).

It was from the Collegiate Institute, however, not the Ladies College, that Redney graduated in June of 1879. With the hindsight of adulthood, she saw her school régime as full of faults, but also as having "the single virtue of room for individual growth along the lines laid down by nature, who is less autocratic than most school boards" (*Globe*, Dec. 20, 1886). "The Collegiate Institute", she was to write, "was a potential melting-pot; you went in as your simple opportunities had made you; how you shaped coming out depended upon what was hidden in the core of you" (*The Imperialist*, p. 76). What was hidden in Redney's core, her drive to become a writer, set her apart from her more mundane school chums, and from the town in general.

In those growing-up years, the rest of Brantford lay slightly beyond the margin. There was a thin, invisible line separating the Duncans, and most particularly Sarah Duncan, from the rest of the small provincial city. It is significant that when she came to write *The Imperialist*, she situated the Murchison home on the very edge of town, which is where her own home stood, psychologically, though not in fact. Her family were, for her, separate and superior:

> They were too good for their environment.... It was a matter of quality, of spiritual and mental fabric; they were hardly aware that they had it, but it marked them with a difference, and a difference is the one thing a small community, accustomed comfortably to scan its own intelligible average, will not tolerate (*The Imperialist*, p. 44).

In the very early years at Central School, Redney had not yet accepted this difference, this distance which grew partly from communal opinion, partly from her own temperament, and very much from the continuing interaction of the two. In the beginning, she had wanted desperately to be exactly like all the other little girls:

> Well do I remember my juvenile wretchedness at being sent to school, out of a perverse parental admiration for rotund little girls, with my skirts distended over hoops of large and unmanageable circumference, when everybody else's little girls wore garments that clung to their ankles. How I envied their drooping state! How I—dare I at this unconceivably remote period confess it!—used carefully to hang the wire abominations up with my hat and lunch-basket, and vie with the limpest of them in the long and classic lines of my dress and pinafore! Children are cruel little animals, and the woes they inflict upon each other are past the comprehension of a grown person (*Globe*, Oct. 23, 1886).

By the time Redney reached her teens, however, she had come to terms with her uniqueness, and the town's disapprobation. What she says of Advena Murchison applies just as well to Redney herself as she stands elsewhere revealed to us:

Advena, bookish and unconventional, was regarded with dubiety. She was out of the type; she had queer satisfactions and enthusiasms.... The inevitable hour arrived when she should be instructed on the piano, and the second time the music teacher came her pupil was discovered on the roof of the house, with the ladder drawn up after her.... She would hide in the hayloft with a novel; she would be off by herself in a canoe at six o'clock in the morning; she would go for walks in the rain of windy October twilights and be met kicking the wet leaves along in front of her "in a dream".... She had taken a definite line, and she pursued it, preoccupied (*The Imperialist*, p.45).

Redney had indeed taken a definite line, and she pursued it, moving surely towards her goals, but the town, in addition to her parents, determined her direction. In fact, Brantford was the macrocosm of Mr and Mrs Duncan's micro-influence. In its allegiances, Brantford was half American, half British, just as, in Redney's own family, her father emulated American ideals of material progress and hard work, her mother upheld British cultural ones of custom and civility. If Charles Duncan's dry goods store was American in its clanging cash registers, Jane Duncan's garden was British in its well-weeded paths and well-wrought urns.

The perfect symbol of Brantford's twin allegiance was the Lorne Bridge, built in 1879 just as Redney graduated from high school, to replace one that had washed away the previous September when the Grand River, as was its wont, flooded its banks after heavy rains. The Lorne Bridge, loyally named for the Queen's representative in Canada, the Marquis of Lorne, had abutments of cut grey limestone from the quarries of Queenston, scene of that former brave show of British strength, but the iron work on the Lorne Bridge, its superstructure, came, fittingly enough, from the Phoenix Works in Philadelphia.[20]

Like those of the Lorne Bridge, Brantford's underpinnings, particularly the cultural and social ones, were British. British to the core, for instance, was the town's love of custom and ceremony. When in July, 1866, the 7th Royal Fusiliers, resplendent in scarlet and gold, had marched into town to protect it from those nasty Irish-American ruffians, the Fenians, they had been led by a fine band playing "Rule Britannia", and the townspeople had cheered and cheered. Young Sarah Duncan must have admired the correct cut of the officers' scarlet coats, the splendid sweep of their mustaches. The Fusiliers stayed for eight months, very much in evidence, forming and reforming with a fine clatter of bayonets, in the Market Square. Their bugle band played a tattoo there each evening, and there were Wednesday concerts as well, in Victoria Park, attended by all the young ladies.[21]

On July 1, 1867, Brantfordites had celebrated Confederation "in a right royal manner. The weather was all that could have been desired, and the day was ushered in by the ringing of bells and the discharge of firearms of all descriptions.... Rule Britannia sung by a chorus of over one thousand voices" (*Expositor*, July 5, 1867). Whenever British royalty or its Canadian representative, the Governor-General, honoured Brantford with a visit, the town showed its love of formal ritual, its patriotic fervour. There were always bands, bunting, banquets at the Kerby House, the town's most sumptuous hotel, banks of cheering school-children, beautiful arches, and flag-draped porches and stores. Prince Arthur, the Duke of Connaught, had come on October 1st, 1869. He went duck-shooting at Long Point, and was escorted into town by the usual proud parade: the Burford Cavalry, the 38th Brantford Battalion, the Six Nations Indian Chiefs, the Fire Brigade, its Hook and Ladder cart gorgeously decorated. Lord and Lady Dufferin had come in August, 1874, he to consent to the 38th Battalion thereafter being known as the Dufferin Rifles, she to lay the cornerstone for the Ladies College. When the Marquis of Lorne and Princess Louise came through in 1879, massed tiers of school-children in Victoria Park sang a special welcome song, printed on satin, in blue and gold, which two little girls then presented to Her Excellency.[22] Redney was an interested spectator of this deference to all things British. From Britain came a sense of form, and of history. In

Redney's restless, life-long search for the ideal setting, Britain beckoned with its stability and traditions.

There was one exotic note in Brantford's British pomp and circumstance, and it too, for Redney, pre-figured future ties. Brantford still had its Indians. It had, in fact, been founded by one: Joseph Brant (1742-1807), that fine, cultured Mohawk who, in 1784, as reward for tribal loyalty during the American revolution, persuaded the Governor of Quebec to give his people 675,000 acres of lush green valley on either side of the Grand River, at the place where they forded. In 1830, the Indians had surrendered the town site to the Crown, and retreated to a Reserve. The town, however, still needed the Six Nations Chiefs, in full war costume of beaded buckskin and feathers, to march in parades and amuse the British royals. In between, the squaws used to come sometimes to the back door of 96 West Street, in three or four coloured petticoats, papooses on their backs, to sell their tin pails of wild raspberries for a pitifully modest sum. Already, in Brantford, as there would be later in Sarah Duncan's life, there were the Rulers, the sub-Rulers, and the Ruled: the British, the colonials, and the Indian natives.

In its social manners and mores, Brantford was also British. In this its first families, the factory owners and leading merchants, set the tone. As they built their brick mansions on the wide tree-lined streets, they were, in their concern for British class distinctions and customs, cementing a way of life that would endure as long as their houses. In 1878, the wealthy élite of Brant Avenue took pains to ensure that the poor could no longer pasture their cows among the immemorial elms and stately homes. They hired "a person to watch the cows and impound them if found on the street" (*Expositor*, May 17, 1878). Free enterprise had its limits.

The Duncans were quite as British as the rest, with their English magazines, their ritual of afternoon tea, when a brass kettle sang above its blue flame and the tea was served in quaint little harlequin cups. By the 1880's, Charles Duncan was making regular buying trips to England for his store, importing fine antique furniture, Chippendale and Sheraton and Hepplewhite, and fine Georgian silver to grace the Brant Avenue mansions of his wealthy customers. Redney must have realized, long before she made her own pilgrimage there, that the patina and polish of life, its aesthetic of social graces, what she calls "the beauty of propriety", emanated from Britain.

One of Charles Duncan's friends who reinforced British ideals in Redney's mind was George Brown, who spent summers with his family at Bow Park, an 800-acre country estate and cattle farm. Bow Park's green paddocks and parading peacocks perfectly imitated the British gentry's leisurely life-style. George Brown was a Scot who came to Canada from New York in 1843. The following year he founded the Toronto *Globe* and eventually rose to leadership of the Reform party. On summer Sundays, the silvery-whiskered Brown, then in his sixties, sat like a dignified laird, surrounded by his farm hands, in his pew at Brantford's Zion Church. At Bow Park, there were delightful groves for Redney to wander through, wildflowers and berries to collect, ponies and horses to ride. Brown's daughters, Margaret and Edith, a few years younger than Redney, were clever, ambitious girls who later would be among the first women graduates from the University of Toronto. While the girls linked arms to stroll about and admire the patrician peacocks on the lawn, Brown himself was likely to be piling up stones in a field, his favourite pastime. On the night of December 2nd, 1879, Redney may have seen the southern sky turn a frightening orange as Bow Park went up in flames, suspected to be the work of a mad arsonist. By the following May, George Brown himself was dead, shot in the leg as he sat at his desk in the *Globe* office by a mad employee, recently dismissed. The funeral was held on May 12th, 1880, and Charles Duncan went up to Toronto to attend it (*Expositor*, May 13, 1880).[23]

Not all the Brantford townsfolk, however, were British emigrants. There were, as well, the United Empire Loyalists from south of the border who had hurried north towards the British flag and offers of free land. If the cultural allegiances, of Brantford were British, the commercial ones were American. Men like C.H. Waterous, owner of the largest factory, the Waterous Engine Works, who had come from Vermont in 1848, brought Yankee bustle and know-how with them,

taking full advantage of "the liberal and stimulating opportunities of a new country" (*On the Other Side of the Latch*, p.
139), a country "where everything was accomplished quickly,
even summer" (*The Imperialist*, p. 108).

Brantford's commercial boom had begun in 1840, when
the Grand River Navigation Canal was completed, giving
Brantford cheap water transport, and accessibility to world
markets. In January, 1854, as symbol of Brantford's commercial ties to the United States, the Buffalo and Brantford
Railroad had been opened, with the two Mayors linking
arms and promising close cooperation and continued good-
will. The railroad brought cheap pig-iron and skilled
working-class emigrants from the United States for Brantford's growing industries. Brantford had achieved city status
two years before Redney finished high school, in 1877, with a
population of 10,000. By then Canada's economic depres-
sion, triggered in 1873 by an American one, was over, and an
era of golden prosperity and progress was just beginning, as
Brantford's factories hummed, turning out stoves, steam
engines, tinware, carriages, farm machinery, pottery.

"We often say that we fear no invasion from the south",
says Lorne Murchison in an impassioned political speech in
The Imperialist, "but the armies of the south have already
crossed the border. American enterprise, American capital,
is taking rapid possession of our mines and our water power,
our oil areas and our timber limits" (p. 232). Already in the
Brantford of Sarah Duncan's formative years, this Ameri-
canization of Canada was well under way.

Not far from the British formality of George Brown's
Bow Park estate lived another Scots family friendly with the
Duncans who gave Redney a different image. Their name
was Bell, and they had come in 1870 to a large Regency
frame house, with porch and French doors, overlooking the
Grand River. The twenty-four-year-old Alexander Graham,
suffering that first summer from ill health, used to lie in his
hammock, coiling *his* ambitious dreams from church spire to
roof-top of the blue-tinged town. Redney must have felt the
excitement, when, on July 26th of 1874, young Aleck put a
receiver near the river bank, looped the equivalent of five

miles of wire between river and house, and asked a church soloist to sing into a transmitter whose wires ran to a grape arbour near the house. She sang "I need Thee every hour", and the telephone clicked into being. Redney also must have observed how Alexander Graham headed south to the land of real enterprise and vision, once he had failed to get backing for his new invention from cautious Canadians. Consequently, as he himself once pointed out to a Brantford audience, while the telephone was conceived in Brantford, in 1874, it was born in Boston, in 1875.[24] Redney, fourteen at the time, carefully noted that matters of communication fared better if they had a Yankee twang.

The hub of Brantford's American-inspired commercial bustle was to be found in Market Square, near the City Hall steps. There, all day long, while farmers shopped in the hardware and feed stores, and their wives sat in the midst of poultry, fruit and vegetables, "skirts tucked close, vigilant in rusty bonnets" (*The Imperialist*, p. 73), the female half of Brantford's commercial élite poked and prodded and pondered which items were small enough to be carried home without losing caste, and which ones had best be delivered to their doors. Redney's mother, basket on arm, made her poised and absorbed progress round the market every Saturday morning.

Growing up in this American-British environment, Redney herself was drawn both to the American Dream of material prosperity and individual initiative and the British one of social and cultural fulfillment—drawn mentally first, then physically, living for extended periods in both countries. If the United States beckoned with freedom and fortune, offering both new directions and material comforts to an aspiring writer, Britain beckoned with social eminence and literary fame: membership in the best clubs, and a modest niche somewhere just beyond the Greats who slept in the Poet's Corner of Westminster Abbey. Redney wanted desperately, and was prepared to work towards, both fortune and fame, towards those American and British ideals upheld by her father and mother, and by Brantford as a whole.

In their day-to-day existence, the townsfolk of Brantford, as Redney was later to realize in *The Imperialist*, had two abiding interests: politics and religion provided all the drama and delight of daily life, and both would help to mould her. The all-pervasive atmosphere of politics, for politics of town, province and Dominion formed the main conversational staple of Brantford, and of the Duncan dinner-table, would later influence Redney's choice of subject-matter in her writing, particularly in her novels. One's political party, like one's nose, was inherited, and accompanied one to the grave. Redney's father was a passionate Liberal, more usually, at the time, called a Reformer or Clear Grit. Her brother, Charles, the model for Lorne Murchison in *The Imperialist*, was later to be active in forming a Young Liberal's Club.[25]

While still a child, Redney caught the habit of mind which would remain with her for the rest of her life: whenever boredom threatened, political fire-works could provide an exciting and absorbing diversion. She may have accompanied her doting father to political meetings which, in Brantford, were always fine dramatic productions. (Brantford didn't have an Opera House, for more orthodox ones, until 1881.) Oratory was a fine art. Politicians who won at the polls knew how to buy votes, but they also knew how to sway and hold an audience, how to squelch hecklers and squeeze out a laugh at the same time. Sheer volume counted; particularly fine were Brantford's Edmund Burke Wood, affectionately known as "Big Thunder", Billy Paterson, "Great Thunder", both fiery Reformers in the federal House, and Arthur Sturgis Hardy, called "Little Thunder" to denote his less exalted position at the provincial level. At the municipal level there was Squire Matthews, Brantford's Mayor from 1869 to 1874, a hot-headed Irishman, always in the thick of the fray at polling booth riots, who, when Council debates grew heated, used to march up and down the table, skirting ink-pots and papers, removing, as the air grew charged, necktie, collar, coat and vest.[26]

Religion, Brantford's other preoccupation, strengthened Redney's moral fibre and, particularly in sexual matters, made her as an adult opt for self-control and self-denial. In religious affiliation, the Duncans were Presbyterians, with that sober, earnest self-discipline which Scots Calvinism

implies. They were staunch members of Zion Presbyterian
Church, where Charles Duncan took an active role and was
for many years chairman of the musical committee, once the
church had progressed from tuning-fork and precentor to
choir and paid organist. Zion Church had been built in 1859,
and the Duncans regularly attended the morning service at
11 o'clock. Their pew was on the right-hand side near the
front, where Charles and Jane sat, heads proudly poised, the
children's in a gradient slope beside them. "The habit of
church attendance was not only a basis of respectability" in
Brantford, "but practically the only one: a person who was
'never known to put his head inside a church door' could not
be more severely reprobated" (*The Imperialist*, p. 60). Zion's
Sunday School was held at 2:30, and Redney's familiarity
with Scripture suggests regular attendance. One's Sunday
schooling was quite as important as the week-day kind;
perhaps even more so, for while the public school library
contained 660 volumes, the combined Sunday School libraries
—there were nineteen in all—contained 6800 books, to sway
the impressionable minds of 3,000 young persons, 800 more
than attended public school (*Expositor*, July 5, 1876).

For the Duncans, as for other families, the Church
provided the main hub for social activities. There were
prayer meetings at Zion on Thursday evenings at 7:30, with
time for gossip afterwards. There were strawberry socials,
held in the church basement, with "literary and musical
entertainment select but brief in order to afford ample time
for social conversation. Admission entitling to one plate of
strawberries and cream, 20 cents, extra dish, 10 cents"
(*Expositor*, July 7, 1875). For the children, there were the
annual Sunday School picnics, which Redney vividly recalls:

> Our earliest recollections are of picnics—torn trowsers and
> soiled embroideries, and 'scrambles' for oranges and unlimited
> raspberry tarts, and the muscular Sunday-school teacher,
> who sent us rocking out into the blue on the big swing, and
> the young lady Sunday-school teacher with the daisies in her
> bonnet, who superintended the making of the lemonade
> under the greatest of the great oak trees (*Montreal Star*, May
> 19, 1888).

Redney liked the sensation of a strong male pushing her "out into the blue" where anything was possible, and felt slight scorn for the gentle lady in the shade who looked after domestic matters. The 1878 Zion picnic had been an excursion to Colonel Perley's Grove in Burford, the young people, sun-bonnets and baskets in hand, having assembled at 10 o'clock at the train station, to take the Great Western Railway (*Expositor*, July 10, 1878). The 1879 picnic, held on July 18th, was more pedestrian in scope: it took place at 4 o'clock on the fair grounds of "West Brantford" with "the scholars going direct to the grounds" (*Expositor*, July 17, 1879).

Zion's pastor, the Rev William Cochrane, was a thirty-one-year old Scot who had come to Brantford from New Jersey in May of 1862, just about the time of Sarah Janet Duncan's christening. After one year in Brantford, he had increased the membership (from 150 to 260) and decreased the church debt. If his zeal had a more saintly cast, he was quite as ambitious and hard-working a Scot as Charles Duncan, and an important enough influence on Redney for her to draw his full-length portrait with a shrewd but affectionate eye in *The Imperialist* in the person of Dr Drummond.[27] Dr Cochrane was a small man, never still, his heels rocking as he talked, his hand busy with the seals of his watch chain, his shrewd grey eyes missing nothing, his laugh hearty and frequent. As minister, he had a special elevated status in the community, where "a particular importance attached to everything he said and did", his life being "sustained on quite another principle than that of supply and demand" (*The Imperialist*, p. 61). The Brantford *Expositor* regularly reported the full text of his long, literate sermons. Among his favourite parishioners was Charles Duncan. They were alike not only in their Scots thrift and high moral tone, but also in their love of books, for in his pillared house on Charlotte Street, Dr Cochrane had a fine library. They were both emotionally reticent, so that "personal sentiments between these two Scotchmen were indicated rather than indulged" (*The Imperialist*, p. 26). Dr Cochrane's diary records many visits to the Duncan home. He regularly, of course, visited every parishioner, every sick-bed. When typhoid struck Brantford in the fall of 1870, he kept on visiting the sick: "If the Lord intends me to catch such a disease . . . when in the discharge of duty, his will be done", he wrote piously in his diary. His young wife Mary died in January, 1871, leaving him with two small children, and when he married the Oakville Postmaster's daughter two years later, Mrs Duncan and the other female parishioners felt a great relief, for he had been, in the interim, the recipient of much genuine solicitude, and many pans of hot scones.[28]

While the influence of Zion Church in Redney's young life, both morally and socially, was profound, there were, as well, important secular social events. Winter ones were usually house parties, where, emboldened by her Secret Purpose and her superiority, clever young Redney liked trying out her wit on her more conventional contemporaries. Her maiden aunt, an admiring audience of one, used to help lace her bodice and slip the silk party-dress over her head, cut square in the neck, *never* low, with modest half-sleeves. Her aunt also knitted "fascinators" to cover Redney's dark hair on the way to the party. Redney describes one such affair in *The Imperialist:*

> It was a clear, cold January night and everybody, as usual, walked to the party; the snow creaked and ground underfoot, one could hear the arriving steps in the drawing-room. They stamped and scraped to get rid of it in the porch, and hurried through the hall, muffled figures in overshoes, to emerge from an upstairs bedroom radiant, putting a last touch to hair and button hole, smelling of the fresh winter air. Such gatherings usually consisted entirely of bachelors and maidens, with one or two exceptions so recently yoked together that they had not yet changed the plane of existence (p. 54).

Redney's repartee sparkled at these parties, for she was still "young enough to be pleased with cleverness for its specious self" (*The Imperialist*, p. 108). Since her father sold fabrics and ran a dressmaking service, she was always more elegantly and fashionably dressed than the other girls. The knowledge of this made her tall figure poised and graceful, with her head held high, her chin tilted at a triumphant angle.

Redney had the usual number of innocent flirtations, received the usual number of "billet-doux in prayer-books at church", the usual number of elaborate satin-and-lace Valentines. She held hands in softly-lit conservatories among the palms and orchids, went along with the fun of fluttering her eyelashes and her downy-edged fan "decorated with marvellous imitations of Watteau" (*Globe*, Nov. 25, 1886). From sixteen to twenty, she confided all her romantic secrets to her aunt. She had nursed an early, unreciprocated passion for a red-haired boy who sat in the front row at school, and had a later "school-boy sweetheart" who inscribed "all over a beautiful pink page" of her autograph album:

> Hast thou a friend? Thou hast indeed
> A rich and large supply
> Treasures to serve your every need
> *Well managed* till you die (*Montreal Star*, Nov. 14, 1887).

Her only all-absorbing passion, however, in these teen-age years, was her writing. Her early romances were never more than the lace-edging round the Valentine and the message itself she regarded with her habitual ironic detachment. She had not been an avid reader and admirer of Jane Austen for nothing. In these early years, Redney much preferred Sense to Sensibility. Only much later, when reality pressed too close, would Romance become for her a remedy and a retreat.

Redney liked the company of boys, but also had a close female friend, a kindred spirit who also had literary ambitions: Pauline Johnson, the half-Indian poet. Pauline had been privately tutored at home by a governess, entering the Collegiate in 1877 for her final two years. Since her family lived outside of town, Pauline boarded with the Curtis family. David Curtis was Collector of Customs for Brantford and his daughter Emily was in the same class as Pauline and Redney. At first Pauline was shy and reserved, a slight girl, with olive skin and one long black braid, whose dark eyes hinted at strong feeling within. As Redney and the other girls, with Emily as intermediary, penetrated her shyness, "Pauley" as they called her relaxed into warm and whimsical playfulness. She often invited them to spend weekends with her at the family home, "Chiefswood", a large, stuccoed mansion sixteen miles out of town, overlooking the Grand River. Pauline's father, Chief George Johnson, son of Smoke Johnson, the famous Mohawk orator, was a cultured gentleman with a fine library and a knowledge of French, German, and various Indian dialects. Her mother, Emily, a cousin of William Dean Howells, the American novelist, was a gentle, elegant woman, fond of lace and tortoise-shell combs. Pauline had a sister, Evelyn, and two brothers, Alan and Beverley. Beverley was tall and handsome — some said the handsomest man in Brant County — and an accomplished musician. He used to play the piano for the girls after dinner, so that Chopin nocturnes drifted out the open French doors to join the night sounds and flower scents.[29] It may have been Pauline, an expert herself, who taught Redney how to paddle a canoe, on summer afternoons on the Grand. Redney soon learned how to paddle it straight ahead swiftly and surely, while Pauline, whose own dreams of literary fame were vague as smoke, listened in awe to Redney's, as practical and perfectly formed as the paddle in her hand.

Redney explained to Pauline, that summer of 1879, as she determined the direction of the canoe with a decisive flick of her paddle, that she had decided to become a journalist. This meant entering a world still almost exclusively occupied by men, which is what she had wanted to do ever since she tore her skirts in apple-trees and played a tough game of hockey. She would get a job on a newspaper, earn her daily bread by her pen, batter her way into all-male bastions, and best the men at their own game.

When she announced this plan to her family, her mother was horrified. Journalism wasn't at all a suitable occupation for a gently-reared young lady, working in a smoky office full of shirt-sleeved men, spittoons and smutty jokes! It was quite as improper as going on the stage! Her mother also pointed out that so far her pen had earned her exactly ten dollars, her Ladies College prize. She should become a school teacher, which is what all the other girls did until they found husbands. That nice Elsie Perley was going to Model School at the end of the summer; Redney should go too. Redney looked to her father, who had always encouraged her writing, for support, but even he thought journalism was going too far. School-teaching would give her financial security, and time to write in the summers. Reluctantly, after much heated debate, Redney capitulated.

So it was on the morning of August 30th, 1879, that she found herself, with twenty-two others, back in the old familiar rooms at Central School, where she had sat years before smarting from the humiliation of hoops and hopelessly muddled columns of figures. As Redney looked around the room, noting that there were only five men, and feeling already the boredom which that old, familiar smell of chalk dust, cheap varnish and stale air aroused in her, she sighed; it was going to be a long two months. But since she was here, she would show them all—including the men—that she was better than any of them, one of a special breed. A new spirit of competitiveness surged within. She had never felt like that in the old Central School days, but she was older now, surer of herself.

Brantford's County Model School, where aspiring teachers earned their third-class certificate, had been established two years before and its curriculum devised by George William Ross, provincial chairman of the Model School Inspection Committee. On that first August morning, the students had been given "materials for note taking" and a copy of each textbook to be used. Redney was only half listening as the Head Master, William Wilkinson, M.A., droned on, explaining that a good teacher was aware that every child had a natural love of activity and a natural lack of method. Good management, he continued, involved "promptness, steadiness, earnestness, geniality, quietness and tact." School discipline, designed for "correction and prevention" was carefully graded, in ascending order of severity, from "1) corporal punishment, 2) ridicule, 3) public censure, 4) demerit marks, 5) detention during hours of recreation, 6) detention after school, 7) suspension and 8) expulsion" ("County Model Schools", *Expositor*, Aug. 31, 1877).

During all of September and October, Redney had no time for her private scribbling. Six days a week she sat in the dusty school, at a desk much too small for her long legs, and conscientiously took notes. There were lectures on how to teach reading, arithmetic, geography, history, grammar and spelling; how to teach recitation; on the characteristics of a good teacher, on moral duties, including good manners. There were five whole lectures on hygiene. The word "duty" kept grating the air like chalk on slate: moral duties, physical duties, community duties, school-room duties of the teacher, school-room duties of the pupils (*Expositor*, Aug. 31, 1877).

George William Ross, Inspector of Model Schools, had paid his formal visit to Central School on Saturday, October 11th, and Redney knew she had impressed him with her bright answers. He had questioned the students from nine to twelve o'clock, then made a long speech, telling them how to be exemplary teachers, and how to conduct recitations (*Expositor*, Oct. 17, 1879). This was the beginning of Redney's life-long friendship with George Ross, and also the beginning of her life-long habit of never missing an opportunity to charm the great and powerful, anyone who might conceivably help her in her ambitions.

George Ross was a clever Scot who had come to Canada in 1832 and pursued a canny and steadily advancing political career. Since 1872 he had been the Liberal member in Ottawa for West Middlesex, and was later to become Minister of Education for Ontario (1883-1899), Premier of the province (1899-1905), then leader of the Senate. Finally, in 1910, he was knighted by King George. He also became director of the Globe Printing Company, leader writer for the *Globe*, and President of the Canadian Authors Association (1899-1901). He was a good person for Redney to know, himself a writer of history, biography and didactic poetry. He was a staunch supporter of Canadian literature, of temperance, of strong Imperial ties, and a splendid orator, an eloquent prophet of Canada's bright future. In his days as school inspector he regularly told the students that "the future greatness of Canada depended upon them." They were going out to make Canada the best country in the world. In strong tones he would say, "Prepare yourselves, prepare, prepare", and with a bright "Good morning" would exit quickly on the last line.[30]

Redney prepared. As October waned and the dark nights closed in early, she spent the evenings in her attic, reading through her neat notes and munching her snow apples. There would be written exams in education, school law, elocution, hygiene. The rest would be oral (*Expositor*, Nov. 2, 1877). When, on October 31st, the Brantford *Expositor* announced the results of the Brant Model School examinations, Redney stood first among the twenty-three candidates. Out of a possible 575 marks, she had obtained 482 (288 was a passing grade), and, along with one man, achieved an A grade. The rest of the class were lowly B's. With perseverance one could best the men. "Sara Duncan" had topped the class. She further emphasized her difference and distinction from common garden varieties by dropping her "h". There were many Sarahs; from now on she was "Sara" in print, still Redney in private.

It was one thing, however, to beat her fellow teachers and to flaunt her superiority. It was quite another to settle into the drudgery of teaching. For that, Redney had no inclination at all. Apart from some supply teaching in Brantford, there is no record of where she taught,[31] but however steady or sporadic her teaching career was during the next few years, she has left a clear record of her dislike. In her day, teaching was the career considered most suitable for women, being the usual stop-gap between school and marriage, and Redney resented this. Young women, she was to write bitterly, are "permitted to pose very gracefully as Saints, and to teach school in almost any country district for two hundred-fifty dollars a year—a 'situation' not without the elements of martyrdom" (*Globe*, Jan. 22, 1887). She also refers to "the large and increasing body that now drags out a miserable existence in the teaching profession underpaid and overworked" (*Globe*, July 24, 1886). School-teaching for Redney was a thorn-bush in her path, like having to mind a baby brother when one wanted to be writing. Her Secret Purpose still drew her, its heady perfume still compelled as strongly as when she had tacked her brother's skirts to the floor. A stuffy roomful of thirty little ones wasn't going to stand in her way. In between marking her piles of papers, she kept on writing poems and essays, sending them off with stamps and high hopes.

How proud she felt, how excited, when on February 18th, 1880, one of her poems was printed in the Toronto *Globe*! It bore only the initials "S.D.", perhaps because of its personal nature, for it was a love poem, a sad, shadowed one, in keeping with her mood at the moment, when blackboards loomed larger than blue skies:

> *My Prayer*
> The white-sailed ship with rope and spar,
> Bound for the land where the blue skies are,
> Passeth the line, so faint and far,
> Dividing the sky and sea.
>
> So let our love, in a glad surmise,
> Sail in the hope of bluer skies
> Beyond the line where the shadow lies,
> Into Eternity.

Although Redney had a special fondness for this, her first printed poem (it reappeared in *The Week*, Nov. 18, 1886, with a new title, "Outward Bound"), it is a commonplace lyric, indistinguishable from those of a hundred minor poets. There is, however, one telling image: "Bluer skies / Beyond the line where the shadow lies". That is unmistakably Redney, directing her gaze towards the archetype, the perfect setting, the perfect everything. Much later, in Simla, she would paint that thin horizon line which divided dull brown cornfield from bluer skies.

Four months later, in June of 1880, Redney was thrilled to have an essay printed in *The Canada Monthly*, one of those many Canadian magazines that bloomed and died quickly; this one lasted longer than most, from 1872 to 1882. Redney called her article "Diogenes on Bric-a-Brac" and gave it a classical form sanctioned by Dryden and other eighteenth-century essayists. It is a dialogue between Diogenes and his young disciple Euphrosyne, on the distinction between the trivia of bric-a-brac and the true work of art. And the miracle

is that in her very first published piece of prose, at the age of
eighteen, "Sara Duncan" has already found her own voice,
the distinctive *persona* that would always be hers in print. It
is a voice whose pertness and precision suggests Jane Austen's,
a voice crisp, arch, playful and very assured. Redney directs
one deft blow at Canadian philistinism in her reference to
"this very practical country, among whose bustling com-
monplaces, the aesthetic is only beginning to find an
existence". She directs another deft blow at the inferiority of
applied to true art: "The artist has a little poem in her heart,
and she embodies it, that it may be a source of enjoyment to
herself and her friends. The decorator of ginger jars is
inspired by nothing of the ideal, and produces a base and
spurious imitation."

Where did Redney learn this pert, vivid style? It
flowered naturally and suddenly from the rich soil of her
Brantford years—those early years when she was more
confident of achieving the ideal setting, the ideal career, the
ideal artistic creation, than she would ever be again. During
those Brantford years she felt clever, witty, energized,
superior. She lived in one of the town's biggest houses and
knew all the first families; she was always superbly dressed;
she had a father who adored and encouraged her; she had
eight younger brothers and sisters who looked up to her and
emulated her; she had topped her class at Normal School.
These were her years of greatest confidence and strongest
drive and her prose style, as vivid and vivacious as she knew
herself to be, is the remarkable ripe fruit of those formative
years.

With "Diogenes on Bric-a-Brac", Sara Duncan, journalist, was launched. June, 1880, was a joyous month: first a
poem, and now an article accepted . . . the school-teaching
year about to end . . . roses unfolding in the sun. In June,
too, there was a happy excursion to Dundurn Park in
Hamilton, where she picknicked with two female friends "in
the jolliest way", under the shadow of Sir Allan MacNab's
Italianate castle, while "Burlington Bay shimmered away
into the blue distance" and "tiny yellow butterflies fluttered
among the gay little wild flowers in the grass" (*Globe*, Aug.
23, 1886). The three girls talked of hard-boiled eggs and the

latest in millinery, of "facts and visions; fixed fate, free will, foreknowledge absolute". Just another school-girl picnic, but with a difference, for these three sprawled on the grass were feminists, although that term was still unknown to them; all three wanted careers more than husbands. One of them was Alice McGillivray, who in 1884 would earn an M.D. from Kingston Medical College, the second woman to graduate in medicine from a Canadian university. The other picknicking friend was the first to do so, Augusta Stowe, who obtained her M.D. in Toronto in 1883, the only girl in the all-male class.

The Stowe family lived in Mount Pleasant, just outside Brantford. Augusta's mother Emily was a remarkable woman, one of several who gave young Sara Duncan a shining image of what women could accomplish. Emily Stowe chalked up several "firsts" for women. She was the first female principal of a Brantford public school, having resorted—didn't everyone?—to school-teaching as the first step on her career ladder. She had obtained her medical degree in the United States, put out her shingle in Toronto in 1867 (just as Redney was starting school), the first Canadian woman to practice in Canada. Emily was also an ardent suffragette, founder in 1877 of the Toronto Women's Suffrage Club.[32] Her daughter Augusta, who in addition to her mother had two aunts who were doctors, and Alice McGillivray, whose sister also went into medicine, were heady friends for Redney. Augusta and Alice sat among the yellow butterflies and talked of the cutting edge of scalpels and male prejudice, of their own iron resolve to succeed in a man's world. Redney gazed at the sparkling blue distances of Burlington Bay, and took heart.

A sombre, more autumnal mood succeeded, if the emotions which triggered her fall spate of poems are genuine, and not just literary artifice. A poem in the *Canadian Illustrated News* for September 11, 1880, entitled "Not Unto Us" and signed "Sara Duncan, Brantford", bemoans the fact that one "can never know, ah, never, / What is false and what is true!" A lyric entitled "It Might Have Been", and signed "Sarah Duncan, Strathroy" appeared in *The Canada Monthly*'s

September issue. Strathroy was George Ross' home town. Impressed with her bright answers at the Model School Inspection, perhaps Ross had recommended her for a teaching post there, or perhaps she was visiting friends. "It Might Have Been" is undistinguished verse, but interesting as the product of an eighteen-year-old psyche:

> *It Might Have Been*
> A baffled, disappointed, worn old man,
> Heavily burdened with a life time's span
> Of dreams and prayers and purpose unfulfilled.
> Humanity hath scorned him, and hath stilled
> His broken cry for pity. Hopeless tears
> Oft thickening in the dim old eyes, I ween,
> Dull the fair vision of what might have been.
> Crowned mockingly with sad, unhonoured years,
> Bespattered with contempt, footsore and lame,
> Weary, full weary with the blows of fate,
> He waits your scornful doling at the gate;
> Be kind, O friend, for Failure is his name!

The *Canada Monthly* printed two more poems that year; "Autumn", by "Sara Duncan, Brantford", appeared in November:

> 'O Stately maiden with dreaming eyes,
> With Summer's secret so wondrous wise,
> Wandering free under gentler skies,
> By the brooks where the water is foaming!
>
> Wrapped in thine own mysterious haze,
> The soul of thine Indian Summer days,
> A golden glory in all thy ways,
> 'Tis bravely apparelled thou'rt roaming!
>
> Alas, fair maiden! The winds are cold,
> And the mists are gray that were all of gold,
> Speed thee away! Thou art growing old!'
> And she saith good-bye in the gloaming!

"A Minister of Grace" by "Sara Duncan" followed in December:

> We call thee Sympathy, in our rude tongue,
> Discerning not thy lovelier, heavn-giv'n name
> Whereby the angels know thee. In no wise

May we command thee—thou art subtly born
Of soul-similitude, or common grief;
Yet souls for lack of thee must daily die!
Thou lurkest in the warmth of clasping hands,
The inner life of human brotherhood,
And often shinest glorious in a tear!
Thou sharest half, and soothest all, their pain,
And from the depths men mutely cry to thee,
All empty-hearted if thou comest not!

Failure . . . It Might Have Been . . . Sympathy . . . Autumn.
What blew these cold winds into Redney's life? Was it the
daily grind in the classroom, all those grubby little fingers
tugging her skirts, while the air filled with dust motes, and
the smell of wet stockings and orange peels? The mystery had
receded, and the margin shrunk to the circumference of a
steel hoop, like that humiliating one under her petticoats,
but this one was harder to step out of. Like Judith Church
in *His Honour and a Lady*, Redney

> knew by intuition that the world was full of colour and
> passion, and when one is tormented with this sort of knowledge
> it becomes more than ever grievous to inhabit one of its
> small, dull, grimy blind alleys, with the single anticipation of
> enduring to a smoke-blackened old age (p. 13).

Becoming a journalist would admit her to that wider
world of colour and passion, but the barriers were formidable. No woman had ever worked in the office of a major
Canadian newspaper. A few genteel ladies scribbled columns
from the safe sanctuary of their plush parlours, but a woman
working *in the office?* Never! Male reporters even covered
the social events, the receptions and balls and weddings, and
described, in wildly inaccurate prose, the ladies' dresses and
adornments.

Redney realized that before she could storm the bastions
she had to perfect her weapons and hone her writing skills to
a sharp edge. She would lie low inside her schoolmarm's
cloak until she was well-armed with published pieces of
journalism. She therefore enrolled at the Toronto Normal
School in January, 1882, to earn her second-class teaching
certificate. At least Toronto was a wider world than Brantford,

and she would have six months there, graduating in June. The only memory which Redney later recorded of that time refers to the "*ancien* — and awful — *régime*" where male professors were humourless and unnecessarily severe, and male and female students segregated on opposite sides of the classroom. Once a piece of blotting-paper, which had blown from Redney's desk to his, was surreptitiously returned to her by a male student as the professor droned on. At the lecture's close, the professor demanded that "the lady who received a communication from the gentleman's side of the lecture room will bring it to the desk". "Horror! Stigma! Disgrace! Clandestine Communication!" is Redney's flippant comment on this ridiculous display of Victorian prurience and patriarchy (*Globe*, Oct. 2, 1886). Redney consoled herself with "unhallowed flirtations with university young men, and the habit of making taffy over her bedroom gas jet" (*Globe*, Nov. 25, 1886). The fact that "*Sarah* Duncan" is listed among the successful candidates who passed the June exams indicates that "Sara" the writer had, for the moment, gone underground.

"Sara" resurfaced in October, 1882, however, as another poem appeared in *The Canada Monthly*. She is still concerned with the difficult upward flight towards the ideal in art:

Conscious
To hate this darkness and to long for light,
Yet grovel closer to our shadowy earth!
Essay, with sparrow's wings, the eagle's flight,
What boon is knowledge of our own unworth!

The final verse, however, strikes a more optimistic note:
The untold sweetness of the flower and song
Hath here a herald. A glad hope that we,
Rejoicing in full noontide, shall be strong,
Whispers the secret of futurity!

Glad hopes had blossomed that fall when Redney and one of her brothers had stayed in Quebec City with a grand-uncle for two weeks. On the way Redney read William Dean Howells' *Chance Acquaintance* and "made her explorations in the spirit of that delightful little novel".[33] One memorable day, with five other young people, Redney had caught the stagecoach at St Roch's for a day's picnic to Montmorenci Falls. There was a similar outing with her brother and cousin Jack to Lorette. While her impressions were still fresh, she "sat down straightway" and wrote two charming pieces, describing these excursions in the light, descriptive vein which she was always to do so well. Some time in 1883, having delivered the one entitled "By Stage to Montmorenci" that summer to the County of Brant Teachers' Convention, and having had it appear in the pages of the local *Expositor*, she was emboldened to send both her sketches, signed "Sara Duncan", to a new magazine called *Outing*, begun that year in Boston, and edited by William Howland. To her great jubilation, they were both accepted, earning her ten dollars each (almost a whole month's teaching salary!) All those earlier rejected essays had cost her two weeks' agony to write. These two were airy nothings dashed off "in two hours", but they had taught her "that she must have some unworn incident, some fiber of novelty or current interest to give value to her work" and among the cobwebs on her attic wall at West Street Redney tacked up the maxim: "Before I say anything I must have something to say".[34]

"By Stage to Montmorenci" appeared in *Outing* in May, 1884. The tone of the article is gay and sprightly as she describes the journey there, crammed into the stagecoach, "a long, narrow, dusty, paintless packing-box". Most of the article is taken up with visual descriptions of scenery and people; her eye is, as it was always to be, a painter's, with her father's fine sense of colour and line and her own definite point of view; her "I" is, as it was always to be, a writer's, with a definite *persona* and her own arch style. She describes the walk through "yellow wheat-fields, starred with ox-eyed daisies and heaven-blue chicory" to reach the wooded ridge, where "lovely, tender, living-green" covers the rocks. She is already recording what was to be, for her, a life-long preoccupation in her writing: national distinctions of character, elucidated metaphorically in setting. The French-Canadians are seen as carefree, close to nature, tolerant, trusting, gossipy, idiosyncratic, and their roadside dwellings reflect all this:

Not one of the odd, little, steep-roofed, parti-colored houses faces squarely upon the road; they are all set at an angle with it, and with one another, and with all the rest of the world. Every house has its irregular little garden, — a charming tangle of exquisite color.

"On Two Wheels to Lorette", which appeared in *Outing* in March of 1885, follows exactly the same formula; only the destination and the vehicle (a calèche rather than a stage-coach) have changed. Redney's aesthetic eye is here even more active as she revels in "great crimson dahlias" nodding over white fences, and the gaily-coloured houses whose designs remind one "forcibly of the Noah's Ark of one's infancy". Both these *Outing* pieces are fine, descriptive journalism: two well-feathered arrows in Redney's expanding quiver.

The spring of 1884 found Redney supply-teaching in Brantford's public schools when regular teachers were ill. (*Courier*, March 6 and March 9, 1884). One of her pupils in a Central School class was her brother Gordon, then thirteen, who remembers his eldest sister as "the strictest teacher I ever had".[35] Perhaps Redney was venting her resentments on her pupils. It was in May that her first article appeared in *Outing*, and here she still was, stuck in a classroom. She wanted to prove herself as a professional writer, not just a Sunday scribbler, someone who could be called upon, as she had been on Friday, April 4th, at Mrs William Watt Junior's "parlor social", to read an essay, sandwiched between the Zion Church choir's rendering of two anthems and Miss Minnie Forde's piano solo (*Expositor*, April 5, 1884).

On May 13th, a news item appeared in the Brantford *Courier* which excited and emboldened Redney: "Editor Sheppard of the Toronto *News* will lecture in Brantford on the 20th, in connection with the Knights of Labor". Edmund E. "Ned" Sheppard was a thirty-one year old Bohemian with a black goatee and sallow skin, who had once worked as a cowboy on the Mexican border and who thereafter always wore top boots of fine Spanish leather and a broad-brimmed hat, even indoors. He had a remarkable collection of cuss-words, as accurate and well-aimed as his tobacco quids which, even from great distances, always hit the cuspidor (although George Ross, when he visited his office, always jumped out of the way, just in case). Ned Sheppard had increased the readership of the evening *News* when he took over as editor by starting a spicy gossip column called "Peek-a-Boo", and by printing the *News* on pink paper, so that little boys pleaded with their fathers to buy it, wanting it for kites.[36]

This was the man Redney determined to ask for a job. She dressed carefully, gathered up her published pieces, scribbled a note on her visiting card, and set off swiftly down the main street towards the Kerby House, before she had time to lose her nerve. Sheppard later wrote an account of their meeting for *Saturday Night*, whose editorship he took over after the *News*:

> I was called down to the parlor of the hotel in Brantford. The card of a young lady was the summons, and I was met by a rather tall and slender miss, whose bright eyes, and freckled face were pleasant to see. The young woman desired a position on a newspaper, and felt sure she could do lots of useful things and write entertainingly of many subjects just then neglected by the daily press. After a short chat, during which I reluctantly confessed that the last lady on the staff of my newspaper had not been entirely a success, I promised to remember her if anything suitable should offer and said "goodbye" (*Saturday Night*, Sept. 6, 1890).

Redney's high hopes dimmed as the days passed and still this Sheppard didn't call her into his fold. She refused, however, to give up; instead she would lower her sights a little. She would apply for a job on her home-town paper. Redney has left her own amusing account of that decisive day in her life when she climbed the three flights of stairs and announced to the astonished editor that "she should be allowed to spend a few hours every day at his office, doing such work as he could give her. The editor, rather reluctantly, accepted her offer "and asked her when she would like to begin. This afternoon", replied Redney, taking off her gloves. She was thereupon given a paste pot and scissors and told to make up the "All Sorts" column, snipping and gleaning from a pile of New York papers.

She went home that afternoon and read the "Sentinel" all over, picked out several other columns which she thought she could manage in it, got up the characters for proof-reading, and went to bed feeling quite capable of taking the paper off the editor's hands at an hour's notice.[37]

Brantford had two newspapers; the one which employed Redney was probably the *Courier*. The Liberal paper was the *Expositor*, begun in 1852 by Henry Racey, an auctioneer. The editor in 1884 was William Watt Jr., a clever lawyer whose wife had held the "parlor social" at which Redney had read her essay. The other Brantford paper was the Conservative *Courier*, begun in 1833 by David Keeler and then called "The Sentinel", which is what Redney calls the paper in her account. There was another reason why it was probably the *Courier* which employed her. "Ned" Sheppard was a typical editor of the day in his reluctance to employ women, but the *Courier* editor, Major Henry Lemmon, was kindly disposed, since both his wife Harriet and his sister Alice wrote for the paper. Alice Lemmon, possibly the first woman journalist in Canada, began writing for the *Courier* when she married its founder, David Keeler. After David died, she married D'Acres Hart and her brother Henry took over the *Courier*. Alice lived to a great age—a bright, energetic woman who was, like Dr Emily Stowe, an important role model for Redney. Alice did editorial work not only for the *Courier* but also for the London [Ontario] *Times* and the St Thomas *Despatch*. Major Lemmon's second wife, an English widow called Harriet Martin, also wrote for the *Courier*.[38] With the first female school principal, the first female journalists, Brantford was a fine forcing ground for early feminists, including Sara Duncan.

For two months Redney busied herself in the office, happily pasting and proof-reading, writing an occasional editorial and descriptions of such social events as the closing exercises of the Brantford Ladies College. But she had no intention of staying in Brantford's backwater long. After a few weeks she determined on a bold plunge south of the border. If Alexander Bell could find success there, perhaps she could too. The United States was more progressive than Canada when it came to female journalists. A few brave

women were already making their mark on Eastern newspapers. Redney therefore placed the following advertisement
in a New York paper:

> a Young Lady of some experience in general journalism
> desires a position at a moderate salary on the staff of a
> newspaper of good standing. Specimens of work forwarded,
> and highest references given.

The advertisement ran for a week, "and at the end of the
week", as Redney later wrote, "not a single newspaper of
good standing, or of any standing whatever" had replied.
Redney received instead a circular suggesting she might like
to hand-colour photographs, which would be forwarded to
her upon receipt of two dollars and fifty cents.[39] In hindsight,
she could afford to be jocular; at the time her disappointment must have been keen.

   One day, while she was still with the *Courier*, a bundle
of coloured lithographs was dumped on her desk. She
opened them curiously; they were advertisements for the
New Orleans Cotton Centennial, a World's Fair to be held in
New Orleans beginning in December of '84, to celebrate the
hundredth anniversary of the cotton industry. Here in her
hands was the colour of that wider world; suddenly Redney
saw that the Cotton Centennial could be, for her, a golden
gateway. She could go, she decided in a flash of inspiration
and excitement, as a special correspondent for Canadian
newspapers. She took the train to Toronto, presented herself
in the office of John Cameron, editor of the *Globe*, talked so
charmingly and convincingly that Cameron agreed to pay
her five dollars for each article describing the Centennial
"with the option of refusing any that he did not like".[40]
Cameron still retained an interest in the London *Advertiser*,
which he had founded with his brother in 1863,[41] so he
contracted Redney to write for that paper too. She was to
write four articles for the *Globe* and ten different ones for the
Advertiser. "Then she went home and told her father of the
chance she had got; and her father, being a wise man,
applauded very heartily, and said he would help her".[42]
Redney's perseverance over the years, so like his own, had
won him over; if she wanted to be a journalist that badly,
then she had his blessing.

Here at last was a magic casement suddenly flung open
to that world which she had seen in fancy beyond the West
Street windows, and a chance to prove how well she could
capture it all in words. Redney packed her bag, folded fifty
dollars into her purse, and on December 4th, 1884, caught
the train for New Orleans.[43] She was not quite twenty-three,
a fine, slim-waisted figure in her smart serge travelling suit,
who drew many admiring glances as she walked along the
platform, pointed chin held high. Her long skirts held in
one hand, she mounted the train steps quickly, with hardly a
backward look. Her heart sang as the train, with a sudden
jerk, pulled out of the station, then glided along through the
silent, snow-covered fields. The engine chugged past the
small grocery store which sold hickory nuts, past the end of
the plank sidewalk, and past the violet smudge of woods,
which marked the farthest margin of Redney's Brantford
world.

2
NEW ORLEANS
"Vistas of Riotous Green"

> A day at whose shining robe we
> would catch if we could with a vain
> prayer for her tarrying. Overhead
> the draped graciousness of infinite
> blue, all around reaches and vistas of
> riotous green.
>
> *Memphis Daily Appeal.*

"Frosty fingered and blue cheeked", wrote Redney from
New Orleans, describing her journey south, she had "glided
out of a bright little snow-draped Canadian city, with
delightful anticipations of warmer things" (*London Advertiser*, Dec. 19, 1884). She had left the Grand Trunk line at
Chicago, stopping over long enough to visit bric-a-brac
shops and a pottery exhibit, then boarding the Illinois
Central evening train for the 36-hour run to New Orleans.
Even a red-faced cockney who occupied the upper berth of
the Pullman sleeper and kept her awake half the night with
his loud snores couldn't dim her happiness to be speeding
south toward the land of real opportunity. "Next morning,
after the invariable scramble for boots, and buttons and
possession of the mirror", she "breakfasted very tolerably in
the new and popular buffet system" on such novel early-
morning fare as cold ham, sardines and raw oysters.

Redney was keyed up, vibrantly alive, as she sat looking out the train window all that day. Behind her were the cold, blue-shadowed boredoms of school-teaching. The land's deep snow cover had gradually thinned to ragged remnants, then there was no more snow at all, only the lyrical roll of Kentucky's brown hills. Redney looked at the Negroes lining the track at each station, holding out their hands for pennies, felt the arm of her own ambition reaching out, ready to grasp. The ideals which had germinated so well in Brantford's nurturing soil, then put forth a tentative shoot in the New York advertisement had now burst into bloom: one single perfect rose. She would be not just Sara Duncan, journalist, but Sara Duncan, journalist on an American newspaper, one of the really big ones. She would use her New Orleans adventure to get herself hired, somehow or other. There were green cascades of elm trees beyond the window, but Redney saw only her name blazoned as byline on a column of type.

The following morning, Redney breakfasted again "upon a variety of things that most of us never saw before" at a restaurant in Hammond, Mississippi. Beyond the windows, summer had suddenly appeared. "Outside the trees are green about the wide verandah, and festive squirrels chase one another along the broad branches". The forest colouring is "glorious in the sun" and "windows are flung open", open to infinity (*London Advertiser*, Dec. 19, 1884). Back on the train, Redney peered out as it rolled into Louisiana. She sees "the first cypress, draped in the famous clinging gray moss", the hard edge of bare black branch veiled in silver embroiderings, in the gauzy stuff of day dreams, but the moss is real here, clinging, not about to disappear. The first magnolia brings "a thrill of delighted discovery", the glossy, dark-green leaves shining with "all the poetry of the South". Now Redney could see the strange jungle growth of the bayous, tangled brown roots and orchids visible at water's edge, snakes dozing in the sun, and sudden scarlet arcs of birds.

At last the dreaming old city itself materialized and Redney descended from the train to matters of baggage and porters. She was as competent and assured as any seasoned traveller as she boarded one of the mule-driven street cars for the journey uptown to the headquarters of the Bureau of Accommodation and Information at 164 Gravier Street. "Warm, moist breezes from the Gulf set the aspen leaves dancing" and "spring-like odors" filled the air. This was an exotic world of evening-party oysters for breakfast and spring-in-midwinter; Redney's blue-gray eyes shone with the excitement of it all. "Fowls and soiled clothing not allowed on board", read the sign in the street car, and there were goats all over the streets "free as air, with a reckless and debauched expression" (*London Advertiser*, Jan. 1, 1885). The street car rattled through the residential area, where through the black-iron lace of high gates Redney could see roses. "Roses are blooming everywhere, roses crimson and pink, creamy and white, red and riotous in every garden" (*London Advertiser*, Jan. 1, 1885). Roses in December — surely anything was possible! Then the street car dodged through the confusion of Canal Street where whips were cracking, teamsters swearing.

At the accommodation bureau, Redney was given a list of names and addresses of residents — mostly indigent gentry — willing to take boarders for the duration of the Exposition. She hopped on another street car, inspected a number of houses on her list, all of which she rejected on the basis of cracked walls or slovenly landladies. Even for a short term, the right setting was important to her — West Street had made Redney fastidious — and for the rest of her life she needed lines and colours to delight the eye and a measure of elegance. "But patience and the industrious mule will finally bring you your heart's desire", she writes happily as she finds the perfect house. It is a roomy, old-fashioned one, with a wide, pillared verandah, magnolias on either side of the front door, honey-suckle everywhere else. Inside are high ceilings, "oil portraits of venerable gentlemen in queues", bedrooms with four-posters and testers (*London Advertiser*, Jan 1, 1885). There are oranges close enough to pick outside her bedroom window, and rustling broad-leaved banana trees. Redney's Southern hostess was typical of the "widows and daughters of the gray-coated officers who fell in '63", people with much "culture and refinement and luxurious tastes", but no money (*London Advertiser*, Jan. 1, 1885). For twelve dollars a week, one got "elaborate dinners and charming society". Redney's own genteel upbringing had made this kind of gracious living obligatory; at once she felt perfectly at home. She enjoyed chatting with her hostess, seventy-five years old, who spent the harrowing Civil War years knitting army socks for Confederate feet, tucking into each one the message: "Never turn the heel of this to the enemy" (*Globe*, Jan. 2, 1885).

Redney settled in happily, not caring that, in the city's garden district, her boarding-house was four and a half miles from the Exposition. It took forty-five minutes to get there by street car, or, alternatively, one could take a steamboat down the Mississippi, leaving at hourly intervals from the foot of Canal Street.

For the official opening on December 16th, Redney as "special correspondent" had been invited to go by boat. She felt a tingle of happy anticipation sitting in her bedroom on the eve of the opening, as banana leaves whispered and she finished off her second *Advertiser* column:

> Joaquin Miller is here, occupying George Cable's house, and writing letters about the city for the *Times-Democrat*. Mrs. Julia Ward Howe is also here, superintending the Women's Department. Tonight the broad streets are waving their gay-colored decorations, crowds are hurrying to and from the Exhibition Grounds, commissioners are frantically crowding 24 hours work into one, and the lovely old Crescent City is quivering to the heart with the excitement of tomorrow's honors (Jan. 1, 1885).

Joaquin Miller was the biggest celebrity in New Orleans, a famous American poet and journalist whom Redney was determined to meet, not only because he could help her move closer to her goal of newspaperwoman, but also because of the mystique and magnetism of the man himself. Joaquin was so notorious that even the Brantford *Expositor* reported his movements over the years. Perhaps when young Redney neglected her Sunday School lesson, she was reading the titillating "Item of Interest" in 1879 in which

"Joaquin Miller says that those who love the beautiful are never bad. And yet, says the Boston *Transcript*, Joaquin loves the beautiful" (Aug. 26, 1879). In June of 1880, Joaquin had come to Canada, visiting Montreal, Toronto and Hamilton, and twice in the "Personal" column the *Expositor* reported on his flamboyant progress.[1]

On the morning of December 16th, Redney dressed with care. At 11 o'clock she stood on the deck of the "Fred A. Blanks", still moored to the Canal Street levee. It was a bright, sunny day with bands playing, streamers flying and a large crowd gathering. Redney felt like a schoolgirl on a Brantford parade day. Instead of the Six Nations Indians, however, there were black deck hands to lend an exotic note.

Promptly at 11:30, the carriage bringing the State Governor and other dignitaries drove up; they came on board and the boat moved down river, as "gay laughter and bright repartee [some of it Redney's] floated to leeward", and the "Mexican band rose and fell, a lovely accompaniment" (*London Advertiser*, Dec. 29, 1884). Pennons fluttered in the Gulf breeze; a French man-of-war and small tugs followed at a respectful distance during the half-hour trip. Redney loved being in the vanguard, loved the importance of being with the press group. As officials and press slowly proceeded down the gangplank and took their seats on the raised platform inside the Music Hall for the opening ceremonies, Redney looked in vain for Joaquin, then forgot him as excitement mounted. On the platform was a telegraph machine, suitably draped. At the appropriate moment, an official whisked off its cover with a flourish: the machine was receiving a message from President Arthur in Washington declaring the Exposition officially open. Ten thousand people cheered, cannons boomed, bells pealed, as Redney thought of Alexander Graham Bell and applauded American initiative in matters of communication.

The seed for the World's Industrial and Cotton Centennial Exposition had come from the Cotton Planters' Association of the United States which wanted to celebrate the hundredth anniversary of the date on which the first bale of cotton crossed the Atlantic. The Exposition was not as big or ambitious as the Centennial one in Philadelphia in 1876, but it was impressive enough to a young girl from a small provincial Canadian city. "Every day, Sundays included", wrote Redney, for six long months "the Exposition will teach its grand lessons in science and art, natural history, and physical geography, national resources and foreign importations, invention and progress" (*London Advertiser*, Dec. 29, 1884). It was the age of Expositions, beginning with the great London one in the Crystal Palace in 1851, all of them based on that comfortable Victorian belief that not only was the world steadily progressing to higher and better things, but that industrialism was largely responsible. Victorians on both sides of the Atlantic, once Utilitarianism had done its work, shared a touchingly naive faith in facts and figures, statistical tables, and absolutely everything with moveable parts. There were some foreign exhibits at the New Orleans Exposition, but they were insignificant compared with the United States' contribution. The exhibition was a nationalist boast of American enterprise and resources. Redney was about to see in operation the great pumping heart of American industry, whose capillaries had long since stretched all the way to Brantford.

On later visits to the grounds, Redney had time to view, and report on, all the exhibits there assembled. She enjoyed the daily street-car ride at mule trot, past orange trees dangling golden fruit, vines climbing greenly everywhere. Finally came the mushroom growth of "restaurants, dime shows, peanut and banana stands" just outside the main entrance, where, having paid one's fifty cents "the world is all before us" (*Globe*, Jan. 12, 1885).

"The world is all before us" .... The Exposition was in microcosm that wider world of colour and passion for which Redney had yearned, that wider world in which, for the rest of her life, she would be a restless Romantic, always pursuing some newly-perceived ideal. The seven large buildings on the grounds were set on a great, flat expanse, horizons clearly visible, blue skies beckoning. There were long mysterious avenues of live oaks veiled in Spanish-moss. To Redney, it was Paradise. "The wild land fresh from the hand of Nature that surrounds the Centennial buildings has been transformed into an Eden of bud and blossom, lake and fountain, shady path and bird-haunted grove" (*London Advertiser*, Dec. 29, 1884).

One fine morning, Redney eagerly followed the crowd walking up the broad asphalt walk to the main building, passing "almond-eyed little Celestials", "red-fezzed turks in braided jackets and full blue trousers" and "Spaniards in slouch hats and slashed velvet" (*Globe*, Jan. 12, 1885). The main building was the "largest ever erected for exhibition purposes", a frame structure covering thirty-three acres, painted lavender and red, with statues of Newton and Washington, an odd but appropriate American coupling, on either side of the entrance, and overhead "a group representing the progress of civilization" (*Globe*, Jan. 12, 1885). Inside, galleries twenty-three feet wide encircled the building and from there Redney could look down on hundreds of bobbing heads, hear the seductive hum of pianos, organs, operating machines and "the throbbing of the big, resonant Seth Thomas bell" (*Globe*, Jan. 12, 1885). All the aisles were fourteen feet wide, except where they were clogged with machinery, and under the huge centre dome was the Music Hall, where evening entertainments would entrance the multitudes.

The exhibits of the forty-four American States and Territories were housed in the Government Building. Inside the building were waving grains, triumphal arches, and a gigantic blue-ribbed glass globe showing the countries of the world with statistical tables "relative to the commerce of each, and the share of the United States therein" (*Globe*, Jan. 20, 1885). It seems fitting, in light of America's vision of Manifest Destiny that the foreign exhibits, a motley collection of tourist souvenirs, radiated out from "the headquarters of the Department of State." As she looked carefully at everything, jotting down details (her notebook was always in hand), Redney was unaware that this was an eerie preview of her future cosmopolitan existence. From Canada were "Montreal souvenirs of winter sports", from Japan a screen showing its "tea, rice and wheat culture", and combining the aesthetic delights and rational insouciance of that country: "As a work of art it is certainly unique; as a medium of instruction about as valuable as Japanese illustrations are apt to be" (*Globe*, Jan. 12, 1885). There were "a couple of porcelain jumbos with three-storey erections on their backs" and "exquisite feather fans" from India, but there was also "a small and very vicious looking idol" (*Globe*, Jan. 12, 1885).

The status of women in the 1880's was evident in the Women's Department, ably managed by Julia Ward Howe, the well-known writer and feminist, but grievously short of funds due to the "miscalculations" of male officials. It was hidden away in one-quarter of the gallery space in the Government Building, sharing it with such educational exhibits as a large hairy mammoth. The women's gallery looked "like a series of sumptuous parlours, profusely decorated with pictures and embroideries ... delicate needlework, decorated porcelain". The women of Louisiana had channelled their full complement of intellectual talents into the creation of a flowered quilt containing 100,584 tiny pieces of silk.[2]

As Christmas drew nearer, Redney's pen raced across sheet after sheet, transcribing all the colour and excitement of her new world in long letters for the *Globe*, the *London Advertiser*, and, less frequently, for her family. She celebrated her first birthday away from home, her twenty-third, on December 22nd, and then her first Christmas. In Brantford, the week before Christmas had meant long hours with her young friends in the cold pews of Zion Church, twisting pine and cedar into swags and ropes and wreaths, until "altar and lectern, and font, and pillar, are dressed in living green" (*Globe*, Dec. 25, 1886). "Living green" in a Canadian December was hard to come by.

In New Orleans, where oranges are found on trees, not in the toes of stockings, Redney spent Christmas Eve with two of her new journalist friends, enjoying Canal Street, where "a wild, exhilarated crowd of men, women and boys" were blowing into tin horns, letting off "fire-crackers, cannon-crackers, torpedos" and "numberless rockets" which streamed up among the stars. Arriving at the levee, Redney and her friends, on a mad impulse, hopped aboard the ferry for Algiers, "a disconsolate suburb of New Orleans across the river. The Mississippi rolled along in its broad majesty . . . the St Louis packet slowly swinging out into the river sent out a broad shaft of light that made a glorious path over the murky water and transformed the dirty village on the other side into a dream of quaint architecture" (*London Advertiser,* Jan. 6, 1885). Any homesickness Redney might have felt dissolved in the promise of that golden light.

January brought frequent warm showers, and a richer green, as news of Redney's journalistic triumphs wafted north. The Brantford *Expositor* was enthusiastic in its praise:

> Since the opening of the New Orleans Exposition graphic, spicy and exceedingly able and clever letters have appeared in the leading Canadian and American papers, bearing the *nom de plume* "Garth". Many have been the enquiries as to the author or authoress. It is an open secret that the authoress (for the writer is a lady) hails from Brantford, where she is well known in literary circles, as possessing a trenchant pen. In New Orleans she is perhaps the most popular of all the newspaper correspondents in the field. Last week a clever article signed "Garth" appeared in one of the morning dailies of the Crescent City. It was brought under the notice of Joaquin Miller the famous American poet of the "Sierras" who forthwith demanded of the editor the name of this rising star in literature. Recognizing her rare ability in this vocation, he has used his influence to advance her interests in the literary world by introducing her to many American celebrities. We are sure that the good wishes of the young lady's friends in Brantford follow her in the path of fame and fortune" (Jan. 14, 1885).

She had managed it! Her own clever journalism had served as bait, as it would many times in her life; she had met Joaquin Miller, met and charmed him, met and used him to advance her career. Her newspaper copy may suggest Southern languor and soft magnolias, but Redney was as sharp and single-minded as ever, making sure that Joaquin introduced her to all the right contacts. She had arrived with assignments from the Toronto *Globe* and the *London Advertiser* — a total of fourteen columns — but somehow she had secured writing commissions from the *Memphis Appeal*, the New Orleans *Times-Democrat* and the *Washington Post*.[3] This was indeed a remarkable *coup* for a young lady whose journalistic experience was limited to two months pasting and proof-reading on a small provincial paper. And if Joaquin introduced her to the right people, her own writing talent did the rest. She adopted the pen name "Garth" for all her New Orleans copy. A woman chooses "a distinctively masculine pen name", she was to write, due to "a dread of that instinctive bias in criticism from which a woman's acknowledged literary effort invariably suffers". It is fitting that Redney, with her androgynous nickname, entered the journalism arena in masculine guise, an equal contender. It is also fitting that she was self-confident enough not to hide completely behind her pen name. On more than one occasion the *Expositor* revealed her female identity, and certainly everyone in New Orleans knew who "Garth" was. The *Expositor* also predicted that this "Brantford young lady" whose New Orleans letters "are read with so much interest throughout Canada" is "destined to make her mark in the American literary world" ("Society Sauce", Jan. 10, 1885). Reading this, enclosed in a letter from her parents, Redney flushed with pleasure, and her resolve to "make her mark" grew firmer than ever.

At the moment, she had her hands full charming Joaquin Miller. He had singled her out for his attentions and she was flattered, if also a trifle flustered. For Redney, Joaquin was the first of several male writers who were father-figures to admire and emulate. She observed Joaquin closely, noting how he mixed only with the notables, how he played to the gallery, how he comported himself in a way that would make good copy and therefore be reported by the press. Joaquin, however, had no intention of staying safely in the father-niche where Redney had initially placed him, preferring a very different role.

Cincinnatus Hiner "Joaquin" Miller was forty-six when Redney met him. He had been raised in Oregon, run away from home at seventeen, gone to work as cook in a mining-camp, and had given himself scurvy from his bad cooking. He had then lived long enough with an Indian tribe to beget a daughter, and be jailed for one night for horse-stealing (a friend sawed through the bars to release him). He had taught school for a while, studied law and been called to the bar in Portland, Oregon in the year Redney was born. Then in 1862 he had written a fan letter to a young poet, Theresa Dyer, whose pen name was "Minnie Myrtle", and, encouraged by her reply, had ridden over to Port Orford, the Oregon town where she lived, curious to see this Romantic ikon in person. He found a willowy brunette. "I arrived on Thursday", said Joaquin, "on Sunday next we were married", having passed the intervening time, according to his bride, "in an atmosphere of poetry."[4]

The following year, Miller bought the *Democratic Register* in Eugene, Oregon and became its editor. His first editorial had been in defence of the Mexican bandit Joaquin Murietta, earning him the nick-name Joaquin, which clearly suited him better than Cincinnatus. When his newspaper was suppressed by the government because he supported the Confederacy during the Civil War, Miller moved to Grant County, where the grateful townsfolk made him a judge in 1866 for leading their posse against a band of hostile Indians. Finding the poetry of her marriage corroding into prose, Minnie Myrtle left Joaquin, taking their two children with her. Miller solaced himself with two published volumes of poetry, *Specimens* (1868) and *Joaquin et al* (1869). In both of these, he extolled in undistinguished verse the glorious Sierra Nevada mountains, which earned him the sobriquet "Poet of the Sierras", although he himself preferred to be called more specifically "Byron of the Rockies".[5]

In 1870, Joaquin made his first trip to England, one of the many "passionate pilgrims" who crossed the Atlantic in those years to embrace their literary heartland. "Byron of the Rockies" went up to Nottingham to lay a wreath on his hero's grave and, when his next book of poetry, *Songs of the Sierras*, appeared, he did indeed, like Byron on the publication of *Childe Harold* (1812), awake to find himself famous, the literary lion of the London season. He had been cook, miner, lawyer, pony-express rider, newspaper editor, judge. For the rest of his life he would be a Poet. Like Byron, he carefully manufactured a public *persona* guaranteed to sell books, affected a certain style of dress, openly wooed clever, beautiful women, and, when he remembered Byron's club foot, limped.

To enhance his public image, he grew his tawny-gold hair to his shoulders, added a beard, clapped a sombrero on his head, stocked up on red shirts, polka-dotted bandanas, cowboy pants with chaps, and boots with jingling spurs. This was to be his costume for the rest of his life, and since he was six feet tall and weighed 190 pounds, there was no danger of Joaquin being lost in the crowd.

The English loved him — to them he represented all the frontier freedom and romance of the American West. On his second trip to England, in 1873, all doors were opened. He had midnight supper with the Shah of Persia, dinner with Tennyson, lunch with Browning, met Swinburne, Ruskin, Dante Gabriel Rossetti, Ford Madox Ford, William Morris, Holman Hunt, and Whistler. When, in New Orleans in '85, to that distinguished list he added one more literary friend, Sara Duncan of Brantford, Ontario, the young lady's ego understandably soared.

Joaquin had been in New Orleans since October, contracted to report on Exposition preparations for a syndicate of Eastern newspapers. He had arrived on Saturday the 11th, and put up first at the St Charles Hotel, where, for five dollars a day he had a room "too small for a bedroom but a little too big for a coffin" (*Washington Post*, Oct. 27, 1884). The next morning, making sure the local press were in attendance, he had sauntered to the foot of Canal Street, stripped, and plunged into the river to escape the heat. Next he moved on to the French Quarter, where he gambled and flirted with the girls, then repaired to church and listened attentively to the sermon. The reporters noted that "he was equally at home in both milieus, and an attention-getter in either place".[6] New Orleans took him to its heart for the length of his stay. After all, he had backed the Confederacy during the War, and declared that "there is more real heart here to the square mile than in any one spot in America. And it is real heart — not show or sham heart, as in Paris. The perfect good manners and ever prevailing politeness here, it seems to me, is real" (*Washington Post*, Nov. 9, 1884) He praised the sensuous beauty of magnolias and Southern women, the dignity of oaks and Southern men, assured both sexes of the success of their Exposition:

> She is rounding rapidly into shape. Like a full-grown tree with its buds ready to burst open in their fullness and freshness, she is just about ready to blossom. This is the home of the magnolia. It is remotely possible — I may be mistaken — there have been deadly frosts out of season — but you can set it down as one of the certain things in an uncertain world that this centennial magnolia will come to full bloom, and will overtop all other like flowers that have yet been (*Washington Post*, Nov. 9, 1884).

New Orleans folk responded by installing him in novelist George Washington Cable's fine house at 229 Eighth Street (they had driven Cable north because of his campaign for equal civil rights for negroes.) Miller was as lionized as he had ever been in London, received by Governor Lowry, invited to all the best plantation homes for dinner, asked to read his poems at select evening soirées, and given a chance to jingle his spurs loudly in the street parade when Buffalo Bill's Wild West Show came to town just before Christmas.[7]

If he was always a poseur, Joaquin was at least a conscious one. Once, when walking down a street with Ina Coolbrith, a clever, red-headed San Franciscan journalist and a life-long friend, Joaquin met another full-rigged cowboy, inspected him carefully and then muttered: "Hell! Another damn fool!".[8]

Redney felt their kinship, for in New Orleans she too was a poseur; for purposes of charming Joaquin and New Orleans in general she had slipped into the satin softness of Southern women, whom she found to be "lovable and loving, asking only to be shielded from the facts of life" (*Globe*, Jan. 2, 1885). The Southern miss "would rather flirt than vote" and is "an unparalleled example of exquisite womanhood" (*London Advertiser*, Jan. 6, 1885). Redney tells her readers that she has begun wearing powder, symbol of the "all-pervasive frivolity" of Southern women, and has become quite as languid as they, taking "her morning coffee in bed without a qualm of conscience" (*London Advertiser*,

May 12, 1885). In New Orleans, the people, as well as the
setting, made it easy for Redney to become a hot-house
bloom, for here that "beauty of propriety" which she had
appreciated at the Duncan dinner table was adopted by a
whole community. Redney never stood on the street car, for
a man always offered his seat; she was assisted getting on and
off; the negro who took her fare always raised his hat. "A
thousand and one little unobtrusive acts of consideration"
create a "balmy influence". "The people address you", purrs
Redney, "and you are verbally caressed" (*London Advertiser*,
Jan. 1, 1885).

Redney observed the Southern belles carefully, perfect-
ing her new flirtatiousness. One moonlit evening when "the
air was warm and heavy with the sweetness of orange
blossoms", and the sound of a hand organ (*London Advertiser*,
May 12, 1885) Redney was escorted by a male friend—
perhaps Joaquin—to an elegant "Creole" party (Creoles
were those white Louisianians of Spanish or French blood).
It was a young people's party, but not at all like those
Brantford ones where the young men stamping the snow off
their boots on the porch came in shyly, almost reluctantly, to
where the bashful maidens formed a muslin phalanx. At this
party the young ladies sat in twos and threes, "their tiny feet
crossed and their arms twined round each other's absurd
little waists in an abandon of amorous friendship" and
openly angled for male attention. There was a Mediterranean
warmth and gaiety new to Redney, a conscious pursuit of
pleasure. She drank "the sweet, seductive anisette" in
thimble-sized glasses, remembered Brantford's teetotal fruit
punch, and slipped easily into flirtatious frivolity. Redney
was like a chameleon, always taking on the temperamental
tone of whatever environment she found herself in.

In Brantford, she had felt the harsh, Calvinist winds
blowing on her from great-grandfather Bailie Duncan, from
her own father, from Dr Cochrane, George Ross, George
Brown—all those hard-working, self-denying, sober Scots—
and her journalism had been correspondingly ascetic. Her
descriptive sketches of Quebec had coolly appraised Nature's
beauty of line and tint, sounding a thin, piping note,

detached, distant. Her New Orleans writing has a richer resonance, deeper chords—the aesthetic eye coupled with the sensual "I". Redney senses the Southern languor, lets it seep into her pores, into her prose, for she has noted carefully that the New Orleans copy of her mentor, Joaquin, throbs with sensual phrases, and she therefore imitated this father-figure in her journalistic path. "A Northern winter is a very mirthful thing, and the sound of sleigh bells is a cheery one", writes Redney now, "but a Southern winter is a beautiful dream—a languorous, throbbing, ecstatic experience" (*Memphis Daily Appeal*, Jan. 20, 1885). She writes of "the tender breath of garden violets", of the air "veritably caressing", of the "incense-laden darkness", of being "verbally caressed" by soft Southern voices. Her New Orleans experience, for various reasons both of setting and personal contacts, brought her as close to real sensuality as she would ever get.

Redney's role as magnolia blossom began as conscious charade, but as her New Orleans stay lengthened, her vulnerability became no longer just a costume but reached her very core. The fact is, Redney was falling in love with the fascinating Joaquin, and not at all relishing the new emotions spilling over the black-iron work of her strong will and self-control.

It began on the January day when Joaquin invited her to breakfast at Cable's house. She wrote a lilting, lyrical account of this event for the *London Advertiser* and it was still glowing in her mind in November of 1886, when she described it again for the Toronto *Week*. The house, to begin with, was the perfect romantic setting:

> The house is a frame one, painted in olive and red, and surrounded by the wide "gallery" that gives its individuality to the Southern home. It is away up in the "garden district" of New Orleans, where the roses blow all the year round, and the tall glossy-leaved magnolias stand graceful sentinels before every door, and the great brown river rolls sleepily past to the blue Gulf farther south, and over all the sun broods, near and lovingly, every long, fragrant, delicious day. There are orange trees in the garden before the house;

by standing tip-toe on the gallery steps one could just reach the fruit Oenone longed so vainly for. And the garden is everywhere bordered with sweet violets (*Week*, Nov. 4, 1886).

Redney resisted the urge to pluck the golden fruit, and instead knocked on the door:

> The door opened and disclosed the poet of the Sierras in full uniform . . . . Joaquin stood before me in characteristic attire. His blue eyes were as eloquent as usual, and his brown hair fell to his coat collar in the accustomed halo. He beckoned and I followed on — on to a pleasant little breakfast room, where sat three ladies in the act of discussing an omelet (*London Advertiser*, April 17, 1885).

"He beckoned and I followed on", for Joaquin was leading Redney, as she knew he would, into that world where she had longed to be: the world of the rich, the talented, the famous. She was introduced by Joaquin to a woman with reddish brown hair, wearing a grey travelling suit trimmed with fur. This was Ella Wheeler Wilcox, the famous poet, author of *Poems of Passion*, "the girl of 25 who long ago built a home for her mother with no tool but her pen", as Redney admiringly put it (*London Advertiser*, April 17, 1885). Redney noted her "strong passionate face that is often but not always beautiful", her quick colour, her girlish ways. She had been married for only ten months and spoke glowingly and at some length of Mr Wilcox's angelic virtues. One of the three women was a nonentity, whom Redney described as "one of those people who applaud and fill up empty chairs . . . and go about the world seeking autographs" (God deliver *her* from such a fate!) The third member of the trio was the notorious Mrs Frank Leslie, widow of the publisher and now sole owner of the Leslie empire of magazines. She was tall and dark with "aquiline features, thin lips, rather prominent dark eyes" (*London Advertiser*, April 17, 1885). She had been the first to publish Ella's poetry. Here indeed were two women whose Secret Purpose had propelled them to the golden fields where Redney wanted to be. Redney had had certain role models to emulate in her Brantford years: strong career women like Dr Emily Stowe and Alice D'Acres Hart but here, for the first time, she saw two mirror images of her ideal self: two women who had earned their own fame and fortune by their pen. Mrs Wilcox was a little too soft, too clingingly dependent on her husband for Redney's taste, but Miriam Leslie, sophisticated, witty, forceful, made an indelible impression.

Miriam Leslie's motto was "tout ou rien", and she always attained her goals, whether in love or in business. Redney notes that "her face had a history in it". It did indeed. She had been born out of wedlock in New Orleans to Creole parents. (The first thing Joaquin had done upon arrival was to visit her birthplace.) At the age of eighteen, she had married a New York jeweller named Peacock, but soon divorced him to marry Ephraim Squier, a writer on archeological subjects who had been hired as editor by Frank Leslie. Miriam began to write for Leslie's twelve magazines, and became the first woman magazine editor in America—proud editor of an illustrated ladies' journal. Leslie fell in love with her, then came to live with her and Squier. When she and Leslie decided that they would be even happier in a *ménage a deux*, Miriam took her husband to a high-class brothel, got affidavits from the five whores who had entertained him, and filed for divorce on the grounds that he was unfaithful. Then she and Frank Leslie married and took off for Europe. She had met Joaquin in Rome in 1873. He probably got himself introduced to the Leslies to further his writing career; he had ingratiated himself so completely with Miriam that this naughty Victorian lady promptly took him to bed. The fact that she was then on her honeymoon didn't deter her one whit. "Tout ou rien" usually meant "tout". It was a liaison which lasted thirty years, and was probably for Joaquin the greatest passion of his life.

Joaquin chronicled the Rome affair with Miriam in his novel *The One Fair Woman* where the "Lady in Pink" is Miriam Leslie. When someone asked why he and Miriam had never married, he replied, "I was single when she was married, and vice versa".[9] When they met in New Orleans in '84, Miriam was between husbands, but Joaquin, though no longer living with her, was still married to Abbie Leland, an

heiress whose father owned a chain of hotels. Joaquin
dedicated his newest book, *Memorie and Rhyme* (1884) to Mrs
Leslie, a collection of autobiographical writings containing a
poem entitled "Miriam" which warbles:

> God's hand is lifting from the seas
> Some Isle of splendour for my queen.
> Some palm-set land in God's right hand
> With opal sea and ardent sky,
> Where only thou and I may land—
> May land and love for aye and aye.[10]

Still, Miriam Leslie was an old, familiar love for Joaquin.
As they sat in the breakfast room of Cable's house, it was
eleven years since they had first "landed and loved". Miriam
was now forty-eight (she always lied about her age and was
then passing herself off as thirty-three) and here seated
beside her was a slender-waisted Canadian miss of twenty-
three whose blue eyes were full of adulation and who was
also very bright, very witty, wearing her new flirtatiousness
like a rose in her hair. Redney noted Miriam's "striking
conversational talent" (*London Advertiser*, April 17, 1885), as
she rattled on about "her 400 employees and her utter
abomination of housekeeping", but there was an acid note in
Redney's comment that her little dog "barks madly at its
mistress' witticisms." It is also interesting that Redney tells
her readers Miriam is about to marry the Marquis de
Neuville. Is this wishful thinking on Redney's part—a way
of dismissing her rival for Joaquin's affections? Miriam
didn't marry the Marquis—in fact she stayed unattached
until 1891, and then took, as fourth and final husband, Oscar
Wilde's brother Willie, who drank too much and wrote
pornography and was young enough to be her son.

As she sat in the sunny breakfast room, Redney looked
and listened, head poised, thanked Mrs Leslie sweetly for
helping her to cold ham, drank the strong New Orleans
coffee, and got in more than a few pert sallies. After they had
finished eating, the others took Redney to meet George
Cable's mother, living in a nearby cottage embowered in
wisteria and sweet olive. Redney found her to be a prim
little New England lady whose "very well-exercised con-

science" didn't fit in with "the dreamy, sensuous life of New Orleans". Well-exercised consciences often got in the way — would that one could leave them up north, along with one's snow boots. Redney's last gesture, as she reluctantly said good-bye to the fascinating Joaquin, was to pluck a dark-leaved olive spray, a romantic souvenir of this memorable day, to bring "sweetly into future days the perfume of a pleasant memory" (*London Advertiser*, April 17, 1885).

Redney was by now very much in love. She sat in the audience at Wetlein Hall on January 13 when Miller, in full evening dress, looking more conventional but as handsome as ever, came to the aid of his friend Julia Ward Howe, struggling to keep the Women's Department of the Exposition going on insufficient funds. He had helped raise $600 by reading his poem "The Fortunate Isles" to wild applause:

> You sail and you seek for the Fortunate Isles,
> The old Greek Isles of the yellow bird's song?
> Then steer straight on through the watery miles,
> Straight on, straight on, and you can't go wrong.
> Nay not to the left, nay not to the right,
> But on, straight on, and the Isles are in sight,
> The old Greek Isles where yellow birds sing
> And life lies girt with a golden ring.[11]

Redney listened to his rich voice, so full of feeling, and was deeply stirred, for Joaquin "recited magnificently, and it was a real pleasure to hear him".[12] The Fortunate Isles — she had been steering straight towards them all her young life, and suddenly they seemed very close.

After meeting Joaquin, a new note of exhilaration crept into her journalism. In Redney's account of attending the California exhibit with him, one can feel the golden euphoria which comes to those young and in love:

> Joaquin Miller took me to California the other day — a limited journey by street car — and I am devoured with a desire to tell somebody about it. He went in his boots and his velvet waistcoat and a sweeping vesture of Western make, which might be denominated an over-coat. His long brown locks were given to the wind, as usual, and were surmounted by a soft, felt hat with a brim which suggested unutterable

things. "One of God's days", he said, as we stepped out into the
sunlight, and it was, God's and Louisiana's. A day at whose
shining robe we would catch if we could with a vain prayer
for her tarrying. Overhead the draped graciousness of infinite blue, all around reaches and vistas of riotous green,
along the car-track white water glistening through ruby
meadows, and everywhere the tender breath of garden violets
(*Memphis Daily Appeal*, Jan. 20. 1885).

At the Exhibit there was a giant redwood slab large enough
for thirty-two people to waltz on; there were jars of honey
"gold and amber and lucent", of candied figs and pomegranates, of wine in pyramids, and a persimmon, which
Joaquin presented to Redney, and which "tasted like ambro-
sia". There was also a huge display of nuts:

> They don't "pick" nuts in California—they shovel them up. If
> you don't believe me ask the Western poet. He is responsible
> for any seemingly erratic statement that finds its way into
> these columns today (*Memphis Daily Appeal*, Jan. 20, 1885).

Redney was certainly in love—but then it was a rare
woman who didn't fall in love with Joaquin Miller. He was,
physically, an incredibly attractive man. What Redney calls
his "eloquent" eyes looked at one intensely from under
bushy eyebrows. They could be blue as violets with deep
feeling, or blue-gray as the sea with dreamy introspection.
Ina Coolbrith once called Miller "the most vibrant man she
had ever known",[13] and he was: vibrant, and magnetic, with
a virile strength as leonine as his tawny hair and beard. At
the same time, with women, he was always gentle, tender,
worshipping. With his long hair and ready tears, he was
quite as androgynous as Redney herself, and she felt drawn
to him because of this.

He was never entirely at ease in the company of men,
being perceptive enough to detect a note of skepticism
towards his posing. "With women alone was he entirely
serene, and then he blossomed out in his entire and very
picturesque individuality".[14] He was fascinating company,
wanting above all to please: "He was truly a pleasure-maker,
and to the extent of his fabulous inventions there was no
apparent end."[15] Perhaps he wooed Redney with his most

romantic gesture for a beloved: sprinkling roses in her path. In *One Fair Woman*, the hero declares his love by telling the heroine he will scatter "roses in her path of life now, even to the end".[16] This metaphoric gallantry Joaquin had first enacted in fact for Lily Langtry, at a London evening party:

> I [Lily] walked upstairs to greet my hostess [Lady Brassey] and he backed before me, scattering rose leaves, which he had concealed in his broad sombrero, upon the white marble steps, and saying with fervor, "Thus be your path in life!"[17]

Joaquin gave a repeat performance for Ellen Terry, years later, when she came to visit him in California.

Apart from their love of roses, Redney and Joaquin were soul-mates in other ways, and she felt the seductive intertwining of their similarities. They both had the Romantic's love of beauty, for, like Redney, Joaquin had an aesthetic eye. He wrote in 1884:

> This love of the beautiful, another name for poetry—this worship of the beautiful, is the best that is in us. Study it every day, when you walk, when you ride, when you rest by the roadside—the flight of a bird, gracefully drooping, curving through the air; the shape and tint of a single autumn leaf; the sweet curved moon in the heavens.[18]

Redney at twenty-three also shared with Joaquin the Romantic's belief in the goodness of man. Miller's philosophy of life was a simple one, the inheritance of his Quaker father's view of the God-in-man. "The main thing", Miller wrote

> is to teach and to prove that all men are good or trying to be good; and that all the world and all things in it are beautiful or trying to be beautiful.[19]

"The world is one great poem", Joaquin wrote in the year he met Redney, "because it is very grand, very good, and very beautiful".[20]

Joaquin and Redney also shared the "romantic readiness" which propelled them forward towards the Fortunate Isles. Joaquin followed the same quest for more colour and magic in life which had brought Redney to New Orleans. "My aspiration is and ever has been, in my dim and uncertain way, to be a sort of Columbus — or Cortez", Miller wrote.[21] Redney, however, as it turned out, would only follow him so far.

For a while, under Joaquin's influence, the realist in Redney was submerged beneath the romantic; she saw all of New Orleans through rose-coloured glasses. There was a seamy side to the city, but Redney was too in love with herself, with this particular setting, with her Poet, with life itself, to notice, or record it. Another writer who was later to become a friend, Charles Dudley Warner, protests that "nothing could be more shabby than the streets, ill-paved, with undulating sidewalks and open gutters green with slime, and both stealing and giving odor".[22] Even Joaquin had a jaundiced view of the French market: "This famous place is dirty . . . . positively nasty. Dirty water flowing all about, dirty people hustling, shouting out their wares, and a smell that rises to heaven" (*Washington Post*, Oct. 27, 1884).

When Redney visited the French market, however, it was all enchanting. She went very early one Sunday morning with a female friend, meeting "in the misty greyness of 6" and taking the one-mule street car. En route she caught a glimpse which, like Brantford's distant woods, suggested a yet wider world:

> We saw, far down, the noble lines of many tall masts and sails reefed in a tender radiance. Ah! the street distances of the Crescent City! Where else, I pray, can you look away and afar to the very brim o' the world, and find ships in port there to take you to another? (*London Advertiser*, March 5, 1885).

At the market there were no bad smells, only fish scales flashing in the gaslight, the strains of many hand organs, and, of course, flower stalls of camellias, jasmine, magnolias, "the poetry of the place" (*London Advertiser*, March 5, 1885).

If Redney was feeling all the golden euphoria of first love, Joaquin was also in love with her; in love, to be sure, for perhaps the hundredth time. Redney reminded him of his first love, Minnie Myrtle, with the same tall, brunette beauty, the same superior talent. "When we first met", he had written of Minnie Myrtle. "she was the better writer".[23]

Certainly Redney's New Orleans journalism is better than Joaquin's, and perhaps he knew it. He liked bright, independent women, like Miriam Leslie and Ina Coolbrith — strong women who knew where they were going. Redney was at her most attractive in New Orleans. As a friend of Redney's once wrote: "the world wore magic colours to her". When she was on an upswing, she had "the power to turn a dull world gay".[24] In this, she and Miller were kindred spirits; he, too, had the ability to gild each moment. "Whether or not he is to be ranked among the very great", wrote his friend George Sterling, "what a success he made of mere living!"[25] When he and Redney met, Miller was nearing fifty, conscious of that spreading bulge under his red sash, of his need for whiskey in the afternoons. He needed a fresh spark, a little hero-worship, someone to gaze at him with "the soft, wide eyes of wonderment, / That trusting, looked you through and through; / The sweet arched mouth, a bow new bent, / That sent love's arrows swift and true".[26]

Joaquin had spent his life in quest of the Ideal, his archetype being the One Fair Woman. There were, to be sure, as many fair women as leaves on the trees, all of them worth pursuing. "What is love?" Joaquin had asked:

> Count the leaves on the trees and count the kinds of trees there are, and mark their changes, their color, their kind: define each well — the development, the decay, the beauty, the glory of their full flower, the pathos of their decline, the pity of the strewn leaves that once lorded and laughed high in the sun — such is love, my innocent boy, my old and cynical sinner, such is love. And the man who says he can hold love or bind him in thongs or lay down law that love will obey and so live with him, is a very young man.[27]

Joaquin was an outspoken exponent of "free love" — daring in his day. ("Doth priest know aught / Of sign, or holy unction brought / From over seas, that ever can / Make man love maid or maid love man?" asks Joaquin.[28]) Wherever it blossomed in life's path, in or out of marriage, love was pure and sacred, to be plucked and enjoyed:

> Come, listen O Love to the voice of the dove,
> Come, hearken and hear him say,

"There are many To-morrows, my Love my Love,
There is only one Today".[29]

Today Miss Sara Duncan was the maid in his path, and she was pretty, pert, and a damn fine journalist.

The climax of his campaign came sometime in the last half of January when Redney accompanied the Poet and others to Florida. Like the breakfast at Cable's house, she describes it twice over in her journalism, once at the time, and again, almost two years later, for the Toronto *Week*, when she was still able to recall every sensuous detail.

She had been lunching on sandwiches, wine and oranges filched from the exhibit in the Florida section of the Government Building, with Joaquin, Miriam Leslie and some others, when Joaquin suddenly said, "Let us go to Florida", and his Bohemian friends enthusiastically agreed. Joaquin wanted to visit the original Ponce de Leon Fountain of Eternal Youth, located near Pensacola. Redney at first hesitated: it would be a most unconventional group, but she knew what marvellous copy it would make for her columns, and she wanted more time with the charming Joaquin. By 8:30 that evening, Redney found herself seated on the train, bound for Florida. The other members of the party, in addition to Miriam (whom Redney calls "Diana" in her accounts) included a young painter and his wife (nicknamed by Redney "Prof. Ochre and Rose Madder"), a young New Orleans journalist ("Theophilus"), with a charming smile, nascent moustache, crushable light felt hat, "and an air of perfumed cynicism". Joaquin, the leader of the little group, exactly old enough to feel the need of a Fountain of Youth, was, of course, "Ponce de Leon" himself. Having forgotten to reserve berths, the six of them sat up all night on the train while the painter deplored the lack of the ideal in French art, and Joaquin put his cowboy boots on the opposite seat, and dozed. At Pensacola, in the clear dawn air, they changed trains, while Redney's tired eyes—she was too excited to sleep—looked out first on the shimmering waters of Pensacola Bay, then on the steamy disorder of thick, jungly growth. At ten o'clock, they arrived at Lake de Funiak, on "the balmiest January morning of my experience". For the

moment, but only for the moment, Redney was floating
through a dream. The lake was "just one mile round, of
sweet, clear water, and sparkles up at the sky like a dropped
sapphire" (*Week*, Dec. 16, 1886). After sleeping in the hotel
for most of the day, the six of them met for fried chicken and
a bonfire under the stars. There was wine and much laughter, witty talk of books and art. Zion Sunday School picnics
were never like this. For the first time in her life, Redney
was among bright, creative people, her kind, who were not
afraid to be individual, even a little odd. But Redney felt a
certain ambivalence towards her new friends; in matters of
social propriety and sexual mores she was still, and would
always be, conventional. She still felt, even in the soft
Southern air, the cold grip of her Brantford Presbyterian
upbringing. She knew exactly what her mother's reaction
would be to a daughter's sitting up all night on the train in
mixed company, travelling in a party whose two "chaper-
ones" were a lady twice-divorced travelling with a man not
her husband, once-divorced and now married. Redney was
therefore defensive about her new Bohemian friends:

> Bohemia is becoming uninhabitable on account of tramps. To
> confess one's nationality is to label one's self a fiend with a
> soiled collar, a facility in borrowing, and a "little thing I
> dashed off before breakfast". Nevertheless, I do boldly pro-
> claim that we, Diana, Ponce de Leon, Prof. Ochre, Rose
> Madder, Theophilus and I, all came originally from that
> much invaded land, where, contrary to all tradition, I beg to
> state that they do occasionally use finger-bowls (*Washington
> Post*, Feb. 1, 1885).

Redney was careful not to report her Florida trip for the
Globe or the *London Advertiser*, but only for the *Washington
Post* and the *New Orleans Times-Democrat*. She was understandably upset—and her parents even more so—when the
Brantford *Expositor* copied it all out from the *Times-Democrat*
for home-town readers.[30] She trusted, without much conviction, that the reference to finger bowls was extenuation
enough.

Next morning, she was tested in the very heart of the fiery furnace when she made the pilgrimage, on horseback, to the Fountain of Youth. It began lyrically enough:

> Did you ever ride nine miles through the pine woods on a mustang pony? Then you haven't exhausted life though you may be twenty-two and blasé exceedingly. Over the soft brown carpet, under the exquisite light green mantle that has surely fallen some tropical night like snow upon the trees, stumbling, cantering, galloping, we followed our gallant knight (*Washington Post*, Feb. 1, 1885).

Redney never felt more sensitively alive to her surroundings:

> We rode mile after mile over the softly rising and falling country under the giant pines, the horses' hoofs falling almost noiselessly on the dry needles, the soft Floridian air veritably caressing us . . . . All the never-ending pine-tree vistas glowed with a strange green fire of new foliage, and the south winds brought us the balm of their resinous breath (*Week*, Dec. 16, 1886).

Redney felt the strange green fire spreading within her, feared it, and, for the moment, chose to ignore it as she pushed on to the cooling waters of the pool. The pines thickened, the underbrush clutched, the resinous scents quickened. No room now for horses, they were walking in single file, Joaquin leading, Redney close behind, the others bringing up the rear. "Denser thicket and suspense" . . . then finally the pool itself, the beautiful silver pool, the Fountain of Eternal Youth, worth the long quest. Redney looked down into the pool, thirty feet down. She could see with incredible clarity, right to the very bottom, every waving green frond, every pebble. She could also see her own reflection. The others chattered and splashed, but she was oblivious, transfixed, staring down as real self rippled into ideal: one clear, concentric image. This was the climax of her Brantford years of striving; she had been heading towards this clear reflection, this shining epiphany, ever since she made up her mind to be a writer and began her steady progress towards riches and renown. She stood poised now on the very lip. Mirrored in the pool's centre was her clear-cut self: Sara

Duncan, brilliant new journalist-star in the American sky, with bolder, bigger stars in a golden ring around her.

Joaquin dipped a cup into the crystal depths of the pool, and handed it to her. It was filled to the brim and she drank it thirstily. She felt confident of reaching all her goals, perceived, with great clarity of vision, a luminous line round every leaf, sharp and unequivocal. Everything clear, everything coalescing. It was a moment she would remember all her life. She would also remember the pony-ride back from the pool. Somehow the others got far ahead, until only she and Joaquin were left, riding side by side, Redney still feeling within her the serene silver pool, round as a mirror, of her new confidence and clarity. Suddenly Joaquin, "her gallant knight", swung out of the saddle, helped her to dismount, urged her towards the strange green fire of the pinewoods, holding her close, speaking soft love-words to this "one fair woman". Redney, however, stood rooted. She would go no further. She was tactful and conciliatory, but unyielding. She remounted, and spurred her pony towards the others, leaving Joaquin behind, reins slack in his hand. Redney and Joaquin may both have been Romantics, but it is here that they part company, that a basic difference becomes apparent. Joaquin was truly sensual—for him it was always an easy, and inevitable progression from white "magnolia's blooms" to the "white bosom" of his current beloved.[31] Redney's sensuality, on the other hand, was fully satisfied with the visual, not needing the tactile. All her life she feasted on the beauty of colour and line; she stayed with magnolia blossoms, admiring them with cool composure. Then, too, there were her Presbyterian scruples to contend with, the cold self-denying Calvinism of Bailie Henry Duncan. She was sexually attractive to men because of the energy and sparkle in her blue-grey eyes, because of the taut grace of her figure, but she was always to use her appeal not to satisfy her sexual longings (for those she would develop certain sublimations), but to satisfy her ideal ones of getting ever closer to her current goal, whatever it might be. She relished Joaquin as mentor, rejected him emphatically as lover.

Only for a moment, as she galloped to catch up with the others, did Redney feel a pang. In retrospect it would grow, and haunt her. What if she had gone with Joaquin? If she had done so, would her life have been different ... and her art? A much older Redney faced the fact that her writing lacked sensual resonance, lacked that rich, deep note of experience "felt in the blood". Perhaps Redney sighed once, deeply, as she galloped back through the thinning pine-woods, conscious that their new foliage was, after all, not so much a strange green fire as a mantle "that has surely fallen some tropical night like snow", snow clinging and heavy as the white counterpane on the spruce trees of Zion Church. She had chosen snow, not fire, and her choice would prove irrevocable. It was a newly sober Redney and a slightly sardonic Joaquin who, with the others, took the train back to New Orleans.

Joaquin had written his final New Orleans article on the Exposition at the beginning of January ("Down the Great River and Good-Bye", New Orleans *Times-Democrat*, Jan. 4). When he had been interviewed at the Cable home on January 18th, he stated that he would soon be returning to his home in Washington (*Times-Democrat*, Jan. 18, 1885), but that had been before the Florida adventure. He was linger-ing now because he still hoped to pluck this newest perennial in his path, this stubborn survivor of the snowy Canadian winter. He was still there for the Mardi Gras which began on Monday, February 16th, and lasted a week, a "gay mad week" with "all the romance which lies behind a mask".[33] If the romance was mostly Joaquin's, the mask was Redney's, firmly in place. She was still playing Magnolia Blossom in public, soft and seductive as ever, but steel underneath. She had got what she most wanted from Joaquin: one foot firmly in the door of the *Washington Post*, Joaquin's home paper, for which he wrote a regular column and for which Redney had written one superb one while in New Orleans. She was well on her way.

Redney captured all the carnival merriment in a long column written February 21st (*Brantford Expositor*, March 2 and 3, 1885), describing how, on the first day, the Carnival King, with Proteus and attendant Dukes, resplendent in

purple and gold, had progressed regally to the Music Hall
where "in truly eloquent style, the poet laureate, Joaquin
Miller", welcomed them to the Exposition, and Redney
watched from the audience, one of a chosen few lucky
enough to get seats because, as she puts it, of "your correspondent's acquaintance with a Duke or two". That evening
a three-hour parade, which Redney enjoyed from the balcony
of the *Times-Democrat* building, made its way to the French
Opera House for the opening ball. Brantford parades of
Burford cavalry and decorated hook-and-ladder cart had
never been like this. There were eighteen floats, tableau
after tableau, "the magnificence of the floats can simply not
be imagined by any one to whom carnival glories are as yet
only dreamed of". The ball at the Opera House, for which
Joaquin exchanged his cowboy boots for dancing pumps,
continues the false note of make-believe:

> Never did the lights flash over a madder, merrier scene—
> Nine-headed monsters of frightful mien glided over the floor
> with exquisite creatures in creamy trains; ice clad demons
> waltzed with fair young debutantes in rosy pink.... Every-
> body danced, and the floor shook with the revelry (*Brantford
> Expositor*, March 3, 1885).

"It is several days over", writes a tired Redney on February
21st. "The splendid flower of the Carnival has burst into its
yearly radiance and faded into lenten grays".

After the Mardi Gras, Joaquin returned to Washington,
and Redney felt deeper regrets. Joaquin's effect on her was
profound, and permanent. He had given Redney pragmatic
help in breaking into American journalism, much encouragement, and some share of his own golden optimism.
Miller's trust and generosity showed in his life-long habit of
planting trees that would never grow tall in his lifetime,
trees for future generations to enjoy. It was while he was in
New Orleans, as he tells it, that

> I picked up a Western magazine with a picture of the house
> which I built and the trees which I planted in Canyon City,
> Grant County, Oregon, when judge there.... The world is
> not greatly in need of more poetry, but it is greatly in need of
> more fruit, more flowers, and more beautiful gardens.[34]

To plant a garden, for Sara Duncan, as for Joaquin Miller, would always be an act of faith. Miller was always to stand, in Redney's creative imagination, for romantic readiness and generosity. ("As great-hearted a man as ever lived", testified a friend[35]). He helped her grow. There was one further gift. Joaquin nurtured Redney's ego with love, approval and gallant attentions. At this point, Redney began to feel as one of her later novel heroines would:

> My egotism is like a little flame within me. All the best things feed it, and it is so clear that I see everything in its light. To me it is most dear and valuable — it simplifies things so . . . . It isn't a source of gratification; it's a channel. And it intensifies everything so that I don't care how little comes that way. If there's anything of me left when I die, it will be that fierce little flame. And when I do the tiniest thing — write the shortest sentence that rings *true*, see a beauty or a joy which the common herd pass by, I have my whole life in the flame and it becomes my soul. I'm sure I have no other! (*A Daughter of Today*, pp. 126-7).

Joaquin had fanned the flame higher until Redney could see it clearly reflected in the still waters of the Florida pool, and again and again, as the years flowed past, in her writing.

Joaquin departed; February turned into March; the wider world beckoned to the restless Redney and she sailed away on one of those tall-masted ships which she had glimpsed in the harbour. She had been invited by the governor, a ruddy-faced Englishman called Goldsworthy, to visit British Honduras, a sleepy British colony ruled by a few whites, mostly Scots, with a thriving trade in mahogany and logwood, and a nascent one in sugar cane, bananas and tobacco. Goldsworthy had been one of the official guests at the opening of the Exposition. Redney may have met him then, or when she paid her visit to the British Honduras Exhibit in mid-January. Whichever it was, her charming personality opened yet another door, and she accepted the Governor's invitation with alacrity. She would be in the company of other journalists. There would be more useful contacts, more scintillating copy for her columns. She packed her bag, ready for a new adventure, and sailed on the

"Wanderer", appropriately named for the first of Sara Duncan's many sea voyages. It was her first taste of life aboard ship and Redney was content:

> For absolute poetry of inertia take a deck chair in the stern of one of those lazily gliding steamers and watch the gulls hover expectantly over, their broad wings flushed with the rosy reflection of the water . . . . It is simple happiness, perfect and without alloy (*London Advertiser*, April 9, 1885).

She had time now to sift and sort her New Orleans memories, to close her eyes and reflect on all that rush of new experiences. The "Wanderer" drifted on, past the low-lying coast of Yucatan, past the green island of Cozumel, and finally arrived at Belize, the capital of British Honduras, a neat cluster of cocoanut palms and white houses. Redney stayed at the International Hotel, with "unassuming exterior" but fine, broad verandahs inviting cool indolence. As soon as she had unpacked, Redney took a stroll about the town, getting her first taste of life in a torrid British colony, noting the disturbing dissonance between British society, so rigid and formal, and the wanton lushness of setting. There were tangled purple creepers everywhere, yellow jasmine flaming out of control over every fence. A little apart, at one end of town, with a clipped green expanse for cricket, stood the barracks of the British officers and men of the West Indian detachment—splendid creatures in red jackets, who reminded Redney of the Royal Fusiliers forming and reforming so many years before in Brantford's market square. At the other end of town was Governor Goldsworthy's mansion, a large white house with impressive gardens; squeezed between barracks and mansion were the natives and their hovels.

The highlight of Redney's stay in Belize was a trip up the Sittee river in that "perfect poem of a boat" (*Globe*, Jan. 20, 1885), which she had loved on sight at the Exposition exhibit, a pit-pan, a dug-out forty feet long and three feet wide. (Many months after the event, she wrote an account of it for the Toronto *Week* of October 1, 1885.) The trip up the Sittee was for Redney pleasant in its green caress, but lacked the emotional intensity of Florida's Fountain of Youth:

The sun shone and the tall tree-ferns waved, and brilliant
birds with strange cries flashed among the green. The water
was crystalline purity itself, sparkling and dashing over
moss-covered stones, here in pale shadows, there in dark,
mysterious pools, but always green and cool and enticing
(*Week*, Oct. 1, 1885).

"Flashed among the green . . . green and cool and enticing",
at this point in Redney's life, the jungle was as bounteous in
its green blessing as her own shoots of creativity. No snakes
among the jungle ropes; not yet.

Redney wrote glowing letters home about this latest
lark, and it was probably her doting father who passed one
on to the *Brantford Expositor*, whose headline on March 20
read: OUR OWN SARA DUNCAN HOBNOBBING WITH
THE GOVERNOR OF BRITISH HONDURAS:

Very few writers have started out upon the literary sea,
encountering less breakers than has Miss Sara Duncan of this
city. Leaving here early last winter in sufficient time to be
present at the opening of the great Cotton Exposition of New
Orleans, she little dreamed of the good fortune awaiting her
and of the smiles that would be bestowed upon her by even
vice-royalty itself. A letter in the *Times-Democrat*, the leading
journal of the South attracted the attention of the literati
gathered at the great Fair and "Garth" immediately became
the favorite of Joaquin Miller, the poet of the Sierras, who
arranged excursions into Florida and did many things for the
diversion of the fair young litterateur, which attested the
interest and pride he felt in her. She has travelled considerably
about the South and has everywhere met with distinguished
treatment at the hands of distinguished people; and she is
now in Belize, the guest of the Governor of British Honduras.
An extract from a private letter written on the 12th inst. says:
"The Governor won't hear of my leaving till the next boat,
the *City of Dallas*, which will take me back to New Orleans
about the 28th or 29th . . . . The dear old fellow has gotten up
two expeditions for me, one to the Caves of Manitee tomorrow, and the other to the Sittee river next week. About
sixteen are going. I have been three times riding on horseback, and for a diversion go gardening with the Governor,
who gives me a basket of the loveliest flowers every morning.
His wife, too, treats me like her own daughter".

Her letters are read with exceeding avidity by the people of the south who have been charmed by the graphic pen picturings of themselves which lack the northern colorings many writers delight to give. With such a bright opening to a young life, what may its future be! May "Garth", glory and fortune be synonomous (*Brantford Expositor*, March 20, 1885).

Already trailing clouds of "glory and fortune" in modest amounts, Sara Duncan arrived back in Brantford on Saturday, April 4th, four months to the day since her departure.[36] She returned greatly enriched from her stay in the city "where the roses blow all the year round". She had reached out eagerly, gathered in new experiences, new friends, new contacts in the field of journalism, new writing skills, new self-assurance. By her own account, she had written about the South "with great acceptance" and "earned her whole expenses".[37] Redney was proud of herself; New Orleans had inspired her, as Quebec had; an exotic setting was the key.

3

Washington, Toronto, Montreal, Ottawa

"A Shining Mark"

It seems to me that one of the most charming characteristics of Miss Cleveland's literary style is its emphasis. She is delightfully emphatic. There is no parley, no consideration of half truths. She forms her conviction, and with swift, sure strokes nails it up, fearlessly, a shining mark.

Sara Jeannette Duncan,
"Woman's World", Toronto *Globe*.

When Redney returned to Brantford at the beginning of April, 1885, flushed with her Southern triumphs, she found the fields still brown, tatters of grey snow still in every shadowed hollow. A chill also hung over her West Street home, for her brother Henry, age twenty-two, was very ill and not expected to live. Her mother's small shoulders drooped, and her step had lost its spring. Dr Cochrane came often to the house and offered up prayers in Zion's Sunday service, his grey eyes compassionate, without their usual twinkle. Just as the first green shoots were showing, on May 9th, Henry died of an "affection of the stomach. He was sent to the other side for treatment, but all efforts were without avail" (Brantford *Courier*, May 9, 1885). Redney suffered

acutely through the ordeal of the funeral, on Monday, May
11th, and Henry's burial in Greenwood cemetery. Her little
sister Bessie Beatrice, who had died on March 1, 1881, aged
three years and one month, was already buried there. A
temporary grey cloud settled round Redney as she felt the
grief of the second family death, the inevitable let-down
after her New Orleans ecstasy, the small steel hoop of
hometown sameness and staleness, her Brantford acquaintances self-engrossed as ever with sectarian and party rivalries.
A bleak little poem in *Week* (Dec. 8, 1887) may have been
written at this time:

> "On the very threshold of life", they cry,
> The door is shut! Poor Soul! Poor Soul!"
> And the mourners in the streets go by,
> And the air is full of a grievous dole.
> And yet for meadow and upland sweet
> Full of the fragrance of deathless bloom,
> Who would not gladly turn his feet
> From the threshold of an empty room.

If life had become, suddenly, an empty room with dusty
corners, Redney was soon busy decorating it with fresh-
blooming plans. She sailed into the Toronto *Globe* office in
mid-May, asked John Cameron, on the strength of her fine
New Orleans copy, to let her write a weekly column, and he
agreed. She would, however, have to be content to write it at
home and send it in—Cameron was adamant on that score:
no woman working in the office. Redney readily agreed; her
secret plan was to use the *Globe* assignments as stepping-
stones to take her south of the border again. Her first *Globe*
column appeared on May 23, 1885, with the newly expanded
signature "Garth Grafton", one she would keep for several
years. Her choice of "Grafton" may have been a further
expression of her "masculine" attributes, for Grafton's was a
well-known men's clothing store in Dundas, a town not far
from Brantford. This initial column describes a Toronto art
show. "Last week", writes Redney with her usual spright-
liness, "I arose and summoned up my adjectives and made a
pilgrimage to see the pictures". Thus began a weekly series,
published every Wednesday, which, from its fourth appearance, was called "Other People and I".

Almost at once, Redney started sending her columns down to her American contacts. Her June 10 column appeared four days later in the *Memphis Daily Appeal*, and her *Globe* column of June 24th, on July 2nd. This latter one she also mailed off to her main target, the Washington *Post*, and to Redney's great delight they printed it on June 28th as a letter to "The Editor of the *Post*, from 'Garth Grafton, Brantford, Ont. Canada' ". It is headed: "On Man's Advice to Women. A Most Intelligent Protest against Officious Interference", and attacks male journalists for perpetually criticizing the female sex in print. "Editors with a missionary spirit", purrs Redney, claws sheathed, "should give our brothers and husbands and fathers a share" of this criticism; "we don't want to monopolize it", being not yet convinced of "absolute male perfection". The *Post* editor obviously liked her wit and tinder, for he printed all but one of Redney's subsequent *Globe* columns, up to and including her final one dated September 2nd. She sent one further column to the *Post*, dated "Sept. 11th, Brantford".[1] No more appeared after that date, because Redney had been hired by the prestigious Washington *Post*, famous from coast to coast, as an editorial writer. Everything she had seen so clearly reflected in Florida's silver pool was hers at last! With great joy and pride she packed her bag again, after her summer hiatus, and as the maples on West Street flamed and the far woods took a deeper violet, she caught the train for Washington. "Miss Sara Duncan, 'Garth Grafton', left today", reported the *Expositor* on Tuesday, October 13th, "to assume a position upon the staff of the Washington *Post*, the leading society journal of the American capital. The best wishes of her many friends go with her". Redney had learned from Joaquin that writers need to keep their names in the public eye; from now on she always kept the press informed of her movements.

As the train sped south, Redney looked out the window, and remembered how her own special American Dream of fame on a US newspaper had floated with her to New Orleans, just beyond the glass. Now it was almost within her grasp. Once arrived in Washington, Redney, with her usual efficiency, found a suitable boarding-house in the downtown area and settled in. Then, on a crisp October morning, dressing with great care in one of the *tailleurs*—man-tailored jacket, long skirt—which would be her favourite costume for the rest of her life, Redney set off for her first day of work. The *Post* building, trimmed in blue limestone, was an imposing one, five stories tall and boasting an elevator, at the corner of 10th and D streets, just off Pennsylvania Avenue (now the site of the Federal Bureau of Investigation). Three months before, the *Post* had suffered a disastrous fire, which had destroyed records and subscription lists, but the building was now rebuilt, bigger and better than ever, complete with young Alex Bell's invention (the *Post* had number 28 of the first 140 phones hooked up in the city seven years before), and electric lights, installed three years previously.[2]

Just inside the front door, Redney was accosted by a uniformed colored boy: "Beg pardon, ma'am, but de gemmen is all busy. Take your card in, ma'am?" When Redney explained that she had come to work there, he didn't bat an eye. Female staff members were no novelty on the *Post*. Colonel Cockerill, the *Post's* managing editor, had hired the first one, Calista Halsey, back in 1878, and the present editor had made Mrs. Lucy H. Hooper the first female foreign correspondent; she mailed a regular column of social, art and theatre news from Paris.[3]

Redney was ushered into the editor's office, curious to meet this man with whom she had corresponded ever since her New Orleans sojourn. Stilson Hutchins, founder and editor of the *Post*, was a forty-seven-year-old man with splendid shoulders, firm jaw, grayish-blue eyes and a deep bass voice. His handclasp was firm but his eyes, from time to time, had the bleak look of cold seas. Stilson was still mourning the death of his second wife. His first wife had divorced him in 1882 for adultery, after twenty-four years of marriage, and the following year Frances Hodgson Burnett, in between writing chapters of *Little Lord Fauntleroy* in her Washington house at 1219 I street, had introduced him to Sarita Brady. He fell in love with Sarita, married her, built his bride a handsome mansion on Massachusetts Avenue.

But Sarita had died in childbirth thirteen months later, so that Stilson was alone once more, and would remain so until 1890.

Stilson Hutchins was a man of granite resolve and ambition, with a glinting vein of sarcastic humour. He had come to Washington in 1877, resolved to start a daily Democratic paper in the capital, had hired a staff of forty men and boys, worked long hours, and watched the paper grow and prosper. When Redney joined the *Post*, it had a format of four pages, one of which was advertising. Since 1880 it had been published seven days a week, the *Sunday Post* a thick issue with special fiction and sports features. Bret Harte, Robert Louis Stevenson and Joaquin Miller were frequent contributors. For the duration of Stilson's editorship, the Democratic *Post* was violently partisan in its political stance. When Republican President Rutherford Hayes, a prim teetotaler whose wife was known as "Lemonade Lucy", left office, a *Post* editorial thundered: "There should be no spot of ground on the continent to give him harborage or shelter . . . . Exit Hayes, the fraud. Eternal hatred to his memory".[4]

The *Post* was also violently segregationist. An 1879 editorial stated that Negroes "are not fit to mingle in refined society", being "rude and ignorant", with "disagreeable" manners.[5] Stilson Hutchins stamped the *Post* with his personality, and while it was opinionated, it was also witty, attention-getting and well-produced, already making the name for itself which a hundred years have hallowed. Redney had reason to feel proud as Stilson welcomed her to the *Post*. She was not an American; she didn't know Washington; she was not a veteran journalist; she was not yet twenty-four. Yet here she was, hired by one of America's important papers, and Stilson had shown his confidence in her ability by slotting her into editorial work, a notch above mere reporting. Reporters earned about seven dollars a week; as editorial writer, Redney probably earned a little more, but not much more, because, of course, women were paid less than men. Her ego suffered a blow when Stilson said that her contributions would be unsigned; he was firm about that: it was a matter of policy.

Redney threw herself into her challenging new job with dedication and delight. She was put in charge of the "Current Literature" column of book reviews, and, as well, wrote editorials on cultural subjects, and occasional leading articles.[6] Since the type was all hand-set by the printers, Redney and other staff writers scribbled their copy onto yellow flimsy, using a stylus, an agate-pointed pencil, which produced a legible copy. Since the *Post* was a morning paper, the staff were usually in the office until it went to press, around three a.m.

The first few weeks were, by Redney's own account, rather terrifying and traumatic, but her great will to succeed and her energy kept her buoyantly afloat:

> Her editor ... was rather an irascible and gouty person, which did not appear in his correspondence, but was perfectly evident when he found that Margery [Redney] had written, and he had unwittingly published, a rather uncomfortable review of a book by one of his intimate friends. Also when Margery talked about "the great unwashed" in an editorial, and he had to be interviewed by a deputation of the Knights of Labor, and assure them that nothing personal was intended. There were things to do, too, that were not easy; the writing, for instance, of a three-column biographical sketch for next morning's paper of a certain State governor she had never heard of before the evening he inconveniently died, and the reporting of a certain grand kermesse, in which fashionable society was deeply interested, to meet the emergency of going to press several hours before it really happened.
>
> But Margery survived all these things, and her growing experience, with certain virtues in the way she writes when she does write well, have thus far enabled the editor to survive them too. Her present work is chiefly book reviewing, in which the instinctive perception of style that once made her think she could write books herself, serves her well, and editorial writing upon literary, artistic, and social subjects.[7]

Even though the bulk of Redney's work for the *Post* is unsigned, it is an easy matter to recognize her distinctive voice, arch and whimsical, the same one first heard in her Quebec sketches, and perfected in New Orleans.[8] By the time she came to Washington, it was habitual. She gave "herself up to the enthralment of speaking with that voice which she could summon, that elusive voice which she lived only, only, to be the medium for" (*A Daughter of Today*, p. 210). She wrote book reviews of William Dean Howell's *Tuscan Cities*, of Henry James' *The Bostonians*, of Robert Louis Stevenson's *Dr Jekyll and Mr Hyde*, of Tolstoy's *Anna Karenina*, and of such ephemera as *Common Sense in the Nursery*, and *Sculpture for Beginners and Students*. Her editorials plump for a new water-works, criticize the chaotic condition of the National Library, and point out Sir John A. Macdonald's "*faux pas*" in hanging Louis Riel.

Redney was caught up in the general jubilation in the *Post* office on the night of November 4th, a rainy Tuesday, when Grover Cleveland was elected President, the first Democratic one in twenty-four years. A great crowd gathered outside the office where the *Post* had hired a band and arranged for the election results to be flashed on a screen, using calcium light from a stereopticon. Inside, there was much cheering and backslapping among the staff; Stilson was euphoric, his bass voice booming excitedly, and Redney loved being part of it all, having become addicted to political excitement in her Brantford days.

She had a brief respite from her labours in November when she went home to Brantford for the Thanksgiving holiday,[9] and found the town buzzing with the news of the long-awaited completion of the Canadian Pacific Railway to the West coast, the last spike having been driven in by Lord Strathcona on the seventh, and the hanging, nine days later, of Louis Riel.

Washington in the '80's, as Redney initially perceived it, was an exciting, and pleasant place to live and work. Here was the ideological heart of the American Dream — the new Washington monument was less than a year old — and in the clean, crisp air was a spirit of individual initiative and freedom. The last twenty years of the century were America's years of phenomenal economic growth and prosperity. The population increased fifty per cent (partly due to the one million Canadians who emigrated to the States) but the national wealth shot up twice as fast. "We live in a new and

exceptional Age", one of Redney's future friends wrote,
"America is another name for Opportunity".[10] These were
the years when the so-called "robber barons", men like John
D. Rockefeller and Andrew Carnegie, were amassing their
fortunes in oil and steel, with help from government in the
form of land grants and protective tariffs. It was every man
for himself. When a reporter once asked Vanderbilt if he ran
his Pennsylvania Railroad for "the public interest", he
blurted out: "The public be damned!".[11] There was plenty of
greedy opportunism, exploitation, and government corrup-
tion, but there was also, in the '80's, a wonderful exhilaration,
a sense of something new and vital being born. As Mark
Twain says in the book which gave this era its name, *The
Gilded Age*, "There is invitation in the air and success in all
the wide horizon".

In Washington, Redney took a deep breath of "the
sense of gigantic enterprise and 'go' " at the heart of American society. Along with their "acceptance of the facts of life",
she noted that Americans had "a subtle hint of consciousness
of power to mould them" (*Those Delightful Americans*, p. 46).
They were all moving single-mindedly towards the "Very
Most Desirable state of existence.... The clearness and
directness of purpose with which they carry this out can only
be called a miracle of nature; it is arrow-like" (*Cousin Cinderella*, p. 154). Observing all those self-made men and women
in Washington, Stilson Hutchins and so many others, reinforced Redney's Scots-Calvinist side, the inheritance from
her father which had once prompted her to sell the family
cherries and her mother's only pair of comfortable shoes.

Now Redney dropped her assumed cloak of New Orleans
languor, shared the greed for material success which marked
The Gilded Age, sharpened the arrows of her 'enterprise
and 'go' ". She was older now, more confident; she did not
need to hide behind a mask: the real-life Redney, always a
realist in money matters, calculating, ambitious, began to
emerge. Now, the fire of New Orleans' lyricism turns to
gritty, realistic ash. "The New Orleans Exposition is again in
its accustomed attitude of bankruptcy", chides Redney in the
Post (Jan. 9, 1886), listing in detail its defects and misman-
agement fiascos. The Exposition was no golden dream after

all, only a financial disaster. It didn't pay; and, in the final analysis, money counted . . . counted for a great deal in the general scheme of things. Redney was quite aware that the only rose that mattered in Washington was the American Beauty variety which George Bancroft originated in his H street garden, to be sold commercially, down the years, for many thousands of dollars.

As Redney walked the Washington streets that autumn, the hard-hitting sound of hammers was all around her: Washington in the '80's was enjoying a building boom. Mansions were going up on Dupont and Scott circles, and along Connecticut Avenue. The first apartment house had shot up in 1879, an impressive four stories, with rents equally high at fifty dollars a month. Sixty thousand trees, newly planted, lined the streets, newly paved. There were libraries and art galleries, few commercial offices, and no factories. Redney particularly liked the lunch rooms, a unique feature of Washington life. There was one on every block, all of them serving excellent coffee and rolls. The popular one opposite the Treasury served its coffee in pint shaving mugs, with sugar kept in two holy water basins chained to the wall, although the clerks who lounged in its wicker chairs had to bring their own sandwiches.[12]

Redney was surprised to see so many young men on the streets and so few ladies: the bulk of Washingtonians, not counting its 60,000 Negroes crowded into wretched slums, were transient males involved in government who came from all over the country and lived in boarding-houses. There were also, Redney noted with distaste, a complementary number of harlots, who also came from all over the country and whose sleazy satin skirts and highly-rouged cheeks shocked her Presbyterian soul. The few properly brought-up ladies who did find their way to Washington, however, were Redney's kind: there were more literary women in Washington than anywhere else in America, except New York. Redney preferred the company of men, and for most of her life had few close women friends, but she did want to meet Washington's brightest female literary stars. The first of these was small, auburn-haired Frances Hodgson Burnett, who had unwittingly condemned a whole generation of little boys to the indignity of black velvet knee breeches and lace collars. Redney had been an admirer of hers as far back as 1880, when she wrote that "Mrs Burnett is an artist surpassed by few in originality of conception or in effective execution".[13] The second star was America's best-known woman journalist, the homely Abigail Dodge ("Gail Hamilton" in print) who turned out spicy political columns sure to be talked about. Redney felt that she had come to the right place, for in Washington, women journalists were not just tolerated; they were revered.

In the beginning, it was a stimulating environment for Redney; she liked, and profited by, Washington society's polyglot make-up. She was able to sharpen one of her chief skills: her ability to deduce and describe character through social conventions. "There is an *embarras de richesse* for the sociologist" here, she wrote. "From California to Maine, elected on a thousand issues, throng the fair representatives of all classes, with their families, their tricks of dialect, their ways of living, their social ideals" (*Week*, Aug. 12, 1886). Redney was shrewdly observing as she mingled with them, stuffing the pigeon-holes of memory with material for future novels.

In the beginning, thrilled with the novelty of a new job, a new environment, Redney was ready to like everything about Washington. Although she was always to be a social élitist, she even relished the fact that Washington's social stratification wasn't nearly as firmly fixed as Brantford's. Washington in the 80's had a distinct social ease, a democratic *laissez-faire* about it. Shanties stood next to mansions; panhandlers jostled senators on the "herdies" (Peter Herdie's eight-passenger, five-cents-a-ride, horse-drawn cabs with yellow plush seats), and the patrician marble floors of the Capitol, swarming with lobbyists, were always brown with tobacco stains.[14] There was none of Brantford's pious parochialism here. There was room in Washington to cultivate and display one's eccentricities. The brilliant men and women drawn to the Nation's capital were truly individual. "Life, liberty and the pursuit of happiness" meant following one's own bent in dress and behaviour. The women, here as in New York, "had clouds of hair about their faces, and looked epitomes of dramatic possibility" (*Those Delightful Americans*, p. 51). Redney felt, as one of her novel heroines would, that she had escaped "for the time being from what one was expected to do into a wide and wonderful region where one could do exactly as one pleased" (*Ibid.*, p. 41). As she walked to work each day that fall and early winter, with her long, impatient stride, Redney inhaled deeply of the heady air, tingling with a sense of new freedom.

If there was room to expand in Washington, there was time as well. Redney noted with surprise that, in spite of the fact that every day laws and fortunes were being made, no one ever appeared to be in a hurry. "The inhabitants do not rush onward as though they were late for the train or the post", wrote one visitor.[15] There was time for croquet, for archery, for idle afternoons boating on the silvery Potomac. There were pleasant Saturday gatherings on the White House lawns, when the red-coated Marine Band played while ladies' ruffled hems swept the grass and gentlemen leaned forward on gold-topped canes to catch the latest political scandal.

Into the midst of this free-ranging and tolerant social group, Redney slipped easily and eagerly. "The social privileges of Washington", she decided, "are probably the most accessible in the world:

> "Where else", says one of the brightest of Washington's many bright women to me the other day, "could I, single, plain, and comparatively poor, without family advantages, find the best drawingrooms of the city open to me, simply by virtue of such brains as it has pleased a compensating Providence to bestow on me?" Truly nowhere (*Week*, Aug. 12, 1886).

As Henry James noted, Washington was a "city of conversation"; its people, as Redney noted, were of "a high order of intelligence", with "independent opinions" and a wide cultural base, either scientific or literary (*Week*, Aug. 12, 1886). Dinner-table talk was clever and cosmopolitan and Redney's witty sallies were returned in kind. There was one topic, however, on which Washingtonians were quite as ignorant as all other Americans. "In Washington", writes Redney acidly, the stock advance toward making a new acquaintance is an inquiry as to one's original locality. If it is Canada, the response is invariably, "Canada! Oh! Montreal, I presume." After hearing this presumption a few dozen times, the Canadian who is not a citizen of Montreal, begins to resent it. Despairing of imparting the locality of the little city I live in when I am at home, I informed one inquiring Washingtonian last winter that I came from Ontario. "Ontario", he said in a puzzled way, "Is that anywhere near Toronto?" (*Globe*, Oct. 9, 1886).

The fine frenzy of Washington's social season began on New Year's Day and ended with Lent. (Redney had seen the New Year of 1886 in with a working assignment: attending a Negro church service where nine hundred Negroes "howled and shouted and screamed with laughter, and the preacher sat down and fanned himself" (*Week*, Feb. 18, 1886). Redney soon had many invitations stuck round her mirror, although she had not yet received the most coveted ones: those to Henry Adams' breakfast parties in his new house in Lafayette Square, or to William Corcoran's oyster suppers, where every guest had his own pail for shucking. Corcoran was the most flamboyant figure on Washington streets, always gloved, no matter how hot the day, always with a red rose in his buttonhole.[16]

Redney attended as many social functions as her late-night work allowed. She would slip into one of her silk party-dresses, wishing she still had her doting aunt to arrange her back hair. Still, she no longer needed her, as she had in her adolescence, to give her ego a quick shot. Redney now had plenty of confidence; she would enter a drawing-room full of Washingtonians with her cheeks glowing from the crisp air, her head high, pause significantly in the doorway, so that she could be seen, and could take a quick survey of the room, noting the figures of importance whom it might be useful for her to meet. She had little time to waste flirting with the debonair young attachés from Washington's thirty legations who turned up at every party. The parties themselves were as original and diverse as the people. There were crazes for guessing-games, soirées where everyone had to dress in a certain colour, bi-weekly "symposiums" at Stilson Hutchins', often with a choir of Negro singers to entertain the guests. There were dinners, suppers, hops, balls at Willard's Hotel. There were Cabinet members' receptions on Wednesdays and Senators' ones on Thursdays and Saturdays. When Senator Jacksons' wife gave a tea on Saturday, February 27th, Redney circulated her *bon-mots* with the sandwiches and *petits-fours*:

> Mrs. Senator Jackson gave a very handsome and largely attended tea yesterday from four to seven . . . . Miss Thom, Miss More and Miss Duncan were the attractive trio who ministered to all in the dining-room . . . . Miss Duncan [wore] white satin and crystal passamenteries (Washington *Post*, Feb. 28, 1886).

The pace was almost too much for Redney. She sighed with relief as Lent brought a welcome surcease: "The whirl is over. Society has abandoned the rotatory and assumed the devotional . . . to Washington society, as a wearied whole, Ash Wednesday will come like a benediction" (Washington *Post*, March 10, 1886).

All this active socializing, however, was secondary. Redney's work came first. In February, she had attended and reported on Congress' International Copyright hearings, had craned her neck for a better view of Samuel Clemens (Mark Twain), dapper in black-and-white tweed, who had pleaded eloquently for copyright law on books:

> His figure resembles a small rectangular cruet, his hair and complexion decidedly remind me of the condiments afore-said; indeed, if Mr. Whistler will pardon me, I should like to label Mr. Clemens in my memory a symphony in pepper and salt (*Week*, Feb. 11, 1886).

The peppery Mr Clemens, as Redney no doubt recalled, had not only refused, in 1878, her friend Alex Bell's request to back his new invention, but had ridiculed it in print in the *Atlantic Monthly*.[17]

In February, too, hard-driving, ambitious Redney took on another writing job in addition to her *Post* duties. She became a regular contributor to the Toronto *Week*, that "independent Journal of Literature, Politics and Criticism" which Goldwin Smith had started in 1883, and which published work by Bliss Carman, Archibald Lampman and others. Redney had written her first column for *The Week* on October 1st, 1885, "Up the Sittee in a Pitpan", that lyrical one describing her Honduras adventure, and Goldwin Smith had recognized her ability. On February 11th, 1886, he printed her "International Copyright. Authors and Publishers Before U.S. Senate Committee", sent from Washington. It was at this point that Redney assumed yet another name, for this article is signed "Jeannette Duncan". Did Sarah / Redney / Sara / Garth want to acknowledge the birth of yet another self in Washington, where all things were up-to-date and cosmopolitan, and where "Janet", her second name, had metamorphosed naturally into "Jeannette"? Her next contribution to *The Week* ("New Year's Eve in Negro Church") was also signed "Jeannette Duncan", but the third one (March 25th) is signed "Sara Jeannette Duncan", perhaps on the urge to reconcile old self with new. "Sara Jeannette Duncan" is the name which will later grace the title pages of her first published books.

In March, Redney attended the Woman Suffrage Convention and had her own feminist leanings strengthened. It was ridiculous that women still didn't have the vote. She went to the hotel reception for the convention's star, Miss Susan B. Anthony, tall and fiftyish in black silk and Redney was surprised to find a woman looking like "anybody's grandmother", with "an expression of benevolent severity, and a decided cast in one eye". Redney points out to prejudiced male readers that the typical suffragette is quite as modishly dressed and coiffed as other women, differing only in "the cerebral development implied in the way she talks in public or print" (*Week*, March 16, 1886).

From time to time, with less and less frequency, Redney paid a visit to the log cabin on Meridian Hill where Joaquin Miller lived. His cabin was two miles from the nearest street-car and stood far back from the road. He had let the grass grow tall and wild; the logs of the cabin were in their natural state. Joaquin was fond of posing in the doorway, draped in a bear skin, which passing sightseers (he was one of Washington's tourist attractions) always wanted to buy.[18]

Now Redney saw Joaquin with new eyes. The sensual, romantic poet had blended beautifully with the silken softness of New Orleans life, but in Washington, where the hard-hitting hammers and cash registers never stopped ringing, he seemed out of place. He made Redney uncomfortable, and also ambivalent about her materialistic goals. Her mixed feelings surface in a later description of Joaquin's cabin with its four little rooms:

> It has been called an advertisement and an affectation and other ugly names, that quaint little house on Meridian Hill that saw the first and the last of every sun that rose and set, and watched all day the silver winding of the Potomac beyond the spires of the city. I never believed it, nor did anybody else who ever tasted the poet's wine—wine of California, yellow as her gold—and listened to his simple creed of life, beside his blazing hearth, and watched the shadows flickering over the skins and rugs and other odd trappings of the low-ceilinged room, and heard the acorns dropping from the single tall old oak that spread over it. The experiment may have been a failure, but listening and thinking within its four walls one half believed that, if people generally were to start upon bottom facts in relation to their lives, they might make better architects. One received a very vivid impression of the flimsy artificiality which most of us make it our aim to construct about us, so soon worn out and ugly and profiting only to vanity. Our elaborate houses, our costly plenishings, our wonderful clothes, what are they under the sun! (Montreal *Star*, Jan. 24, 1888).

Redney wrote this description of Joaquin's cabin two years after the fact, and it reveals a repeating pattern in her life: more and more, for Redney, romance, nostalgia, sentiment, were separated from the relevant events by a long gap in time. The greenest fields were always behind her, or ahead of her, never beneath her restless feet.

Redney sat in Joaquin's cabin sipping his golden wine as the sun set and his blue eyes kindled, and remained unmoved, her New Orleans infatuation over. Joaquin had served his purpose: he had paved the way for her entrée to the Washington *Post* with practical counsel and an introduction and recommendation to Stilson Hutchins. Redney didn't need Joaquin any more. She was now as busy as the rest of the world upholstering her life, and the acorns from Joaquin's oak tree, as Redney listened, hit the roof with metallic chinks, like so many coins.

The fact is, Redney had found a new father-figure, William Dean Howells, the master of American fictional realism. At the end of February, Mr and Mrs Howells, and daughter Winifred (two years younger than Redney) had come to stay at her Washington boarding-house for a month. Howells, like Redney, was a wanderer and nomad for most of his life, and was then living in Boston in a house he had bought on Beacon Street, but Mark Twain was suggesting that they "should both go to live in Washington".[19] Howells may have come to Washington with that in mind, (although he didn't move there as it turned out, but to New York in 1888), or perhaps he had come for Grover Cleveland's inauguration, which took place on March 4th.

Redney had been a fan of Howells' realistic approach ever since *A Chance Acquaintance* had inspired her Quebec articles. She was, naturally, dying to meet this famous author. First, however, she met his boots:

> One journeys up in the hostelries of Washington, and up, and farther up, until an inquiry for the whereabouts of Gabriel seems a reasonable demand for information. On my heaven-wards pilgrimage the other night I paused, my hand upon the banister, my attention fixed upon two dark objects that the lowered gaslight dimly outlined . . . . It had been a night of wassail and progressive euchre, but I had achieved distinction in neither. On no reasonable ground could I accuse myself of any optical delusion whatever. . . . It had been for some time currently reported in the gossip of mine inn that our next distinguished guest was to be the Master of American Realism. The air was athrob with it, the landlady radiated it, we all expected it. There was nothing especially realistic about these boots; they were buttoned boots, dusty and undistinctive. But it flashed upon me that these were the apartments newly garnished and set aside for the occupancy of the notable person aforesaid. These, then, were the boots of the Modern Novelist. In all human probability the Modern Novelist was within. I hereby confess that I deliberately

listened that I might report the snoring of the Modern Novelist. But the beating of my own heart was the only sound I heard (*Week*, April 22, 1886).

In New Orleans, an article of Redney's had served as bait to hook a famous writer: her *Times-Democrat* column had landed Joaquin. Now it happened again. The *Post* published an interview by Redney with Howells' boots so clever that he asked to be introduced to the bright young lady who had written it.[20] It was the beginning of a long friendship, fed by occasional reunions down the years in Europe when their paths crossed. To get them started, there were common meeting-grounds: Howells' father had been American Consul in Toronto from 1878 to 1883; his sister Annie lived in Ottawa, married to a Canadian, and Redney's Brantford friends, the Johnsons of Chiefswood, were cousins.

Redney observed Howells closely as he sat down to ham and eggs in her boarding house. He was the exact antithesis of the flamboyant Joaquin, being "very well bred, without a single discernible 'fad' or oddity" (*Globe*, July 14, 1886). No jingling spurs for him; he "dresses precisely as all the men you know do" (*Week*, April 22, 1886). Nor was he six feet tall with flowing hair. He was short and rather heavily built with greying hair brushed forward over his broad forehead, a heavy moustache, and rather "massively cut" features. "It is a humorous, sensitive, refined face, but I should say that the characteristic it expresses most strongly is intensely absorbent rather than keenly observant", notes Redney (*Week*, April 22, 1886). During the month of March, Redney had many chats with the Howells at Washington parties. At one given by Senator and Mrs Morrill, on Sunday, March 20th, the Howells were "the centre of gravity and hilarity" (*Week*, April 22, 1886), with Redney hovering persistently on the periphery.

Gradually, Redney was drawn into Howells' centre of gravity, ideologically speaking. As the *Post*'s book reviewer she was well aware of the current battle of the books: whether American novelists should opt for Romance or Realism. Should a writer be true to an ideal of life, or to life itself? The Romance-Realism War, mainly conducted in newspapers and magazines, and rumbling on to the end of the century, was just now in its hottest phase. Following the publication of Howells' *The Rise of Silas Lapham* (1885), the Romance buffs referred to its realistic material as "dirt" and "poison",[21] and Howells countered by condemning Dickens, Thackeray and Reade for airily spinning novels that "befool and debauche us",[22] reserving his deadliest darts for women's sentimental novels, where, if the heroines didn't "burst into tears" or "choke with sobs", they were too often filled with notions of self-sacrifice which Howells saw as weakening and blinding.[23]

Howells and the Washington environment conspired to draw Redney away from romance, towards realism; the ongoing conflict within her took a decisive turn in Washington, but she would never be completely in one camp. In her own life, the realist usually sat at the controls; in her writing, she vacillated from realism to romance, and the latter, as time passed, tended to surface in her fiction in awkward and pathetic little fantasy-leaps. In her journalism, once she had thrown away her New Orleans mask of Magnolia Blossom, she plunged into the bramble-patch of daily existence and stayed there. Throughout her journalistic career in Washington and subsequent cities, there was the usual Canadian preoccupation with documentary detail, plenty of it, a tradition going back to such pioneer diarists as Catharine Parr Traill.[24] In Redney's newspaper copy, after she left New Orleans, there are few imaginative flights towards the ideal, fewer emotional forays. Everything is black-and-white, not just the newsprint; no more roses, no more vistas of riotous green.

This is an urban, very practical Redney: observing people interacting in the social cosmos, concerning herself with current political and social issues. It seems significant, given her divided allegiance, that in her city-journalist phase, while she was in actual practice writing realistically, in theory she still sided with romance as a necessary ingredient in novels, leaving the door open for herself later in her career. "The modern school of fiction", she writes in 1886, "may bear the blame of dealing too exclusively in the corporealities of human life, to the utter and scornful neglect of its idealities" (*Week*, July 15, 1886). "Gentlemen of the realistic school", she writes in 1887, are "mistaken in your idea that you go the whole distance and can persuade the whole novel-writing fraternity to take the same path through the burdocks and the briars" (*Week*, Jan. 13, 1887). Almost a year later, she takes the same stance:

> A cabbage is a very essential vegetable to certain salads, but we do not prostrate ourselves adoringly before the cabbage bed in every day life, and it is a little puzzling to know why we should be required to do so in art galleries and book stores, however perfect the representations there of cabbages (Montreal *Star*, Dec. 5, 1887).

She was then deep in the cabbage-patch herself, ignoring the scent of roses from the other side of the fence.

By June of 1886, Washington was hot and sticky; the social whirl was over and Redney's initial enthusiasm and excitement had evaporated. The office was like an oven; she had to keep wiping her palms on her hankie as she pushed the stylus across curling yellow sheets. The noise of hammers—did they never stop building something bigger and better?—seemed to invade her head. Even the flurry of Grover Cleveland's wedding on June 2nd, the union of a young girl and an entrenched bachelor of forty-nine, couldn't shake her out of her apathy. Since April the *Post* had been speculating in print almost daily on this romance between the President and Frances Folsom, twenty-one-year-old daughter of his former law partner, and when the wedding finally occurred the *Post*'s headline read simply "MARRIED!"

Redney grew restless. She was experiencing another instance of what was to be a repeating pattern in her life: first, the idealization of a shining mark, a clearly-perceived goal (in this instance, an editorial job on a foremost American newspaper). She had worked her way towards it with great energy and drive, and the momentum of her enthusiasm had carried her through the first weeks after she reached her goal. Gradually, however, boredom was seeping in and the golden vision was spoiled by irritating motes of everyday reality. Redney lost her momentum, slowed to a halt, paced restlessly back and forth. Eventually, a new shining ideal would hang like a Chinese lantern in her mind, and the whole cycle would repeat . . . and repeat.

By June, 1886, the realities of Washington life were a
constant frustration. Redney saw now that American society,
which at first had appeared to be sparked by freedom and
initiative, got its impetus from brashness and greed. America
bludgeoned its way forward to everything bigger, but not
necessarily better. Redney began to feel the lack of British
taproots, of social strata clearly defined, of historical traditions. Her thoughts, as she sat sweltering at her desk amid
the dust and din, winged north to West Street's cool shadowed
garden and well-wrought urns. She longed for the dark-
green waters, smooth as glass, of the Grand River, flowing
beneath the Lorne Street Bridge. She felt suddenly (and this
too would be a repeating pattern) homesick for Canada, its
quiet modesty, habitual moderation, and British civility. It
was her tragedy that only when she was somewhere else,
looking at Canada from a long way off, that Redney felt most
Canadian.

This first wave of nationalism hit her in Washington,
along with the furnace blast of heat. Redney handed in her
resignation to a surprised Stilson, gave notice at her
boarding-house, packed her bag and left Washington, never
to return. This, too, would be part of the pattern: this
constant circling back, from wherever in the world her
restless feet had taken her, to Canada and her idyllic West
Street home.

Now, once again, Redney found herself sitting on a
train looking out the window as reels of landscape rolled by.
Her dreams seemed always to hover between parallel rails,
for as the train carried her home, a new goal began to glow
in her mind. In Canada, in those happy Brantford years, she
had been one-of-a-kind, had felt her uniqueness. In Washington, on the other hand, there had been too many
competing women journalists, too many good ones; she
couldn't really shine there. But back in Canada . . . . She had
always wanted entry to a man's world. What if she succeeded
in landing a job *in the office* of the *Globe*, the very first
Canadian woman to be so hired by a leading newspaper?
That would be something to be proud of! As a breeze of cool
northern air blew through the open window and ruffled her
hair, Redney felt a rush of sudden excitement.

Back home in Brantford, Redney decided that before launching her attack she needed a quiet green space in which to plan her strategy. On July 2nd, her father left on a seven-week buying trip to England, and Redney went for a week's holiday with another young lady and "the youth", probably a sister and brother, to the "Sand Banks", near Picton, on Lake Ontario's beautiful Bay of Quinte. She arrived by steamer on a Friday night to find a rambling, log resort-hotel, with a plank-walled dining room full of lake breezes and garish "chromos".[25] She relaxed in a hammock on the wide verandah, bathed in the clear lake, walked among the pines and rocks, concentrated on her new goal.

Then, her holiday over, she put on her most becoming *tailleur* and presented herself before John Cameron at the *Globe*. She waved her sheaf of first-rate Washington copy at him, and he capitulated. He agreed to hire her to work in the office, writing the "Woman's World" column on a daily basis. Up to that time it had been a scissors-and-paste affair, penned by a homebound female.

She had done it! Like Alice McGillivray, like Emily and Augusta Stowe, she had chalked up a "first" for Canadian women: the very first to work in the editorial department of a leading Canadian newspaper. "Here in Canada", wrote Redney later, "nothing, comparatively speaking, has been accomplished by women in journalism", for "there are difficulties in the way which look insuperable at first and can only be surmounted by the exercise of the divinest kind of patience" (Montreal *Star*, Jan. 25, 1888). Like so many Canadians before and since, she had had to prove her abilities in the United States first, but now here she was, gleefully ensconced in the *Globe* newsroom, a noisy, paper-strewn place where the local misfits dropped in to talk, play poker, share a bottle. The office walls were hung with "old voters' lists, ante-dated city maps, ancient witticisms and cobwebs" (*Globe*, Jan. 12, 1887). Redney swept away the cobwebs, put fresh flowers on her desk, sat there in her neat "tailor-made", chin held high. Her first "Woman's World" column appeared on July 8, 1886. The column was unsigned until September 3rd, when "Garth Grafton" became the regular signature.

Gradually Redney's charm and ability exacted a grudging deference from the men whose territory she had invaded. By October, she was feeling enough at home to tease her proof-reader in verse:

> Stay thy dire destructive finger,
> Leave one unmolested line,
> Over which my soul may linger
> In sweet knowledge that 'tis mine (*Globe*, Oct. 21, 1886).

Redney moved into a boarding-house at 239 Jarvis Street, south of Carlton, in an area of Toronto where "rents are reasonable, and street cars convenient, and the milkman's bell twangeth earliest in the morning" (*Globe*, March 30, 1887). At Mrs Monro's, the hall carpets matched the room-rates: rag on the cheapest floor, the third, where Redney had a room, all-wool on the second, and Best Brussels on the first. There was a cat, "a kitchen maid called Katisha", and other young people boarding there whom Redney found congenial.

After Washington's jarring jumble, Redney liked the fact that Jarvis Street's class stratification was as rigidly defined as Mrs. Monro's: blue-collar workers at the south end near the lake, commercial middle-class around Carlton in terraced brick houses like Mrs. Monro's, with iron basement railings and tiny grass plots. From Carlton north to Bloor Street stood the mansions of the wealthy merchants and entrepreneurs, houses much larger than their Brantford counterparts. There was, for instance, the twenty-five-room mansion "Euclid Hall", bought by Hart Massey in 1882, with a conservatory for orchids, a greenhouse for grapes, and a fountain in the front hall with goldfish in the splash-pool. At Mrs William Cawthra's new mansion, built in 1884, even the stables and coach house were of cut stone to match the main dwelling.[26] Redney only had to walk north on Jarvis to savour its elegant ambience, its wide grassy verges, stately elms and flowering chestnuts, to admire the silk-hatted gentlemen and ladies with parasols, riding by in polished broughams and victorias or strolling along the shady sidewalk.

The social strata were more clearly defined, and the society itself was much more homogeneous than Washington's. Toronto had a population of 105,000, mostly emigrants from Britain and Ireland, whose numbers had earned the city its label, "the Belfast of Canada". Since January, 1886, Mayor Howland had been its civic head, and he was very busy earning for Toronto its second and longest-lasting nickname: Toronto the Good. When he wasn't teaching his Bible class or visiting the poor, Howland was closing brothels, gambling joints and drinking dens, banning little boys from ball-playing in parks or bathing naked in the bay, and seeing that the Sabbath was kept as it should be.[27] That he was eminently successful in the latter endeavour is evident in Charles Dudley Warner's account of Toronto on a Sunday:

> The city, though spread over such a large area, permits no horse-cars to run on Sunday. There are no saloons open on Sunday; there are no beer-gardens or places of entertainment in the suburbs, and no Sunday newspapers.[28]

On Sundays one went to church; there was nothing else to do, and there were plenty of large churches scattered throughout the city. Redney probably attended St Andrew's Presbyterian, at the south-east corner of Jarvis and Carlton, a fine building erected in 1878. In the afternoons, she sometimes walked in Queen's Park, where The Good of Toronto, fresh from a formal church sermon, strolled on the grass and listened attentively to the informal, open-air preachers. "It is a multitude that is eminently creditable to any city, a clean, fresh, brisk, well-clad multitude, workers all of them, honest, well-meaning", writes Redney in one of her first *Globe* columns (July 13, 1886), feeling the full force of Toronto's saintly, soap-scrubbed image, and feeling also a certain relief that there were no hordes of harlots, tottering on their high heels.

The pressures of a daily column kept Redney on the run, jumping on and off street cars as she rushed round the city, gathering copy. Most of her Toronto reporting was in her realistic Washington vein, tramping through the burdocks and briars. She usually had a companion on her assignments, who in her columns is labelled "Theophilus" if male, "Seraphima" if female. Wednesday, September 1st found Redney back-stage at the Grand Opera House on Adelaide Street, whose manager was, surprisingly, a woman: Charlotte Morrison, who had played Lady Teazle in Sheridan's *School for Scandal* in 1872, while the playwright's grandson, Lord Dufferin, watched from out front.[29] Redney attended, and reviewed, many theatrical productions, thereby catching the footlight fever which would culminate in her own play-writing attempts. On this particular night, she stayed back-stage for the whole performance, among the "painted pieces of sliding scenery, packing boxes . . . 'supes' in green velvet, carpenters in anxiety, stage manager in a fume" (*Globe*, Sept. 2, 1886).

On Wednesday, September 29th, Redney made her first visit to a place which would gradually take on deep psychological significance for her: a nunnery. This one was Notre Dame des Anges on Bond Street, and the nuns' rooms were "narrow, bare, guiltless of carpet or ornament". "What years of fast and penance, and sore chastening of the spirit has it required to efface every footprint of life and love and vanity from these pale faces?" asks Redney thoughtfully (*Globe*, Sept. 30, 1886). She looked at their narrow white beds, their blank white faces, and felt the first faint *frisson* of their chill asceticism.

Redney dutifully attended a Mission Meeting of the Elm Street Methodist Church, visited the Sick Children's Hospital, and the Kindergarten attached to the Normal School, where the children were "flapping their arms in a circle pretending to be butterflies and not aware what good exercise it is" (*Globe*, Dec. 13, 1886). How good it felt not to be in charge of them all, day after tedious day! Redney attended the prize-giving for University Company "K" of the Queen's Own Rifles, held at Convocation Hall on the university grounds, where such prizes as a blue porcelain lamp and a biscuit jar were presented to the worthy, while the Glee Club sang "The Canadian Boat Song" and Miss Gunther rendered the difficult march from *Tannhaüser* on the piano. This event exactly captured the tone of Toronto society in the '80's: a rather childlike and chaste parochialism.

Redney herself sought out a few kindred artistic souls with whom to socialize. She always attended the Saturday afternoon receptions of Lucius O'Brien, Toronto's best-known painter, for which he sent out "exceedingly *chic*, little brown paper invitations" (*Week*, Feb. 3, 1887). Since she was writing a woman's column, Redney felt compelled, occasionally, to pick through sewing-basket trivia in search of items. Tongue-in-cheek, she reports the latest fashion in brooches: a live bug attached to a thin gold harness and chain—free to roam one's shoulder or hat (*Globe*, Aug. 17, 1886) and the latest crazes for hand-painted black satin nightdress cases, and patchwork counterpanes made from worn-out kid gloves (*Globe*, July 16, 1886).

In addition to her *Globe* column, Redney was still writing for *The Week*, and after her return to Toronto formed a friendship with the owner and editor, Goldwin Smith, another father-figure "to whose kindly encouragement she was much indebted".[30] Goldwin Smith was an Englishman who had been Regius Professor of Modern History at Oxford, had emigrated to Canada in 1871, married William Boulton's widow four years later, and settled happily into the Boulton home, the Grange. "Fortune made for me", writes Goldwin smugly, "almost an England of my own in Canada", for the Grange is "the counterpart in style and surroundings of a little English mansion".[31] It was George Brown's Bow Park estate circumscribed to an urban setting. The Grange had its spacious lawns, spreading elms and devoted servants (the butler stayed for fifty-two years). The servants lived at a respectable distance from the house in four vine-covered cottages on the grounds. Goldwin was Toronto's ultimate intellectual, thrust onto every platform as Exhibit "A", to prove the city's distinction and culture. He reinforced for Redney her Brantford ideals of British traditions and literary distinctions.

Beginning on September 2nd, 1886, Redney had a column in *The Week* called "Saunterings", signed "Sara Jeannette Duncan", and beginning October 28th another one headed "Afternoon Tea" and signed "Garth Grafton". Both columns covered current cultural and social events.

Her journalistic style in *The Week* is sometimes surprisingly heavy and prolix. Perhaps the stately Goldwin intimidated her. "While we are largely governed by the social traditions that obtain in England", writes Redney, deeply entangled in an ivy-covered Latinate style,

> we are so far from the autocratic code of insular dictation, and so near the somewhat lax and liberal system that prevails among our cousins of the Republic, that repressive austerities are somewhat softened among us with the result of a decided gain in individuality" (*Week*, October 14, 1886).

From time to time, Redney left the Toronto scene for Brantford, chronicling these visits for *Globe* and *Week* readers. She stood in the Market Square crowd on October 13th as Lieutenant-Governor Robinson unveiled the bronze statue of the city's founder, Joseph Brant, while Dr Cochrane offered a suitable prayer, and W.F. Cockshutt read a poem of Pauline Johnson's which she was too retiring to read herself. Special platform guests were a group of North-West Indian chiefs, in full feather, there to observe how meek and mild the local Indians were, just in case they themselves were contemplating another Rebellion.[32]

On the following day, Redney visited her old school chum Pauline. While Redney had been seeing the world, Pauline had been living quietly at home ever since high school graduation, helping her mother and writing her poems in her spare time. Her father had died in 1884 and, unable to support the expense of Chiefswood, Mrs. Johnson and Pauline moved into lodgings in Brantford's unfashionable North Ward. Redney found her friend as beautiful as ever, "charmingly bright in conversation". Pauline showed her a scalping-knife made by her father from a deer's foot, but Redney, name-dropping deftly to impress *Globe* readers, regretted that Pauline had no photo of her relative William Dean Howells "who spoke in terms of the liveliest interest of his 'Indian cousins' when I met him last winter in Washington (*Globe*, Oct. 14, 1886).

By now Redney's journalist *persona* is decisive, opinionated, steely. In reviewing a book of essays by Rose Cleveland, Redney writes:

It seems to me that one of the most charming characteristics of Miss Cleveland's literary style is its emphasis. She is delightfully emphatic. There is no parley, no consideration of half truths. She forms her conviction, and with swift, sure strokes nails it up, fearlessly, a shining mark (*Globe*, July 22, 1885).

In all her Canadian journalism, Redney, too, formed her conviction and nailed it up fearlessly. She saw herself as a Canadian Matthew Arnold, setting up high cultural ladders for Philistines to climb. "In our character as colonists we find the root of all our sins of omission in letters", writes Redney. "So long as Canada remains in political obscurity, content to thrive only at the roots, so long will the leaves and blossoms of art and literature be scanty and stunted products of our national energy" (*Week*, Sept. 30, 1886). Her *persona* is consistently that of a cultivated, conservative, cerebral, well-bred social critic. The New Orleans romantic, all sensual impetuosity, has disappeared and the Jane-Austenian ironist has emerged. The November meeting of the Canadian Institute, in spite of the fact that her friend George Ross graced the platform, was a dull affair, writes Redney, picking up her hammer, so that "at the close of the programme, notwithstanding the Institute's obvious attraction in the shape of creeping things with stings and wings, souvenirs of the North American Indian, and the whole Canadian animal kingdom stuffed, the audience went home with great unanimity" (*Week*, Nov. 18, 1886). "As Pygmalion", she writes, reviewing a performance of a Greek play, "Mr. R.D. McLean displayed a magnificent physique but histrionic abilities that were rather ox-like...Leucippe dropped his h's, which they never did in Greece, and Chrysos and Daphne, though old comedians, and good ones, gave their classic sentiments disagreeably through their noses" (*Week*, Nov. 4, 1886). She was revolted by the spectacle of a boy's head being used as target in a Centre Island amusement park: "No, it wasn't a dummy. I heard it swear. A few more such disreputable shows and the Island will become unfit for the resort of respectable people" (*Globe*, Aug. 17, 1886). Redney objected to the way strangers lean over and kiss any baby going by in

its carriage (*Globe*, Oct. 29, 1886) and to the low level of
ladies' décolleté as both "unhealthy and immodest" (*Week*,
Feb. 10, 1887). Being a thorough-going élitist she approved
of Upper Canada College, a private school for the sons of the
wealthy, because its ivy-covered walls protect them from
"the rabble of the earth" and "the great unwashed" (*Globe*,
Oct. 23, 1886). A reader who wrote to her gets a sharp rap on
the knuckles for beginning abruptly with no salutation:
"You are not addressing air, but an individual when you put
a query to Woman's World—an individual who will be glad
to hear from you again, but who hopes that in the meantime
you will have learned better manners" (*Globe*, Sept. 29,
1886). Redney hit the nails on the head, cleanly, sharply,
driving them in again and again, showing Toronto the Good
that in matters of breeding and culture it still had much to
learn. She spoke from the secure vantage-point of her own
genteel upbringing, with an autocratic Lord Chesterfield-
like father whose tone Redney was already reproducing in
print as she would later in private life. If she shared Jane
Austen's astringency, she also shared her moral imperatives,
firmly in place. There is no fumbling, no red-hot fury. It is
all cool and cunningly ironic, as in her description of the
ladies' fancy-work exhibit at the National Exhibition:

> It is difficult to preserve the unities in worsted. Every
> oriental, for instance, was provided with a beautiful china
> blue eye.... But if one leaves the unities out of considera-
> tion, and the vanishing point, and perspective, and drawing
> and color considerations, the work was beautifully done.
> From the standpoint of stitches there was absolutely no fault
> to find (*Globe*, Sept. 9, 1886).

Redney also firmly nailed her feminist's manifesto to
the door, temporarily abandoning her conservatism. The
'80's in Canada, as in the United States, saw the emergence of
the New Woman who wanted to vote, pursue a career,
smoke, ride a bicycle, talk politics and play golf. Over the
years, Redney herself would do all these things, and didn't
see why other women shouldn't, if they so desired. "The
woman of today is comparatively self-sufficient", she announces proudly, thinking of her own weekly pay-cheques,

"the woman of tomorrow will be, perhaps, superlatively so" (*Globe*, Sept. 2, 1886). "Men cannot possibly understand the shrinking sense of humiliation with which the average woman asks her husband to deplete his pocketbook for her", observes Redney (*Globe*, Nov. 16, 1886). "Careers, if possible, and independence anyway, we must all have, as musicians, artists, writers, teachers, lawyers, doctors, ministers, or something" (*Globe*, Nov. 12, 1886). She looks forward to the day when "a conscientious married person will be able to bring up her children, and vote, and cultivate the true and beautiful, and walk in the fear of the Lord and not of the cook" (*Globe*, June 10, 1885).

She takes plenty of pot-shots at the traditional female stereotype: woman as domestic, dumb and docile. Being inept in the kitchen herself, she has good reason to resent the role division which makes meal preparation a woman's task, whereas "man's share has been the consuming and the criticizing" (*Globe*, May 27, 1885). She takes exception to the old adage that women should conceal their cleverness from men:

> Why we should "carefully conceal" it passes my comprehension.... It is difficult to see why we should be requested to refrain from making Aristotle a third party to a *tête-a-tête*, or introducing the binomial theorem into general conversation any more than our fellow B.A.'s who wear the additional distinction of whiskers (*Globe*, Aug. 5, 1885).

And she is equally contemptuous of that other old saw which states that since men like to talk about themselves, women should encourage them to do so, listening mutely:

> Every man who constantly unburdens himself in the bosom of his family of an uninterrupted essay on the Ego of his existence is a public nuisance and a private bore, and his presence on this planet ought not to be encouraged, much less his peculiarity (*Globe*, June 24, 1885).

Part of Redney's clever feminist strategy was to keep the rose in her hair as she strode forward into a man's world. She herself was always perfectly decorous and lady-like, feeling that one needn't bash down the door keeping women from full emancipation with strong-arm methods; one can open it slowly and carefully, and keep the hinges oiled with charm. Redney always kept a nice balance between the flirtatiousness she had adopted in New Orleans, and the firmness she had acquired in Washington. In her columns, as in her life, she found a comfortable (and typically Canadian) compromise of clinging-ivy and sturdy-oak intertwined. "Cannot the higher mathematics co-exist with frills? Can't we be professional and dress for dinner? Is there a natural law forbidding the assimilation of puddings and politics?" she asks. "I don't think so:

> Loss of the least womanly grace means loss of power. Recognizing this, let us with the wisdom of serpents and the anti-thetical innocence wear not one glove-button or yard of embroidery the less, tolerate not the least diminution of courtesy or disregard of conventionality because of these latter-day privileges of ours (*Globe*, June 17, 1885).

When a reader questions whether the writer of "Woman's World" should be addressed as "sir" or "madam", Redney replies crisply:

> I don't see why that doubt should haunt you as to my identity with the clinging vine rather than the sturdy oak of humanity. If the sentiments that have appeared from time to time in this department of Woman's World have ever been other than vine-like and feminine, I greatly deprecate the fact. Upon this score let me set your vacillating opinion forever at rest. I cling (*Globe*, Sept. 23, 1886).

This is not mere rhetoric, but Redney speaking from an acceptance of her own feminine preoccupations, particularly those of dress. "For centuries women have been concentrating their energies upon dress", she writes wisely. "A decade or two during which women have been given other things to think about will modify only slightly this all-absorbing interest" (*Globe*, June 3, 1885). "I simply couldn't have gone to see my relation in a hat and gloves that didn't match", says one of her heroines. "Clothes and courage have so much to do with each other" (*An American Girl in London*, p. 25). For Redney, clothes were always a psychological and aesthetic bolster, as well as an expression of her androgyny. She was as hard-working and career-minded as any man in her man-tailored jackets, but she kept a hand free to manage the sweep of her skirt: an iron hand in a pearl-buttoned glove. Christmas, 1886, found Redney celebrating with her family, for the first time in three years, at home in Brantford. She took a week's holiday from the *Globe*, while a man wrote her column. "It is quite wonderful", she observed upon her return, hammer tapping gently, "with Kenshaw as the guiding divinity, our little sphere swung no more erratically than it did" (*Globe*, Jan. 5, 1887).

But by the time February's dirty slush and interminable snows had arrived, Redney had lost her energy, and felt the familiar grey cloud of her apathy and restlessness descending again, as it had in Washington. She had been in Washington for seven months when the gritty realities spoiled her shining achievement; now she had been working in Toronto for exactly seven months. To be sure, some of the disfiguring dirt, quite literally, had been there from the beginning. She had complained early on in print of the mud at the corner of King and Yonge Streets, through which she had to wade every day on her way to work:

> The mud is simply awful, and the awfulness of Toronto mud is quite beyond description. It lies in wait for you on the crossings with viscid maliciousness, every street car hurls it at you, and you are bespattered by every passing carriage (*Globe*, Sept. 24, 1886).

Then too, riding Toronto's street cars, inefficiently run at thirty-minute intervals by Toronto Street Railway, is "an experience, equally composed of fear, horror and disgust" where "you get the benefit of at least twenty personal odours", writes Redney, aquiline nose wrinkling, "bad tobacco, bay rum, musk, onions, corned beef and cabbage, hair oil, imperfect ablutionary habits" (*Globe*, Sept. 20, 1886).

By November, four months into her job, she began to feel "departed summer in one's soul" (*Week*, Nov. 18, 1886) and by mid-December she takes note of the snow "in all the little hollows . . . of the ragged ruin that was once the garden hedge:

> And at the foot of the orchard, in the marsh . . . there lie
> between the hummocks small and fragile-looking patches of
> ice, murky mirrors for the sere desolation of the flags and
> cat-tails (*Week*, Dec. 16, 1886).

Snow was settling slowly but surely in the corners of Redney's
mind, lying, heavy and cold, on her imagination and initiative. The mirror of the self which had been so clear, so
compact, in Florida, as she gazed into the Fountain of Youth,
was murky now with separate ice patches: Sarah Janet, Sara,
Jeannette, Sara Jeannette . . . .

By February, her restlessness and boredom were intol-
erable. Being the first woman in the *Globe* office was a stale
victory now, cobweb-hung. A new plan began to buzz in
Redney's head as she swept the dead flies from the grimy
windowsill. She persuaded editor Cameron to send her to
Montreal to cover the Winter Carnival, held the second
week of February. She didn't tell him her Secret Purpose:
she intended to look for a new job while she was there.

Redney caught a night train for Montreal, a twelve-
hour run, chasing her dream of a new self, a new setting,
along the tracks. Her first sight of the city on the St
Lawrence imaged her own end-of-winter emotional stasis:

> [Montreal is] a city the hem of whose garment is bordered
> by the broadest, bravest green ribbon of a river . . . . But now
> it is winter in the city, and the mountain wears the patriarchal
> snow that befits it, and the heaven the church-spires point to
> shines very clear and cold above them, and the great river
> vexes itself under strong bonds (*Week*, Feb. 24, 1887).

The Montreal Winter Carnival was a Canadian counterpart of the New Orleans Mardi-Gras, thought Redney,
standing a few days later in the frosty air, watching the
Carnival's climax, the storming of the Ice Palace, a magnificent turreted structure in Dominion square, opposite the
Windsor Hotel. It was then that she felt the first sparks of
new energy shooting up within her:

> Up from the ranks of the attacking party flew the first rockets
> of the assault, answered by a perfect "rain" of coloured
> missiles from the Lansdowne tower. Faster and faster they
> flew from besiegers and besieged, curving high and gracefully

in mid air, and falling in thousands of fiery stars. Within the castle walls burned mysterious fires, that shed weird and fearful glows of rose and green upon them, and were awesomely suggestive of the work of destruction the enemy was ruthlessly accomplishing. At last, with a grand up-firing and up-flashing came the *dénouement*—the king of the carnival had capitulated and his stronghold was in the hands of the people (*Globe*, Feb. 9, 1887).

On Wednesday, February 9th, the day of the Ball at the sumptuous Windsor Hotel, there was a terrible snow-storm. It was "a storm which baffled one's powers of locomotion. I had never seen such a storm", writes Redney in awe (*Globe*, Feb. 16, 1887). The snow heaped itself in huge drifts "immediately across the sidewalk that led anywhere one wanted to go", but Redney, arrow-straight and resolute once more, pushed ahead through all obstacles. She dressed carefully for the Ball in "pale green silk *en traine*, ostrich tips and pearls",[33] then had to pile on cloak, boots and scarves to make the hazardous trip by sleigh through the snowdrifts to the hotel. The ballroom supper rooms were filled with smilax, laurel, potted ferns, and above the dais placed for the Governor-General, Lord Lansdowne and his wife, was a nine-foot coronet of roses.[34] Redney felt flushed, beautiful, kept her eye on the roses. When she learned that the millionaire New Yorker Erastus Wiman, former Canadian, was there with his daughters, Miss Wiman in white satin, Miss Mattie in red tulle, Redney made up her mind to meet them. A millionaire with wide journalistic contacts could be useful to her. Before the dancing ended at 3 a.m. she had met and charmed yet another father-figure who would advance her career, and for good measure had ingratiated herself with his daughters as well.

After Carnival week, Redney returned to Toronto, mission accomplished. On April 2nd she wrote her last regular column for the *Globe*. (Twelve more signed ones would appear between May and October.) Ethelwyn Wetherald, another ambitious female journalist, would take Redney's place. Between May 26th and September 13th articles signed "Garth Grafton" sprouted sporadically in the

Montreal *Star*, and after a restful summer in Brantford and
Toronto Redney moved to Montreal to begin her new job as
regular columnist for the *Star*. Behind her she had left her
shining mark on the *Globe*. The fame of the woman's
department, according to a younger colleague, "was made by
'Garth Grafton'."[35] Redney cleaned out her desk, and made a
pilgrimage to West Street, where her youthful ambitions for
fame and fortune had flamed highest. From Monday, April
11th until the 19th, Redney was at home, watching the first
peony-shoots sprouting red and green under the dining-
room windows and warming her spirit at the familiar hearth.
Then, on April 20th, she was off again, having charmed
Erastus Wiman so successfully that he had invited her to
visit his sumptuous estate on Staten Island, New York, just as
Governor Goldsworthy had invited her to British Honduras.

Here, thought Redney, as the train pulled into New
York City, was the very vortex of that American "enterprise
and 'go' " which had caught her up in Washington; swirling
and surging round her was "the crowded, vivid, provocative
life that seemed so to stir one's nerves and infect one's veins"
(*Those Delightful Americans*, p. 217). She found the same brash
greed as in Washington, but here the pace was faster, "as if
the city were in the throes of an uncontrollable hysteria, and
shrieked without a pause" (*Ibid.*, p. 43).

"Chaz" Wiman, who welcomed Redney to his adopted
city, had been caught and held in the mad maelstrom of New
York since 1866. He was now fifty-four years old, a stocky
little man with mutton-chop whiskers and an expression of
"shrewdness, sense and determination in every lineament of
his face".[36] For Redney, he was the epitome of the self-made
man. Born in Churchville, Ontario in 1834, he had worked
as farm labourer at the age of twelve for fifty cents a week, as
newsboy in Toronto, then as an apprentice type-setter,
working ten to sixteen hours a day, and increasing his pay
from $1.50 to $5.00 a week. In 1854, George Brown of the
Globe hired him as commercial editor, but he was so competent that R.G. Dun soon lured him into his mercantile
agency. "Chaz" was on his way, moving up from manager of
the Toronto office to Montreal and then to head office in
New York. In 1881 he had been named President of the

Great North Western Telegraph Company of Canada, and a director of Western Union. "Do not drift, but steer. Have a defined motive in full view", advises "Chaz", in "Hints for Young Fortune Hunters".[37] Like Stilson Hutchins, he demonstrated to Redney what an iron drive could accomplish in The Gilded Age. Eventually Erastus became an American citizen (in 1897), but he was, even before that, a vocal advocate of commercial union between Canada and the United States: "If a great future is in store for the United States", he wrote, "the supplies which come from Canada are the one essential for success".[38]

"Chaz" had certainly shaken things up on Staten Island once he had settled there. He looped a railway round its periphery, improved the landings for ferries chugging the six miles from Manhattan, formed the Staten Island Amusement Company, hired Buffalo Bill as star attraction, imported a $40,000 electric fountain from England.[39] The interior of the island, fortunately, had not yet received his Midas touch, so that it was still a pastoral landscape with orchards and Dutch farmhouses two hundred years old. For Redney, seeing it for the first time as she was driven to his mansion, it was Brantford's mixture of rural peace and mercantile bustle writ large.

She definitely opted for the latter, admiring what Wiman had done for this island once "sleepily connected with the great city":

> Then came Mr. Erastus Wiman and Staten Island was revolutionized by "Rapid Transit". Boats leave South Ferrry every twenty minutes now, all running to the point on the island nearest New York. Trains meet them, speeding along through the woods and fields, to twenty different points (Montreal *Star*, Sept. 13, 1888).

She was impressed with the Wiman home, a Queen Anne red-brick wonder with wide piazzas and beautiful grounds, and enjoyed the Wiman girls, both of them "clever and interesting" (Montreal *Star*, Sept. 13, 1888), with her own love of literature and art.

The Wimans seem to have accompanied Redney back to Toronto, for they were with her when she was one of the

thousand Torontonians presented to Lord Lansdowne at a
Government House reception:

> Miss Sara Jeannette Duncan (Garth Grafton) was presented
> to His Excellency at his request. Miss Duncan was more than
> once seen in the company of Mr. Erastus Wiman and his
> daughters (Brantford *Expositor*, May 26, 1887).

Finally, as the brisk October air came, Redney packed
her bag, said her farewells and caught the train for Montreal. She found Montreal—then Canada's largest manufacturing centre, with a French-English population of
200,000—a wider, more cosmopolitan world than Toronto
the Good. By November 1st, Redney had found a boarding-
house and had begun a regular column for the *Star*. She
would continue to send weekly articles back to Goldwin
Smith's *Week*; after November 24th, all her signed work for
The Week bears the signature—yet another variation—"Sara
J. Duncan".

The Washington *Post*, the Toronto *Globe*, and now the
Star: the shining marks were piling up. The *Star*, owned by
Hugh Graham, boasting "the largest circulation of any
Canadian newspaper",[40] had begun in 1869 so modestly that
the coppers and nickels received by the newsboys the previous night were used to pay for the next day's supply of
paper, and the office boy bought one day's supply of coal at a
time, fifty cents' worth, drawing it to the office on a hand-
sled, to work the press. The *Star* had prospered enough to
build, for $175,000, its imposing quarters on St James Street,
housing both the Daily Star and its adjunct the *Family Herald
and Weekly Star*.[41]

Redney considered herself a veteran by now, and
slipped easily into the office routines. Under the name
"Garth Grafton", she turned out an almost-daily column,
similar to her *Globe* one, called "Bric-a-Brac". She had once
defined "bric-a-brac" as a collection "infinitely more valuable for the character behind it, of which it is generally the
expression than for any inherent beauty",[42] and, as with
"Woman's World", Redney stamped "Bric-a-Brac" with her
own arresting mark.

"The first thing one looks for on arriving in Montreal", she notes, "is lodgings and a laundress; the next is an alpenstock. By the time the first two are satisfactorily got we don't want the alpenstock. We are accustomed to the hills, and like them" (*Week*, Nov. 10, 1887). She puffed up Westmount's steep grades, recompensed by the "loveable, habitable-looking, fine, old houses" (*Week*, Nov. 10, 1887). She found her favourite snow apples, but here they were called *fameuses*. She developed a taste for oysters, which turned up everywhere: at the fruiterer's, the fishmonger's, the grocer's, the confectioner's, even at the stall of the little woman "who sells odds and ends of buttons, lace and the evening papers" (*Week*, Nov. 10, 1887). Redney was relieved to find that no one laughed at her halting French, but even more relieved that "the knowledge of English among the French of Montreal is much more universal than among their cousins of New Orleans" (*Star*, Feb. 23, 1888).

Montreal's winter, on the other hand, was a severe shock; it was longer and colder than Toronto's and there was far more snow, a continuing impediment to Redney's steel-edged will:

> "There are no circumstances which can overthrow or circumvent the passionate resolve of a noble, earnest soul", writes Ella Wheeler Wilcox . . . . Mrs. Wilcox has evidently never spent a winter in Montreal. If she had she would have seen hundreds of noble, earnest souls starting out upon the routine of their daily duties with as passionate a resolve to arrive at the scene of them as she could possibly imagine, and being utterly overthrown and distressingly circumvented before getting as far as St. Catherine street (*Star*, Dec. 23, 1887).

She advises her female readers to carry a cane, with a sharp prong on its end, to point the way for rescuers when one is buried in a snow bank, to gauge the depth of water one must wade through in a thaw, but mainly to act as a "stay and support upon icy pavements" (*Star*, Nov. 28, 1887).

As in Toronto, Redney travelled—precariously—around the city in search of copy. She dined in the Presbytère of a French Catholic Indian mission and visited the Brothers of Charity Industrial School, where, waiting in the reception room, she cast an irreverent eye on the portraits of one Pope, two bishops and a private individual who "is not well represented". Monsieur Berthelot, who donated the building "might have been immortalized in a better laundered collar" (*Star*, Dec. 20, 1887).

Her Montreal mood is imaged in the snow and in the Catholic nunneries which she visited. It was in Montreal that an idea of renunciation, of withdrawing emotionally from the world, began to appeal to her romantic sensibility. She was deeply moved by her visit to a Carmelite nunnery, a grim building

> with a very high thick stone wall. I have never seen so impassable a wall around a prison as this which confines inmates who have imposed a life sentence on themselves. The building is the worldy face of the cloistered cells of the Carmelites, and the wall is built about their garden (*Week*, Nov. 10, 1887).

Inside were fifteen sisters who had taken vows of "the most literal renouncement of the world possible to a human being":

> The face of a Carmelite nun is never seen after her entrance except by her immediate relatives, and then only for half an hour once a month, through heavy gratings. Her hand is never touched save by her sisters. From behind the little door that is barred upon her on the day of parting with our pleasant world she never comes again.

Redney approaches that door with awe:

> We ring, and the sound reverberates within, hollow and chill. A nun dressed like those of the convent opposite opens the door, and, after a whispered conference with our French friend, admits us. The hall we stand in is narrow, cold, and ill-ventilated, and we shiver as we pass along to a small, bare room with an opening in the wall about four feet square. From the iron bars which guard it project spikes half a foot long. On the other side of the opening is another barred network, and behind that hangs a black veil.... This is where the Carmelite comes to get her pitiful sight of some one she loved in the days before she became a "favourite soul" (*Week*, Nov. 10, 1887).

It was late afternoon, grey and chill and shadowed, as
Redney left the convent, hearing a "dirge" which swept

> through the gloom from somewhere behind the altar and
> beyond the knowable. It sinks and swells in its inexpressible
> mournfulness, as waves might beat on a desolate shore. It is
> the call—the cry—the chant of the Carmelite nuns (*Week*,
> Nov. 10, 1887).

That cry of desolation and renunciation would echo permanently in Redney's mind.

At the beginning of January, 1888, Redney took a few
days' leave from the *Star*, and went to Kingston to see her
friend Dr Alice McGillivray, then Professor of Obstetrics at
the new Women's Medical College. Redney sat in Alice's
office, the doctor's name painted in black letters on the
outside of the window, and talked "of the present and future
opportunities of women" (*Star*, Jan. 14, 1888). After January
14th, Redney's "Bric-a-Brac" column appeared only twice a
week. Montreal was already beginning to pall. The relentless cold continued, often well below zero; the snow drifts
mounted. She had, since childhood, suffered winter attacks
of bronchitis, and had a racking cough which she could not
seem to shake. The height of winter doldrums, as for most
Canadians, came for Redney in February; as in the previous
February, her restlessness and boredom grow insupportable
and she plotted yet another move.

Her mother was perturbed to receive a letter from her
head-strong daughter at the end of February announcing
that she was about to move to Ottawa, after only four months
in Montreal. A rare frown no doubt creased Jane Duncan's
forehead. If only Redney would find a good husband and
settle down! What Redney did not tell her mother was that
she had invaded male territory even further; she was to
serve as one of the *Star*'s parliamentary reporters, one of two
women in the all-male press gallery.

Redney had difficulty finding an Ottawa boarding-
house since the Parliamentary Session was about to begin.
She looked at a dozen, charging from $16 to $30 a month,
many of them "small and closetless" in houses without gas,
furnaces or even bathrooms. Finally she found one down-

town at 28 Albert Street, but it was not up to her usual elegant standard. In addition to her parliamentary reporting, Redney continued to write her "Bric-a-Brac" column twice a week for the *Star*, and also sent a weekly "Ottawa Letter" to *The Week*. Perhaps enough hard work would keep boredom at bay.

After Washington, her own nation's capital looked uncouth and unplanned, "like a handful of blocks a child might have dropped on the floor" (*Star*, Feb. 29, 1888), with streets of narrow red-brick houses, "painfully ugly...without balcony or verandah", not so much a city of homes, but "rather of temporary abiding places" (*Star*, June 9, 1888). She was anxious, however, to gain *entrée* to Ottawa's artistic circle, if it had one. One of her Montreal acquaintances, the painter William Brymner, a gruff but kindly artist not in the first rank but "much respected by James Morrice and Maurice Cullen",[43] writes to his Ottawa friend, Achille Fréchette, on Redney's behalf:

> A Miss Duncan has gone to Ottawa. I had the cheek to tell her that I was sure you would be glad to know her and said I would write and ask you to call. She wrote for the "Week" last year and now she is employed on the "Star" and writes in that paper as Garth Grafton. I met her at dinner at W. McLennan's here & since then she has been in my studio and I spent an evening at her house or rooms. I think it will not bore you to know her and by calling you will do me a favour.[44]

Achille Fréchette, then forty-one, was an amateur painter who had studied with Brymner and who worked in the House of Commons translation bureau. He was a distant cousin of Wilfrid Laurier, who was often a guest in his home. In 1877 Achille had married Annie Howells, William Dean's sister. She and Redney would have much in common, for, in 1872, hired by *Inter-Ocean* in Chicago, Annie had been one of the very first American woman journalists to work in the office, rather than at home (shocking her brother William, who despatched a disapproving letter). The Fréchettes lived on MacKay Street in New Edinburgh, an Ottawa suburb, close to Rideau Hall. Their circle of friends included young poets Archibald Lampman, Duncan Campbell Scott and

Wilfrid Campbell, while Achille's brother Louis was French-Canada's best-known poet.[45] It was a set of people among whom Redney could feel at home.

She felt rather less at home in the Press Gallery. She and her female colleague, Eve Brodlique of the London *Advertiser*, who had been in Ottawa for the 1887 session and was back for the 1888[46] decided it would be best to invade the Press Room only long enough to collect their papers and blue books from the lockable boxes ranged round the walls, one for each scribe. The men members, who affected frock coats, flowing Byronic ties and wildly original whiskers, were courteous enough, but the air in the Press Room was so blue with smoke that Eve and Redney preferred to work in the Parliamentary Library. It was a quiet, beautiful room where afternoon sun rayed out from the central dome, striking brass gasoliers, gilded bindings, luminous pine and Redney's white pages, as her pen ran a race with the clock hands above her, before six o'clock closing.

The men of the Press Gallery were a genial, happy-go-lucky bunch. The aristocrats among them were those attached to morning papers; only the Montreal *Star* "among afternoon journals compared favourably with the morning newspapers".[47] There were, besides Redney, two other reporters representing the *Star*, E.J. Chambers, and Alex Pirie; the latter, then in his second year as editor-in-chief of the Toronto *Telegram*, was in Ottawa for this session only. Representing the Toronto *Globe* was John Willison, five years Redney's senior, whom she deliberately cultivated, forging a lasting friendship with him, recognizing in him a young man on his way to the top. Willison had begun his newspaper career working for John Cameron on the London *Advertiser* for $3.00 a week as proof-reader and reporter. (In 1890, he would become editor of the *Globe*, in 1902 of the Toronto *News* and in 1910 Canadian correspondent for the London *Times*.) Other members of the gallery included the urbane and polished Molyneux St John of the Montreal *Herald*, and three men who were "young, eager and brilliant, Roden Kingsmill, John Garvin and W.J. Healy".[48]

Redney enjoyed the pomp and ceremony of Parliament's opening at the end of February, its "real splendor and
genuine impressiveness", forming a link with Britain's historic past "in which we have not yet forfeited our right to a
share" (*Star*, Feb. 29, 1888). However, as she sat, day after day
in the Press Gallery, looking down on the heads of the Prime
Minister, Sir John A. Macdonald, and the other members,
while the Eton-jacketed pages ran softly from desk to desk
over the green carpet, Redney soon grew bored, "deeply,
exhaustively, laboriously" bored,[49] and also slightly appalled.
There was plenty of "slander and scandal"[50] in those days
and a small-boys frivolity in the House that shocked her.
The "honourable gentlemen of the Opposition aim large
and forcible paper-balls at the occupants of the Treasury
benches, and the missiles are returned with unearned incre-
ment attached in the shape of mucilage and pen-holders"
(*Week*, April 19, 1888). During one particularly uproarious
all-night sitting, the members threw a cricket-ball back and
forth across the House, and when Sir John rose to close the
debate they yelled: "Give us a song instead!" Sir John
obliged with "God Save the Queen".[51]

If Parliament quickly bored her, there was, to be sure,
plenty of opportunity, in Ottawa as in Washington, to study
character as environment had moulded it. There was "the
legislator with his polished manner from Nova Scotia . . . the
legislator with the long hair from Quebec, the legislator with
the salt of the land as his opinion of himself, from Ontario,
the legislator with the broad and breezy manner from the far
West" (*Star*, June 9, 1888).

There was also an active social scene, with Lord and
Lady Lansdowne's entertainments at Rideau Hall the central gem, but after Washington's splendours it all seemed
rather second-class to Redney. The Lansdownes and Redney
were destined to meet often in the years ahead. The fifth
Marquess of Lansdowne, married to Maud Hamilton, daughter of the first Duke of Abercorn, was a slight, sartorially
elegant man, with a reserved manner, who loved translating
Greek verses and salmon fishing. He had accepted the post
of Governor-General of Canada in 1883 because he had
inherited a family debt of £300,000 and needed the money.

The Lansdownes held large winter outdoor parties in Rideau Hall's grounds, and invited Redney, just after her arrival in Ottawa, to one of these, held on Tuesday night, February 28th. Having curtsied to her host and hostess, she was free to admire the ice palace which had been standing since December, more modest than Montreal's, wherein the band played, keeping their gloves on and thawing their brass instruments round a stove. She skated on the two skating-rinks, ringed with fairy lamps, whizzed down the two long, icy troughs of toboggan slides, loving the speed, the wind in her hair, the feeling of rushing forward into the unknown. The men wore blanket coats and knickerbockers, with sash, stockings and toque in the colours of their snow-shoe clubs, scarlet, purple, sky-blue; they looked, and behaved, like children, their whiskers turning white with hoar-frost as the evening wore on. Supper was served in the curling-rink, where the temperature was quite as low as outdoors, so that while the tables shone with the fifth Marquess' best silver candelabra and plate, there were fir branches instead of flowers in the vases, and all the waiters wore heavy fur-coats and caps.[52] "The uncanny blue and rose and green burnings" of the Chinese lanterns hung "in the branching vistas" of the fir trees reminded Redney of the ones hung in the West Street garden for summer parties, when there had been dew-spangled grass underfoot, not deep, defeating snow, and when the green "branching vistas" suggested hope and possibilities.

Redney also went to evenings of amateur theatricals at Rideau Hall. It was a rush, for she had to eat an early dinner, then pray for a prompt cabman, for guests had to arrive by 7:30. The Ottawa cabs were cosy, jingling affairs with cabby dressed in coonskin coat, cap and mittens, one buffalo robe draped on the seat, another round his passenger's knees. Once inside the viceregal mansion, there was a crush in the hall, then a mad scramble for seats as soon as the doors of the dining-room opened. Everyone wanted to sit directly behind the sofa reserved for the Lansdownes and their party; somehow, Redney always managed it. However, she found herself stifling a yawn more and more frequently at these predictable affairs.

She found the same chaste and childlike provincialism in Ottawa as in Toronto, with the difference that the setting was colder and snowier. It irked her that because she represented a Liberal paper, she was not invited to Conservative functions, for there was absolutely no social mixing between the party in power and the opposition. This meant that she did not get to shine at the poshest parties, nor before the real power-brokers. For Liberals, there were only the Saturday night receptions at the Grand Union Hotel, where the Honourable Leader of the Opposition, Alexander Mackenzie, held court on a sofa in the middle of the room, and Redney listened to the "unstatistical jokes" of her Brantford friend, Billy Paterson, who had been in Parliament for twenty-odd years and knew everyone (*Star*, April 19, 1888). It also annoyed Redney that the lack of a husband barred her from intimate Rideau Hall dinners; "young ladies... whatever their social position in Ottawa, who are without the claim constituted by a husband's official position" were not asked, and that was that (*Star*, March 12, 1888). Redney wanted the centre spotlight, as always, not a dusty stand in the wings, and this Ottawa denied her.

On May 2nd, Redney put on her finery for a farewell Ball at Rideau Hall, for Lord Lansdowne was moving on to greater things: to the most coveted post Britain had to offer its deserving peers, Viceroy of India. Like so many other nobles, Lansdowne had served his apprenticeship as Canada's Governor-General and was now ready for the biggest plum. On May 15th, Redney got dressed up for the final reception for the Lansdownes in the Russell Hotel. "The evening was divided between farewells and ices", reports Redney laconically, too apathetic now to write a long description (*Week*, May 24, 1888).

Redney, too, was getting ready to leave Ottawa, after a miserable spring spent watching slashing rains obliterate the view from her Albert Street windows and wishing she was somewhere else, where she could feel the sun spreading golden warmth and promise through her blood. On June 14th, after only three months' residence, she said good-bye, not at all reluctantly, to Canada's cold capital and, stopping for a short stay in Montreal, circled back, once again, to her Brantford home.

Her summer mood there was elegiac. One July day, Redney sat, hunched and pensive, in the West Street orchard where, earlier,

> the grass was in flower, and had foolish dreams . . . like a girl's heart. And every evening as the sun went down there came from the West a lovely purple glow and lingered in the grass, which was still then and rejoiceful. Sometimes the light had a rosy tinge, sometimes a golden underglow.

Suddenly, there was a chill in the air and the "soul of the summer is gone . . . . The sun went down and left no purple glow in the tall grass, and when I looked I found that every tiny grassflower had dried up into a wrinkled little ghost of itself" (*Star*, July 21, 1888).

And so, at the beginning of September, Redney was back in New York, on another visit to the Wimans. Standing in the South Ferry waiting room, she felt again that "extra drop of nervous fluid in Americans" (*A Daughter of Today*, p. 127) as they swirled round her, buying peaches and milk shakes, getting their shoes shined, knowing exactly where they wanted to go. "Do not drift but steer", was Mr Wiman's creed, and all America's, but Redney's arm was tired, her writing arm . . . so many weed-beds of trivia to push through, so many columns churned out, all of them forgotten in a day. Certainly she had proved herself as a journalist, but journalism would never bring her lasting fame. She needed a different form . . . Redney leaned over the railing of the "Robert Garrett", the ferry taking her to Staten Island, looked out over the choppy blue-grey waters as bits of garbage and old newsprint sank slowly out of sight, kept her eye fixed on the far horizon. Yes, she needed a new kind of writing, new scenes and challenges.

The Wiman coachman met her with a fine pair of mottled black horses, drove her to the Wiman mansion as she leaned back on the padded seat, passing green orchards and long, waving meadow grass. Mattie greeted her at the door, just back from England and India, bubbling over with the excitement of her trip. She talked ecstatically of Ceylon, its tropical richness and its flamboyant flowers, as she and Redney strolled arm-in-arm, about the grounds where "tall

rubber plants and palmettos make pleasant Eastern nooks"
(*Star*, Sept. 13, 1888). During her stay, Mr Wiman arranged a
party for Redney and invited all the important New York
journalists: the small, cheery Mr Ford, editor of *Harper's
Weekly*, Bill Nye of the New York *World*, Miller of the *Times*,
Curtis of *Harper's Magazine*.[54] Suddenly Redney felt energized, effervescent as the champagne bubbling in her glass,
with these famous men laughing delightedly at her pert
sallies. She could feel their interest and approval as she
talked to them, glass held high, of her new, shining vision.

She had followed her star to Washington, to Toronto, to
Montreal, to Ottawa, hammering out shining marks along
the way. Now she would follow the rails right across the
country, to the Pacific's rim. From there she would sail
round the world, following the sun; she wanted a bigger
field than North America, richer greens, rarer flowers. In
the East she would gather an armful of exotic experiences
and bind them together in her liveliest prose. She would
write her first book.

Sara Jeannette Duncan's mother. Courtesy of Mrs K. Duncan.

The family home at 96 West Street, Brantford.

The entrance hall at 96 West Street as it looks now.

Sara Jeannette Cotes in early 1890s.
Courtesy of Public Archives of Canada. C-46447

99 Gower Street, London, where Sara Jeannette Duncan boarded in 1890.

Joaquin Miller.

Courtesy Metropolitan Toronto Library Board.

Sara Jeannette Duncan in her court dress, 1890.
Courtesy Mrs Wilma Duncan.

Sara Jeannette Cotes in 1901. Courtesy of Metropolitan Toronto Library Board

Sara Jeannette Cotes,
circa 1904.

Courtesy Brant Historical Society.

23 Barnett Wood Lane, Ashtead, Surrey.

17 Paulton Square, London.

Sara Jeannette Cotes in 1909.
Courtesy Metropolitan Toronto Library Board.

Everard Cotes.
Courtesy Dr John Cotes.

Pauline Johnson.
Courtesy Brant Historical Society.

Sara Jeannette Cotes, circa 1920.
Courtesy Metropolitan Toronto Library Board.

4
World Travels
"Taking the Image as It Comes"

Let the direction go, . . . and give the
senses flight, taking the image as it
comes, beating the air with happy
pinions.

Sara Jeannette Duncan,
The Pool in the Desert.

Redney herself is going to tell most of this chapter. Her
own account of her trip round the world is fine descriptive
writing, vastly entertaining. She described her odyssey first
in a series of articles for the Montreal *Star*, then revised them
to form a serial in *The Lady's Pictorial*, a London magazine,
and finally, her first published book, bearing the rather
cumbersome title *A Social Departure: How Orthodocia and I
Went Round the World by Ourselves*. The title, however, is the
only cumbersome thing about it. It has a consistently racy,
conversational tone; one can hear Redney's distinctive voice
throughout: here and there slightly weary and sardonic,
particularly in the second half, but mainly breathless and
animated, with laughter bubbling just under the surface.
Here she is, for instance, recounting one of the trip's most
euphoric moments, near its beginning, a ride on the cow-
catcher as the CPR train sped through the Rockies:

Now, I have no doubt you expect me to tell you what it feels like to sit on a piece of black iron, holding on by the flagstaff, with your feet hanging down in front of a train descending the Rockies on a grade that drops four and a half feet in every hundred. I haven't the vocabulary—I don't believe the English language has it. There is no terror, as you might imagine, the hideous thing that inspires it is behind you. There is no heat, no dust, no cinder. The cool, delicious mountain air flows over you in torrents. You are projected swiftly into the illimitable, stupendous space ahead, but on a steady solid basis that makes you feel with some wonder that you are not doing anything very extraordinary after all, though the Chinese navvies along the road looked at Orthodocia and me as if we were. That, however, was because Orthodocia's hair had come down and I had lost my hat, which naturally would not tend to impress the Celestial mind with the propriety of our mode of progression. We were intensely exhilarated, very comfortable and happy, and felt like singing something to the rhythmic roar of the train's accompaniment. We did sing and we couldn't hear ourselves. The great armies of the pines began their march upwards at our feet. On the other side the range of the stately Selkirks rose, each sheer and snowy against the sky. A river foamed along beside us, beneath us, beyond us. We were ahead of everything, speeding on into the heart of the mountains, on into a wide sea of shining mist with white peaks rising out of it on all sides, and black firs pointing raggedly up along the nearer slopes.[1]

"You may choose", says Redney scornfully to *Star* readers, "to be dragged along in an inlaid box upholstered in silk plush all the days of your earthly pilgrimage if you like, but for me I would ride on the engine always" (*Star*, Nov. 3, 1888).

For the first half of her trip, Redney was metaphorically riding on the engine, ahead of everything, pursuing the vision of herself which she has had since childhood: a front runner, outdistancing nine younger brothers and sisters, all of them smaller and slower, outdistancing her classmates in the Brant County Model School, outdistancing other Canadian journalists, setting records, getting there first. She was also pursuing a vision of herself more recently formed: that of the single woman, daring and adventuresome, who leaves her home to travel in search of new experiences. This kind of woman would preoccupy Redney in nine of her novels, beginning with *A Social Departure*, and would provide her with her favourite fictional plot. As one of her heroines puts it, they all travel, as Redney herself did, "to gather up remarkable experiences" (*Vernon's Aunt*, p. 112).

As a writer, Redney wanted to play it safe, to repeat the winning formula of her earlier journalism: to travel to new scenes, then to describe them vividly in print. She had done this first in 1884 with her trip to Quebec and her two articles about it in *Outing*; she had repeated her success in New Orleans, in Florida, in British Honduras. She had grown dependent on the rich stimuli of a continually changing panorama. When she stayed in one place too long—in Washington, Toronto, Montreal or Ottawa, the tedium of the daily round tarnished first her sensibility, then her prose. The moment when Redney had gazed at her reflection in Florida's silver pool had been a prophetic one, a clear prediction of a pattern: she always looked outward, never inward, for her identity and for her inspiration. She needed an external mirror for the self. As Redney sat in the cow-catcher speeding toward new sensations, the old routines left behind along with her hat, she saw her writer's life gleaming ahead of her in an easy, straight line: find an exotic new scene, observe its detail, describe it in print. It worked for her journalism; it would work for her books—or so she thought. Redney sat in the cow-catcher "projected swiftly into the illimitable, stupendous space ahead", as she had been momentarily on the Ottawa toboggan slide, not knowing what she would find but eager, "intensely exhilarated", singing loudly as she went.

Because she was travelling in search of "remarkable experiences", Redney was deliberately "going round the world the wrong way" (*SD*, p. 182), not just because she was travelling from west to east rather than in the more usual direction, but because she was a conscious innovator, an original, riding ahead of the usual travel conventions. Her modes of transport were often unorthodox: cow-catchers, catamarans, donkeys, camels, even an elephant. She went to

places at the wrong time of year when the weather was a trial.
In Tokyo she deliberately chose lodgings away from the
foreign residents' section of the city. At least once she
retraced her steps in an impractical way, doubling back over
territory already covered. Going round the world the wrong
way was the only way (for her) to go.

Mrs Grundy would certainly consider it "the wrong
way"—to go unchaperoned was shocking indeed! In fact,
Redney dedicates *A Social Departure* to that self-same para-
gon of prudery: "This volume", she writes archly, "as a
slight tribute to the omnipotence of her opinion and a
humble mark of profoundest esteem is respectfully dedicated to Mrs. Grundy". "It is very American", explains Redney,
"for young ladies to travel alone but not such a common
thing in my part of the continent that it could be acceded to
without a certain amount of objection on the part of...
friends and relatives" (*SD*, p. 8). Rather than travelling with
a mature person "with the habit of wearing black alpaca and
unknown horrors which she would call 'goloshes' " (*SD*, p. 8),
Redney proposed to travel with a young journalist friend no
older than herself; Mrs Duncan raised objections: "It was the
height of impropriety ... unheard of that two young women
should go wandering aimlessly off to the other side of the
globe!" but Redney "exercised forbearance, valour, and magnificent perseverance" and, as usual, prevailed (*SD*, pp.
9-10).

Redney was going "the wrong way" in another sense—
with no Baedeker in hand, no desire to be edified and
enlightened. "Instruction was entirely a secondary object
with us" (*SD*, p. 91) she writes. Baedekers and set schedules
interfered with the serendipities of travel; it was better to
travel by whim. "We had been so grievously embarrassed by
kind-hearted people who wanted to know our plans in
detail, with dates attached", says Redney, "that we refused to
entertain a single plan or date or detail" (*SD*, p. 11) and thus
they sped away. Accompanying Redney was Lily Lewis, the
"Orthodocia" of *A Social Departure*, a friend from Montreal
days. Lily was a fellow journalist who wrote for the *Montreal
Star* and for *The Week*, sending a regular "Montreal Letter"
to the latter from her home base. Now she had arranged to

send *The Week* articles about her world trip under her usual pseudonym, "Louis Lloyd", and would send back several to the *Star* as well.

Lily had grown up in Montreal, the daughter of John Lewis, a Welshman who came to Canada in 1841 as surveyor of Customs for the port of Montreal. Her mother was Matilda Caroline Snowdon, daughter of Colonel William Snowdon, a Scot who had ridden with Sir John Colborne at the head of the British troops at the battle of St. Eustache in the 1837 rebellion.[2] Lily came from the same sort of genteel, well-heeled family environment as Redney, except that her Celtic heritage was Welsh-Scottish rather than Irish-Scottish, and her family Anglican rather than Presbyterian. The image of Lily which emerges from Redney's *Star* articles and her own in *The Week*, is of a young lady as soft and bending as her name, less sophisticated and self-assured than Redney, quite willing to let the latter be the dominant member of the party, even though Lily herself had been abroad before, visiting Paris in June of 1887 (*Star*, June 8, 1889). Redney claims in *A Social Departure* that she had to protect Lily "from extortionate cabmen and foolish bargains in curios" (*SD*, p. 55) and certainly it is Redney, not Lily, who sits in the cow-catcher of their relationship.

"People must travel round the world with their friends to know them", says Redney (*SD*, p. 384), suggesting that perhaps she and Lily were not well-acquainted before the trip, yet their friendship seems to have worn well for the twenty-month period of continued intimacy. They were alike in many ways; in addition to their common profession, they shared a sense of adventure, a youthful *joie de vivre*, an interest in the visual arts and a keen sense of humour. One of Lily's most endearing traits was her ability to laugh at herself. Sitting on the floor of a store in Nagasaki, "chattering à la phrase-book" in Japanese, Lily didn't mind at all when the clerks were "convulsed with laughter. I laughed too. One loses so many laughs by not laughing at oneself" (*Week*, Aug. 9, 1889). The girls did occasionally argue good-naturedly about whether a particularly choice morsel of copy should go to *Star* or *Week* readers. Lily, complains

Redney, "had a bad habit which I can look back upon
forgivingly now but which was very trying at the time, of
exclaiming whenever she found anything particularly delec-
table 'That's mine!' " (*Star*, Aug. 31, 1889). Lily seems to have
been more democratic in her political views than Redney,
for they had "a bitter altercation ... as to the ethics of a
British India". Redney was all for the imperialist yoke,
whereas Lily sympathized with the poor Indian, robbed "of
his holiest emotion — patriotism" and they ended the argument by craning their necks "out of opposite sides" of their
carriage "further than ever" (*Star*, Oct. 16, 1889).

Their itinerary went like this: they travelled by train
across Western Canada to Vancouver, by ship to Japan,
Ceylon (visiting Colombo and Kandy), and India (visiting
Calcutta, Madras, Bombay and Agra), by ship to Suez, by
train to Cairo and by ship back to England via Brindisi,
Malta and Gibraltar. They were in Japan from late November, 1888 until late January, 1889, in Ceylon for most of
February, in India until March when they moved to Egypt
for several weeks and by mid April, 1889, they were in the
Mediterranean en route to England, arriving, as Redney
states in the body of one *Star* article, on "May Day".

Redney wrote thirty-six articles for the *Star* describing
her world tour: five appeared in 1888 (the first one datelined
"Sept. 24, Moosomin" appeared Oct. 20), twenty-three in
1889 and eight in 1890. All articles up to and including the
one for November 20, 1889 were signed "Garth Grafton"; the
Dec. 12th one is signed "Sara Jeannette Duncan (Garth
Grafton)" and the Dec. 20th one, "Sara Jane Duncan (Garth
Grafton)"; all eight articles for 1890 are signed "Sara Jeannette Duncan".

The datelines on Redney's articles are deceiving; two
articles in different issues of the *Star* are both dated November 1st, 1890, yet one is head-lined "Colombo" and the other
"Calcutta". The *Star* article datelined "Calcutta, Aug. 15,
[1889]" describes a vice-regal party which, according to *A
Social Departure*, took place six months before, on February
28th, 1889. The *Star* article for June 3, 1890, datelined
"Southampton, May 1" appeared a year after the fact, for

Redney arrived in England in May of 1889.[3] This time lag may have been Redney's fault, taking a long time either to write up her impressions or to mail them, or it may have been the *Star*'s, letting her copy gather dust on the editor's desk. Certainly there was no feeling in journalistic circles then, as now, that an item had to be "hot". Lily's description of Hong Kong as it appeared to her in January, 1889, appears in *The Week* in March, 1890, more than a year later.

Apart from datelines, however, Redney's *Star* accounts are factually accurate, and closely correlate with *A Social Departure*, which Redney claims is "a faithful chronicle of the ordinary happenings of an ordinary journey" (*SD*, p. 40). The very detailed descriptions of scenes and people in both published accounts suggest that she kept a daily journal of her trip, written up on the spot and later expanded and polished into versions suitable for publication.

She and Lily began their great adventure on September 17th, 1888, the *Star* reporting in its personal column that "Miss Sarah Jeannette Duncan (Garth Grafton) of the Montreal *Star*, left Brantford yesterday for a tour of Japan (*Star*, Sept. 18, 1888). As always, Redney was ecstatic to be travelling again, particularly to be headed for the exotic East. Lily and Redney between them had four portmanteaus, two large trunks, two shawl straps, and a green trunk entrusted to them for delivery in Japan by a Canadian acquaintance, a cursed green trunk with a mind of its own about its destination and a habit of disappearing whenever it was wanted. The girls also had letters of introduction to be presented along the way. They said their final farewells in a state of high excitement "out of the car window in the noisy lamp-lit darkness of Montreal station" (*SD*, p. 11) and sped westward on the splendid new Canadian Pacific, completed three years before. Travelling by whim, the girls had told their relatives that "we would get out occasionally and wait for the next train where the landscape looked inviting" (*SD*, p. 11) and they did in fact stop over at Winnipeg, Moosomin, Regina and finally at the "Great Glacier" in the Selkirks, where they stayed at a luxurious Swiss-chalet hotel and climbed the glacier as far as they could go.

On the morning of the third day, feeling rather stiff and dusty, they reached Winnipeg, then a city of 25,000 with very wide streets and solid public buildings. Redney was surprised to find how civilized it all was. She met Lily's brother Lansing, a wiry little man with neatly trimmed beard, who had advanced ideas about female suffrage and a flashing Welsh humour. He was then thirty-four, newly married to the daughter of Sir Henry Newell Bate of Ottawa, and had been in Winnipeg for eight years working with single-minded ambition in the insurance firm of Drummond Brothers and Lewis, serving briefly as acting mayor of Winnipeg and as *aide-de-camp* to two Manitoban Lieutenant-Governors. Redney enjoyed being a guest at Katharine and Lansing's gracious table.[4]

Beyond the province of Manitoba, however, civilization abruptly ended, for the Northwest Territories (comprising Assiniboia, Alberta and Saskatchewan) were still largely unsettled. Moosomin was a distinct shock. The only hotel was an unvarnished frame house and Redney and Lily's room impossibly small and ill-equipped. Fastidious Redney recoiled, abandoning her earlier plan of spending time on a Northwest farm. She and Lily made fun at dinner of the local young men "who slouched in to dine as if edging a way through brushwood" (*Week*, Oct. 25, 1888). Things improved in Regina, however, whose "short but solid-looking main street" was lined with brick houses (*Star*, Oct. 27, 1888), for Regina boasted a population of eight hundred and the whole town, in its own modest Canadian way, pulsed with some of Washington's energetic optimism.

The girls were squired around Regina by "genial" Nicholas Flood Davin, editor of the Regina *Leader*. Redney had met Davin in Ottawa where he was, from 1887 to 1900, the Conservative member for West Assiniboia, one of Sir John A's protegées, the best Conservative orator in the House. Davin was a brilliant and erratic Irishman, forty-five years old, with a wide moustache and shrewd grey eyes.[5] He had trained as a lawyer in London, England, served as war-correspondent in the Franco-Prussian War, emigrated to Canada in 1872 and been hired as *Globe* editorial writer by George Brown. Two years later he had switched to the practice of law, so that when the disgruntled employee who had shot George Brown came to trial for murder, Davin defended him brilliantly, but unsuccessfully. In March, 1883, Davin had founded the *Leader*, the first newspaper in Assiniboia. He was also a regular contributor to *The Week* and fancied himself as a poet. For Redney and Lily, he was a vastly entertaining and lively companion, rolling out, in his rich brogue, an unending stream of amusing stories.[6]

Before leaving Regina, Redney and Lily took tea with a British homesteader in a drawing-room full of antiques, gilt-framed mirrors, family portraits, even a Broadwood piano, so that Redney found herself listening "for the roll of wheels through South Kensington or Regent Park". She did not know it at the time, but this Englishman, "half adopting the customs and clothes of the foreigners, half clinging to his own, and not especially happy in his state of transition", was a foretaste of those transplanted to India whom Redney would, over the years, have ample opportunity of observing. Like the sweet william and mignonette at his door, this British gentleman-farmer was "a familiar garden flower solitary in alien soil" (*Star*, Oct. 27, 1888). For Redney he would become a haunting image.

Back on the train as it left Regina and sped west, Redney met another literary father-figure who would influence her. Lily's account of this meeting not only gives us a fine close-up of Redney but also reveals how Lily habitually stayed in the background:

> Our train had just left Medicine Hat . . . when Garth Grafton came up hurriedly, excitedly, with that peculiarly feminine interrogatory exclamation: "*Do you know, do you know,* my dear, who the tall, gray-haired man is to whom I've been speaking?"

> > I confessed my ignorance.
> > "That man is Charles Dudley Warner!"
> > "Charles Dudley who?"

> "Charles Dudley Warner. Well, think of it, just think; the author of the delicious *My Summer in a Garden* and *Backlog Studies* and—and—oh! You *must* know. Well! I was standing

on the platform, and the Assistant General Manager came up
and asked us into his private car. Mr. Warner was there, and
repeated the invitation, so we're going. [Lily confesses to
total ignorance of Warner] "Not know Warner!" continued
Garth aghast. "Not know Warner! Why, you might just as
well say you don't know Longfellow, or Emerson, or —
anybody. Have you heard of Lowell? Have you heard of
Whittier? Perhaps you would like me to tell you who Mark
Twain is? Not heard of Charles Dudley Warner! and I've
been saying we are his most ardent admirers. Well, I don't
care; *I* am, at any rate, so you must just get out the best way
you can.

Garth is a Canadian *doublée d'une Americaine* . . . . Garth
knows lots of American *litterateurs* more or less personally. I
don't think I ever spoke to a genuine author in my life; I
mean one who has had his things printed without paying for
it . . . . Mr. Warner then came in and repeated his invitation.
Garth, hugely pleased, was on the point of going out, when a
premonitory motion of my foot withheld her. We promised
to join the party anon. [Lily then asks for information about
Warner] . . . but Garth got up suddenly and wouldn't wait
any longer. I rose also. My mouth twitched into a ghastly
smile. I knew how the whole thing must turn out. We should
enter and get luxuriously seated, and have miles of prairie to
look at, and then — then Garth would talk Washington and
New Orleans. Garth always talks Washington and New Orleans
when she can; it is her fox's platter . . . . No. Garth didn't start
Washington, but she started something worse — Commercial
Union . . . . Our interviews *à trois* usually pass this way. Garth
having been some years on American newspapers, always
distances me (*Week*, Dec. 14, 1888).

No doubt Redney's head was still echoing with Chaz
Wiman's cogent arguments for Canadian-American commercial union, heard round the Wiman dinner table the
previous month, and now trotted out to impress Charles
Dudley. She and Warner would "talk New Orleans" because
he, too, had been there during the Exposition, loving the
city, as Redney did, for "preserving more of the old and
romantic than any other American city".[7] The two of them
would have plenty to talk about, while poor Lily sat mute.
What Warner, listening delightedly to Redney's chatter,

didn't know, was that she had given him one of her hammer-taps in print, bristling because he had, after three days in Montreal, declared in *Harper's Magazine* that the moribund state of Canadian letters was due to the cold climate (*Week*, Sept. 30, 1886), nor did he know that she had borrowed the title of one of his books *Saunterings* (1870) for her *Week* column. Like Howells, Warner was one of Redney's literary idols, having "made a specially sunny place in a certain bookshelf I knew of" (*Star*, Nov. 3, 1888). Her own style has something of his ironic humour and his gentle, Addisonian kind of social satire. She was thrilled to have this unexpected opportunity to bask, and burgeon in Warner's bright beams.

Charles Dudley Warner's forte was the familiar essay and he had published many books of personal travelogues and sketches, first coming to fame in 1870 with *My Summer in a Garden*, a book which Redney would later use as model for one of her own. It is a charming book in which Warner's basic optimism and trust, like Joaquin Miller's, finds expression in his love of growing things. Warner was a tall, bearded man of fifty-nine, with longish grey hair, remarkable blue eyes which Redney tells Lily she must despair of ever accurately describing in print, and a charming smile which "began at the heart and worked upwards" (*Week*, Dec. 14, 1888). He came from an old New England family and lived at "Nook Farm" in Hartford, Connecticut, next door to Mark Twain.

Like Joaquin Miller and Nicholas Flood Davin, Warner had practised law for several years before becoming a newspaper editor—in his case, of the Hartford *Evening Press*. He was currently editor of the "Drawer" column of *Harper's Magazine*, and would eventually take over its "Study" column from William Dean Howells.[8]

Charles and Redney had an instant rapport and she was thrilled to be adding another literary lion to her list of acquaintances. In addition to their love of New Orleans, they shared a passion for flowers, a belief that women had the right to full emancipation[9], but shouldn't sacrifice their feminine attention to clothes. "Love itself", Warner was to write, "could scarcely be expected to survive a winter hat worn after Easter".[10] He liked bright, cultivated women, believing that "neither persons nor plants are ever fully themselves until they are cultivated to their highest",[11] and he is charmed with Redney. Perhaps he was thinking of her when he wrote that: "The Canadian girl resembles the American in escape from a purely conventional restraint and in self-reliance, and she has, like the English, a well-modulated voice and distinct articulation".[12] As Redney talked on in her own low-pitched, pleasing voice, Warner was spellbound to such an extent that he came round to her point of view in their only area of disagreement. As the train sped west into the mountains and the rainy weather which had plagued them in Winnipeg gave way to bright sunshine for the remainder of the trip, Redney was earnestly disagreeing with Warner's view that Canadians have no "national identity". Redney told him tartly to interview a few—they can be "approached without great difficulty by any person having a slight familiarity with the language"—He will thereby discover that Canadians do indeed have "entirely distinct characteristics" (*Star*, Nov. 3, 1888). By the time his *Comments on Canada* appeared in 1889, Warner had come round to Redney's view: "One can mark already with tolerable distinctness a Canadian type which is neither English nor American", he observes meekly.[13]

Redney was deeply moved as the train snaked through the mountains, "the snow-capped mountains, in their stern, remote, inaccessible beauty" (*SD*, p. 51). Here was a further margin and mystery than any she had ever glimpsed, and a new image of the ideal loomed permanently in her mind: snow-capped, inaccessible, shining and perfect. At last, in the third week of October, the CPR train pulled slowly into the Vancouver station and Redney sighed happily: "There is a satisfaction that is difficult to parallel in getting as far as you can go" (*SD*, p. 51). The travellers liked Vancouver so much that they decided not to catch the *Batavia* for Japan the next day, as tentatively planned, but to wait for the next ship out, due in two weeks. They stayed at the Hotel Vancouver, where Charles Dudley Warner had also registered, finding it "in point of comfort, elegance of appointment, abundant table service, not excelled by any in Canada".[14]

The Hotel Vancouver had other attractions for Redney and Lily, however, beyond Warner, for they were enjoying the combined French delights of the cuisine, and the company of three young men who had come to Vancouver from France to buy property. One of them had "golden hair", one was "tall and bronzed" and the third beguiled them with Chopin on the grand piano in the upper hall, reminding Redney of summer evenings at Chiefswood when Beverley Johnson's fingers had sprinkled Chopin to the soft twilight. The Three Musketeers invited Redney and Lily on an overnight duck-shooting party and they eagerly accepted, Redney declaring, with her habitual desire to best the others, that ducks were all very well but that *she* intended to shoot a bear! Lily gives a full account of this lark in *The Week* (Dec. 28, 1888). They took a steam yacht up the Fraser River, spent the night on "bracken couches" in an abandoned cabin. The next day's shooting, where Redney "aimed ever so much more scientifically than I did", according to the modest Lily, yielded only one duck and not a glimpse of a bear.

There was another happy excursion to Victoria on board the *Yosemite*, this one with Charles Dudley Warner and a party of his friends. To Redney, Victoria looked like "a dear old maiden aunt in curl-papers...very set in her ways" (*Star*, Nov. 10, 1888).

Vancouver, on the other hand, was Regina in the Pacific, a booming, bustling town two years old with 18,000 inhabitants, many of them land speculators. "It exhilarates one to be in a place whose vigorous young vitality is so strong as to get into one's blood" enthused Redney (*Star*, Nov. 10, 1888), feeling the consonance of self-and-setting which habitually fuelled her best writing. Blocks of buildings were springing up amid the charred stumps and skunk-cabbage swamps, and the sound of hammers was drowning out the chorus of frogs. Redney decided that "there is an American spirit in the place" which buoyed her up just as Washington's had, in her initial stage of high energy.

By the end of the first week of November, Redney and Lily felt ready to leave Vancouver for the Orient. By this time they were such relaxed travellers, so content to drift rather than steer, that they almost missed the ship, the first of many instances of their habitual tardiness. The two-week passage on *The Duke of Westminster* was "horribly stormy, and we had head winds all the way" (*Week*, Jan. 11, 1889). There were a dozen passengers aboard, including two young English aristocrats, one the grandson of a Duke, whom Redney observed closely. It was her first encounter with a type she would later capture in print.

The girls landed at Yokohama around November 22, and after the tedium of a sea voyage, the colour and novelty of Japan lifted Redney's spirits at once. In "quaint Japan", she writes, "one laughs more than anywhere else in the world" (*SD*, p. 65). Knowing it would be an adventure they could capitalize on in print, the travellers decided to rent a house upon arrival in Tokyo:

> We had kept a dolls' establishment before, and it would be interesting to renew our extreme youth by doing it again, this time in the capacity of the dolls. Perhaps, too we could get a more satisfactory idea of the national life if we sat on the floor for our point of view. And straightway we went to look at three modest domiciles from which the householders had gathered up their cushions and departed (*SD*, p. 76).

After inspecting all three, they decided on the third one on the hill of Kudan, near the Imperial Palace. The house, as big as a "bon-bon box", exactly suited Redney's mood, relaxed and floating, open to new experiences, ready for anything. "Dignities and classifications in the matter of our apartments were purely arbitrary", she writes, "the side-board and the dining-table and the piano being a-wanting and the bed and toilet arrangements put securely away in the wall, we might sleep in the dining-room, dine in the *salon*, and receive in the bedroom with equal comfort and propriety" (*SD*, p. 92) The girls engaged five servants to look after them since servants came cheap in Japan, "a gentle, smiling fluttering set" (*Star*, Feb. 5, 1889), and began a varied social schedule which included "at homes" on Saturday afternoons, a garden party given by a Japanese gentleman who read of their arrival in the newspaper and wanted them to meet his two sons just returned from an American college, a charity bazaar, and a tour of the Mikado's new palace three days before he moved in.

Redney was supremely happy in Japan, for two reasons. Firstly, more than any place she had ever been, Japan satisfied her highly developed aesthetic sense, her hunger for beauty of colour and form. Beauty blossomed everywhere in Japan, particularly the beauty of man-made art. For one who firmly believes that "in all our complex system of giving pleasure to ourselves there is little that imparts a keener joy than simply to stand in the presence of the beautiful as man has created it" (*Globe*, Jan. 28, 1887), Japan was a constant delight. "One's eyes", Redney was to write later, acknowledging her visual bias, "have given one more and keener pleasure certainly than any other organ" (*On the Other Side of the Latch*, p. 71) and in Japan Redney's eyes had a feast. She visited Japan at a time when there was a Western craze for its decorative arts, sparked in part by Gilbert and Sullivan's *The Mikado*, which she may well have seen in its Toronto performances of 1885. There isn't "any place out of Paradise so fascinating to the feminine soul", Redney had written while still in Canada, "as the Japanese shop of this continent" (*Star*, Nov. 28, 1887), and a whole column of her "Woman's World" series is devoted to a lyrical description of a consignment of Japanese ceramics (*Globe*, Dec. 18, 1886). "The undeniable fact", she confesses, "is that we spent a great deal more time" in Japan "in the shops than anywhere else" (*SD*, p. 137). These were "the long, happy days" when "all the dainty fantastic life about us pressed sharp upon our senses" and where "the acutest joy was centred in the buying of a teapot" (*SD*, p. 108). Redney had always needed visual beauty as a spur for her imagination; now as she wrote up her travel adventures each night in her journal, her imagination soared like one of Japan's golden kites and the words unwound effortlessly from the spool of her experiences. In Japan, the recording "I" became even more dependent on the seeing eye; Redney bought masses of curios to keep her inspiration permanently around her.

Another reason Redney was happy in Japan was because she had been raised on Oriental images in her Brantford childhood. "Who does not remember marvelling over the lovely ladies on the thin olive green box of her grand-mother's 'flowery Pekoe'?" she asks (*Star*, Nov. 28, 1887). Three wild geese flew with long necks outstretched over the Mikado's moat "just as they flew always across a tea-tray, that I knew long before I went to Japan" (*SD*, p. 104), and a group of Japanese matrons startled her because they talked: "We had known their facsimile postured gracefully upon fans and tea chests for so many childish years, during which they never spoke at all, that their low voices seemed a strange and unnecessary part of them" (*SD*, p. 110). The whole Japanese world, not just its art, led Redney back to a child's world where one lived only in the present, on a level of pure sensation, innocently and impulsively.

There was one aspect of Japanese life, however, which angered Redney, and that was the position of women. A visit to a Geisha girl, made in the company of a friend, Taro-San, a government official, raised her feminist hackles. "The culture of a Japanese lady", confined as it is to social graces and flower arranging "is like a very minute and wonderful growth of flowers within the compass of a finger ring" she writes (*Star*, April 6, 1889). Here was a constricting metal hoop smaller than anything in Western society. The feminist who had aired her views in "Woman's World" resurfaced now in a *Star* column in which she interviews a Japanese novelist:

> Society is composed of men and women and cannot develop in any way the world will turn its head to look at, without the equal, even the predominating influence of the latter. Japan is only beginning to take women into account and her social system is yet on a plane which makes imperial concubinage an honor, and legalizes the sale of daughters, by their parents, to lives of infamy. So long as ... her novels reflect these conditions, the modern schools will not receive an impulse from the fiction of Japan (*Star*, April 3, 1889).

The position of women, however, was Japan's only drawback; the rest was a dream, an idyllic interlude, and Redney was understandably loath to leave. She held Japan's heart in her hands, as she departed, in the shape of a red camellia:

I carried a budding camellia branch, with one conscious red flower open-eyed. I mused upon it, thinking how curious it was that a flower could grow and blow to be just the decorative essence that it seemed, and nothing more (*SD*, p. 171).

Suddenly the camellia was "red and white. I looked up—the snow had come" (*SD*, p. 171). Japan had been a beautiful kaleidoscope and had inspired some of her finest writing.

She left Japan in January, 1889, on her first "P and O" (Peninsular and Oriental), a steamship line for which Redney had nothing but praise, after having "sailed with intense joy and satisfaction upon seven of the ships of the P and O" (*SD*, p. 19), and finding on all of them the same unfailing "kindness and courtesy, and even protection" (*SD*, p. 409). As in Japan, life aboard ship allowed Redney an escape from the real world; there she was always cocooned in comfort and carefree indolence, and she would become addicted, as the years passed, to the Shangri-La of P and O life. Laziness, decides Lily, as they sail for Ceylon on the *Sutlej*, after brief stops in Hong Kong, Singapore and Penang, "isn't often made as seductive as on a P and O steamer. When we weren't disporting ourselves in a marble bath, we were toying with delicious iced things in the *Sutlej*'s salon, or dreaming Eastern dreams in the sleepy afternoon stillness or burning incense to the solemn stars" (*Week*, March 28, 1890).

They must go ashore in a catamaran, decided Redney upon arrival at Colombo. All the other passengers were going in the steam launch, but she preferred this "small wet wooden half egg", without even a seat, "because it was an innovation, and we were opposed on general principles to the ordinary and the commonplace" (*SD*, p. 203). This time, however, the girls overreached themselves: "I suppose that two more water-logged passengers never disembarked at Colombo. We advised each other warmly as we wrung each other out, to travel in future with our luggage in the steam launch" (*SD*, p. 204). It was hard to reform all at once, however, so they decided not to stay at the Grand Hotel with all the other tourists, but at the Galle Face, "a quaint old castellated looking concern in a clump of cocoanuts by the sea about half a mile from town" (.*Star*, July 6, 1889).

One day while Lily sat reading in their high-ceilinged room with blasts of hot air and an occasional crow blowing in through the open windows, Redney indulged in a characteristic gesture:

> Suddenly Garth came in on tiptoe and put something between me and the pages of the pamphlet of statistics. It was a flower. It was a very large flower, with a multitude of velvety rounded petals, pearly pink, like the lining of a shell. I took it up in my hands. . . . Its perfume was fine and strong. I bent lower over it with a sort of rapture. . . . It was the heart of India that I held. Between me and the pamphlet of statistics Garth had put a lotus (*Week*, Dec. 27, 1889).

If Japan's aesthetic heart had been a red camellia, India's sensuous one was a lotus. "The separate phial of perfume at the end of every stamen" (*SD*, p. 219) drew Redney seductively towards the ideal in art just as the vases and teapots had in Japan. It was on the train to Kandy in central Ceylon that Redney got her second portent of India's secret heart:

> Here and there a little lake lay in the jungle, giving back strange blooms of yellow and scarlet. . . . Far away to the right of us a jagged blue line of mountains ran along the sky. A whole panorama of the tropics stretched between them and us . . . full everywhere of that throbbing, sensuous life that sends young leaves forth in great curves and dips, that puts a flame into the hearts of flowers and a flash on the wings of birds (*SD*, p. 229).

The jungle seemed to shoot up almost as one watched, new growth instantly sprouting from spongy decay. Could one do that, wondered Redney, staring out the train window, in one's art . . . from rotting branch to orchid, real to ideal, all in one quick, creative leap? "Let the direction go", cries an artist in one of Redney's short stories, "give the senses flight, taking the image as it comes, beating the air with happy pinions" (*The Pool in the Desert*, p. 188). Beginning with her discovery of the exotic East, this became Redney's favourite formula for writing.

During this trip, she was continuously "wrought up to an immense keenness of sense and brilliancy of energy"

(*Path of a Star*, p. 253). She felt more alive, more vibrant, than she ever had before. Her senses surged dramatically in Kandy's Botanical Gardens, where "marvellous butterflies floated sensuously from flower to flower" and "a lizard like a streak of green fire darted from the shadow of one great plant to the shadow of another" (*Star*, Aug. 31, 1889). New Orleans' vistas of riotous green prompted Redney's first creative spurt; these tropical gardens seemed to promise full flowering. Redney marveled that the palmetto of Canadian "home conservatories", there cossetted indoors through the long winter to counteract the white sterility without, here arched "in its beautiful youth straight from the soil" (*SD*, p. 235).

At the end of February, Redney and Lily reluctantly left Ceylon and sailed on another P and O, the *Coromandel*, up the Bay of Bengal and the Hooghly river to Calcutta, where they engaged rooms in a boarding-house for the next month. They were delighted with their large rooms, curtained in pale Indian muslins, complete with dressing-room, balcony and bath, and at once, according to the usual tourist practice, they each engaged a servant from a collection lined up on the verandah. For the equivalent of twelve cents a day their choice, Ram, a fat Hindoo, and Arumzan, a tall Moham-medan, brought them *chota hazri* ("little breakfast" of tea and toast), stood behind their chairs at table, raided the kitchen on their behalf, ran errands, rode the box of their *ticca-gharri* (India's horse-drawn public conveyance) and squatted out-side their door awaiting orders the rest of the time. These brief experiences with Japanese and Indian servants were a useful apprenticeship for Redney who would one day have a houseful to handle on a permanent basis.

Not even Ceylon had prepared Redney for the amaz-ing, entrancing, stupefying, dazzling, disorienting assault of India upon her senses. It was a kaleidoscope of infinite complexity, spinning colours, strange garden growths, strang-er birds and beasts, strangest gods. It was new life in a newly created world. Even the homeliest, simplest objects, the oxen drawing the carts, the crows squabbling in the gutter, were extreme, exotic, for the little buff-satin oxen had humps, the crows were blue.

Redney's aesthetic eye blinked, and blinked again,
unbelieving. The colours in the street-crowds were like no
other dyes she had ever seen; they radiated the very sun's
intensity. These were the archetypes of colour, the deep,
primal paint-pots from which all others were taken. There
were tulip-gardens of turbans: vermilion, crimson, orange.
There were satin trousers of fuchsia and purple, waistcoats
of peacock blue and emerald, saris of sulphur yellow and
chartreuse. The light gilded everything, so that even bare
brown arms and legs were polished bronze, or dusky topaz.
Surely the East had enough colour to inspire her indefinitely;
Redney's pen raced, recording what she saw in her journal.
Images flamed and flashed on every page.

It seemed strange and jarring to Redney, however, to
find in this great, gaudy setting, as she had found in British
Honduras, the high palings of English social forms. Nevertheless, when she and Lily met "a memsahib who knew
people" (*Star*, Nov. 20, 1889), Redney was British enough and
snob enough to enjoy driving up to the Memsahib's cool
portico, its white pillars twined with bougainvillea, for her
Sunday at-homes and tennis parties, being bowed in by
red-and-gold liveried servants. This same memsahib chaperoned the girls to parties, and introduced them to her
friends.

Redney quickly sized up the Anglo-Indian type, those
Britishers transplanted to India's strange soil. Her descriptions of them in *A Social Departure* hinted at the satiric skills
she would later perfect in her novels, where not only
Anglo-Indians but also Canadians, Americans and Britishers were pinned to the specimen board through their exact
centres. She found the typical Anglo-Indian extremely hospitable, lacquered over "with a coat of indifference", fatalistic,
"blunt with his antipathies", treating all natives with a
"hearty contempt". Unless she was a woman of resources, his
wife spent her time in "flirtations—mild little flirtations
which she tells the Heaven-Born about, or flirtations to the
nth, which she does not" (*Star*, Dec. 20, 1889).

One morning soon after their arrival in Calcutta, when
Redney was escaping the heat on the cool upper verandah of
their boarding-house, a large, square white envelope was

handed to her by a servant "with more than the usual amount of scarlet and gold". The card inside informed the ladies that the Aide-de-Camp-in-Waiting was "commanded by His Excellency the Viceroy" to invite them to an "Evening Party on the 28th of February at 9:30 o'clock" (*SD*, p. 266). It was to be the last evening party of the season, before fashionable Calcutta migrated to Simla for the hot weather. The Viceroy was Redney's Ottawa acquaintance, Lord Lansdowne, who had been in Calcutta since the previous December, but who found tiger hunts a poor substitute for Canada's excellent salmon fishing. This square, white card, which Redney held in both hands and read excitedly, would change her life.

On the appointed evening, the *ticca-gharri*, with Redney and Lily inside, the most decrepit and dirty *ticca-gharri* in all Calcutta, according to Redney, drew up at the Viceregal mansion. Copied from Adams' design for Kedleston Hall, built by Lord Wellesley who had shocked the East India Company directors with his extravagance, Government House was a truly royal residence, surrounded by six acres of lawn and garden. It presented to the world a buff-coloured expanse, solid and symmetrical, of central portico and dome, tall Ionic pillars, four extensive wings. Redney, feeling royal herself, ascended the double flight of steps, which were imperially wide, a couchant sphinx on either side. To the left and right stood tufted palms, ivy tightly and tenaciously clinging to their trunks: India and England intertwined.[15] Redney and Lily, arrayed in as much finery as three countries' wear-and-tear allowed, hurried through the wide halls to the dressing-room, for last-minute primping with the other chattering young ladies, and to meet their *memsahib* chaperone. Redney was flushed, excited as she walked through the crimson-carpeted ante-chamber to the ball-room itself, then drew in her breath at the splendid sight. A hundred gas jets shone back from the polished teak floor; an orchestra was playing at one end, but since this was merely an evening reception and not a ball, there was no dancing. Guests were strolling about, helping themselves to ices and champagne cup from a long buffet decorated with roses and ferns. To Redney's delighted gaze the company assembled was the human counterpart of the tropical opulence of Kandy's Botanical Gardens: "As to the humanity gathered there, that met and parted, and bowed and smiled, and talked and passed on, I suppose for actual brilliancy, that sparkles in a jewel and glows in a rich fabric, and flashes where contrasting civilizations meet and mingle, nothing like it could be formed out of the capital of the Indian Empire in the whole world" (*SD*, p. 270). There were three celebrities in the crowd: the Archbishop of the Greek Church in lace and purple velvet, the conquering hero of Burma, General Sir Harry Prendergast with "a red face and bushy side whiskers" and a German prince, "a tall, fair creature with a wasp-waist all in the bluest of blue uniforms" (*Star*, Nov. 2, 1889).

It was as perfect a setting for romance as any novelist could wish, and it was here, either in the brilliantly-lit ballroom, or on one of the shadowy verandahs "looking out upon the mystery of a tropical garden" (*SD*, p. 270), that Sara Duncan was introduced to Everard Charles Cotes. He was twenty-six years old, tall and blond, with a fair skin rather sunburnt, and a fine bearing. Like her father, he was the kind of man one notices in a crowd, with a courtesy deeply instinctive and sincerely felt. He told Redney that he had come out from England four years ago as assistant to the Superintendent of Calcutta's Indian Museum, described his work there as entomologist, examining insect pests which farmers sent to the Museum for identification, and in every spare moment compiling the first *Catalogue of the Moths of India*, a huge work almost finished after three years' intensive labour.[16]

As he fetched her champagne and ices and then steered her through the crowd with a gentle pressure on the elbow, Redney observed Everard closely and felt drawn to him. Because of her strong visual bias, she always needed an exotic setting to germinate feelings of romantic love, as in New Orleans where she fell for Joaquin. In India she had a setting even more sensual and striking. Everard had the kindest blue eyes she had ever seen, with many fine, faint laugh-lines at their outer corners. There was something in his thin face and taut posture which suggested a greyhound's elegance and bearing.

Everard was equally enchanted with this pretty, poised Canadian girl whose conversation sparkled like her eyes. One met so few unattached young ladies in India — most of the English ones were spoken for before they landed — but to meet one so charming! Everard stuttered now and then as they talked, his face flushed with the discovery of such a prize, such a rare specimen, for at the Viceregal party of February 28th, 1889, Sara Duncan had reached a height of self-assurance. Surely the feelings of one of her heroines at a similar Viceregal function were Redney's own:

> She was full that night of a triumphant sense of her own vitality, her success and value as a human unit. There was that in her blood which assured her of a welcome, it had logic in it, with the basis of her rarity, her force, her distinction among other women (*Path of a Star*, p. 200).

In the flame-and-flash setting that was India, Redney revelled in her own rarity and force. Once more, as in New Orleans, self and setting bloomed together in a fine feeling of wholeness, and self-worth.

Redney was still radiant next evening when, with Lily, she attended one of the highlights of the Calcutta season, the investiture Durbar at which the Viceroy bestowed various Imperial dignities and decorations on the worthy. The Durbar was held in a large tent on the Viceregal grounds, "with carpeting spread all the way from the dressing rooms in Government House, for the protection of satin-clad feet" (*Star*, Nov. 2, 1889). Redney enjoyed the pomp and circumstance, describing in detail how they were seated and given programs, large folios in red and blue, by handsome Lord Frederic Hamilton, Lady Lansdowne's brother, a friend from Ottawa days whom Redney had applauded in Rideau Hall theatricals. Later Redney saw the Lansdownes informally when they invited her to tea, where, seated in her huge, cold drawing-room, Lady Lansdowne "spoke with especial warmth of the quaint home-likeness of Rideau Hall" (*Star*, Nov. 2, 1889).

For the rest of her Calcutta stay, Everard, usually known as "Evey", and Redney were constantly together. With Everard, there was none of Joaquin's quick flood of emotional flamboyance; Evey's English reserve intrigued and challenged her:

> With his eyes upon her and his words offered to her intelligence, she found herself treating his shy formality as the convention it was, a kind of make-believe which she would politely and kindly play up to until he should happily forget it and they could enter upon simpler relations. She had to play up to it for a long time, but her love made her wonderfully clever and patient; and of course the day came when she had her reward (*The Imperialist*, p. 70).

Joaquin had spread his whole personality before her with one grand flourish of rose-petals; Everard revealed himself slowly, almost reluctantly, and demonstrated his love obliquely, with a thousand small thoughful acts, unexpected kindnesses and cossetings. Redney was very moved, then deeply in love, not with that mercurial flutter which she had felt for Joaquin, but with a love deeper, more deliberate. For the first time in her life, having previously thought of herself consistently as a committed career woman, Redney now began to think of marriage. What would life be like, cocooned forever inside the warm giving-and-caring of Evey's love?

With her persistent prompting, Evey modestly told her about himself. He had been born at Newington Rectory in Oxfordshire in 1862 where his father, Septimus, was rector. The Cotes family traced its lineage back to Norman times and Sir Roger de Cotes. Everard's father had been the seventh, as his dignified name implied, of the seventeen children of Peter Cotes, most of whom had died without issue, but not before they had served their King and their God with dedication and distinction. Among Evey's uncles, his father's brothers, were Christopher and Robert, who fought under Wellington in the Peninsular War; William, who served in the British Army in the Indian Maratta campaign and died in Bombay; and George, who had topped his class in the Indian Civil Service entrance exams only to die young of an Indian fever. Peter and Digby, like their brother Septimus, had entered the Church. Thanks to the liberality of another Uncle Digby, Colonel Digby Peddar, married to a sister of Septimus', Everard had had a "public school" education, first at Cowbridge School for Boys, then at Clifton College in Bristol, where he showed his scientific bent by inventing, among other things, a device for detecting icebergs in the North Atlantic. There had been, to be sure, a Roger Cotes, professor of astronomy at Cambridge, of whom his friend Isaac Newton said when Roger died young of tuberculosis, "had he lived we would know something of astronomy".

Evey had gone on to St Catherine's College, Oxford, to read zoology and row in his College Eight, walking the ten miles back home to Newington every Sunday to read the lesson in church. He spent a year in France and Germany becoming fluent in both languages, then, in 1884, had come out to the Indian Museum. The first thing he did upon arrival was to wire the five pounds still in his pocket back home to the family at Newington, where a rector's stipend had to provide for three sisters and a young brother.[17]

In early March, 1889, Redney reluctantly said good-bye for the time being to Evey and Calcutta to continue her tour, but she left her heart behind. It is precisely here—as Redney boarded the crowded *Khedive*, a P and O old salt built at Greenock eighteen years before, to backtrack to Ceylon via Madras—that one notices a change in her narrative voice. The sparkling, euphoric tone of the earlier part of *A Social Departure* now becomes subdued, a little sardonic. The first burrs of reality begin to appear amid all those lotuses and orchids. In love with Everard, Redney was looking at India, not so much with a tourist's eyes as with those of a possible future resident forced to root herself in this strange soil. She notices, for instance, that on board the *Khedive*, bound for England, are "a large percentage of invalids, mostly ladies" (*SD*, p. 305), who were going home because India's climate had permanently ruined their health. Redney's drive through Madras left her with the impression of "the awful filth and apparent depravity of the place, with its imported 'public buildings', towering above, and the keen commiseration that we felt for such English people as fate ordained to live there" (*SD*, p. 307).

In Bombay, India's less romantic side continued to oppress her: the dirt, the poverty, the crowding, the unsavoury smells. Even the hotel was bad, for the girls had

> a tiny place in a tortuous passage, with disjointed wooden shutters opening on a court behind, grimy and dismal, and largely decorated with the cigar ends and torn papers and empty beer bottles of the last inhabitants. The bed might have been made of old red sandstone. The atmosphere was unsavoury. The passage was dark; we were in constant terror of stepping on native servants asleep outside their masters' rooms (*SD*, p. 311).

Since they were now short on funds, the girls decided to economize by not engaging servants to fight in the kitchen for their share of food. This meant that they often went hungry at table; one night they secured only a dish of potatoes and the next night nothing at all except the menu. Their Bombay hotel was much closer to the norm of Indian hostelries than their pleasant Calcutta one had been. A British newspaperman travelling in India a few years later found its hotels "unspeakably vile", most of them looking like "a haunted house crossed upon a byre" with rickety furniture, bad food and non-existent management, "the only things barely tolerable" being "the personal service and the bedding, both of which you bring with you".[18]

Redney's tone got shriller when she visited Bombay's Towers of Silence on Malabar Hill, five round, white towers with hollowed stone troughs inside, where the Parsees laid their dead. The dark, sardonic shadows here were cast by vulture's wings—no "happy pinions" these. In Parsee funeral rites, vultures play a key role:

> Then one by one there flapped heavily out of the branches, dark, hideous birds, with fierce hooked claws and featherless heads and necks. They began to come in twos and threes, then in half-dozens, and settled closely together in high-shouldered rows, heads looking over, along the top of the stone parapet of the nearest tower. They knew the funeral was coming long before we did (*Star*, Feb. 1, 1890).

Redney's account of the whole procedure is much more explicit in the *Star* than in *A Social Departure*, whose readers would be predominantly female and presumably more squeamish. The *Star* account is grimly realistic:

> They carry the body, swathed in a sheet, to its receptacle, and lay it there without any clothing whatever.... Then the corpse-bearers go away, and the vultures come, and in ten minutes there is a clean picked skeleton where they left what had been a man or woman the day before (*Star*, Feb. 1, 1890).

Redney and Lily watched while a dead child was laid inside the tower; "the air seemed full of the flapping of dark wings, and hoarse cries.... We turned away in loathing, sorry we had come, and unable to rid ourselves of the imaginative carnage behind the great round wall" (*Star*, Feb. 1, 1890). Sunday-school classes in Zion Presbyterian Church were no fit preparation for the Towers of Silence.

Hoping to erase the memory of the Towers, the girls decided to visit a different kind of memorial to the dead: the Taj Mahal in Agra. But Agra was two days away by train, and most European tourists would never dare to go at that time of the year; acquaintances in Bombay, says Redney, consciously dramatizing, "told us of unacclimatised Europeans who travelled in the hot weather, and were taken out dead at the end of the journey" (*SD*, p. 320). Redney and Lily were keen to try it.

Armed with palm-leaf fans, plenty of lemonade and their own bravado, Redney and Lily survived the train trip, but Redney admits that they arrived in Agra "dusty and eyesore and deeply begrimed" (*SD*, p. 328). Indian trains were an ordeal at any time of year, let alone in the hot weather. They travelled at a leisurely twenty miles an hour or less, stopping for the occasional cow on the track. There were no restaurant cars, so that one either got off and ate in the dirty stations or took a picnic basket. The carriages had bare bunks without bedding and filthy washbasins.

For Redney, the long, hot train ride had added a telling image to her growing store. It is, characteristically, a floral one; flowers float continuously through Redney's mind, but the flame in this one threatens:

Now and then we saw, solitary in some tangled space, a tree
with thick black, misshapen boughs, leafless, but bearing
large flame-red flowers in thick profusion, a kind of magnolia . . . . As we saw the tree it had a strange fierce air, as if its
flowers consumed it (*SD*, p. 324).

"A kind of magnolia", but not the New Orleans kind—green
flames kindle, red ones consume. "Solitary in some tangled
space" sounds a plaintive, and a prophetic note.

"We would not go to see the Taj", Lily and Redney
decided next morning after breakfast, in a rare fit of conventional conduct, "until the starlight of the early evening with
the prospect of the moon at nine o'clock" (*SD*, p. 331).
Redney was richly rewarded for waiting. There was, first of
all, the white marble magic and mystery of the Taj itself, its
dome indescribable, suspended between heaven and earth,
simple, sublime, the very shape and substance of the ideal:
"We had eyes only for the strange dream-thing that the
garden made sanctuary for", Redney writes, "rising phan-
tasmal at its further end, beyond the roses and above the
palms" (*SD*, p. 340).

There was, secondly, waiting for her in the moonlit
garden, there among the roses, Everard, who had, to surprise her, made the long, hot, dusty journey from Calcutta.
He may have been a scientist carefully cataloguing moths,
but he had romance enough to know how important the
right setting was to his beloved. It was there, where "to that
subtler consciousness which receives it the Taj tells its own
untranslatable story of Love and Death" (*SD*, p. 341) that
Everard asked Redney to marry him.[19] She had once described her ideal man as one "who possesses in equal proportions
culture, and common sense, and courtesy, and philosophy,
and discrimination, and appreciation (*Globe*, Nov. 5, 1886).
With the Taj Mahal's ideality and tenderness above her, and
Everard's beside her, Redney said yes.

Redney was twenty-seven years old, and her decision to
marry Everard Cotes was no sudden whim. It was based, as
much as anything, on her restless nature. She was, first of all,
eager to try on the brand-new role of wife. Secondly, Evey
offered a gateway to two worlds which held great appeal for
her. The first one was the mysterious East, glinting and

sinuous; Redney was mesmerized by it as it continually slid and slithered into surprising new shapes. She had, to be sure, seen the first dark shadows of its underbelly, but those she chose to discount. Thus far, the East had inspired her best writing, and she was confident that she could grasp it all, define it all, given time, in her books. She also felt sure that it would never bore her, never turn into just another dull alley. She is like her heroine Judith Church who decided to marry John for similar reasons:

> When he asked her to marry him, the wall at the end of the alley fell down and a breeze stole in from the far East, with a vision of palms and pomegranates. She accepted him for the sake of her imagination (*His Honour, and a Lady*, pp. 13-14).

The second gateway which Evey offered Redney was permanent entry to the civilized world of British custom and ceremony which her Brantford upbringing had taught her to revere. Like the promise of Brantford's woods, like the New Orleans vistas of riotous green, Evey imaged a wider world of new quests and challenges, a world in which Redney would be warmly enfolded in his deep, abiding love.

   In every love-relationship, there is one who loves and one who is loved; in this case, Everard was the one who loved and Redney, with her writer's intuition, knew that his love would be loyal and lasting. She also knew that she could dominate and control Evey as she had her younger brothers and sisters, as she had Lily. She knew that she could propel Evey along the path of her direction and desire, that, beside her, he would be consistently considerate and adoring. In bearing and manners, he reminded her of her beloved father and she wanted very much to rest on the strong arm of his approval and unqualified love. Convention triumphed; Redney chose marriage, capitulated to "social position, assured income, support in old age, the strands in . . . the bond that holds us all" (*The Pool in the Desert*, p. 210).

   For the next few days, a radiant Redney, leaning on Evey's arm, walked about Agra, but what she saw most clearly were not the tourist sights, but the mirage of their happy life to come, suspended in the hot air above the pavement. Then Redney said a reluctant goodbye to Evey and returned to Bombay with Lily. Poor Lily had felt limply redundant with the loving couple, and was glad to be leaving Agra. In the third week of March, the women sailed to Suez.

From Suez they took the train to Cairo. Redney had now arrived in her travels at the farthest edge of childhood's magic carpet, for Cairo was "the city of the genii, and of our dreams, always furthest away of all the cities in the magical distance beyond the rim o' the world, which edges the fields of home" (*Star*, May 17, 1890). And, like all tourists, the pair visited the Pyramids, but, unlike all tourists, they did it with a difference. They decided that they would see them by sunrise, which necessitated tiptoeing from their hotel at three in the morning; they would travel by donkey as far as the Sphinx, and by camel to one of the Great Pyramids which they would, still true to form, climb to the very top.

On the first of May, 1889, Redney arrived in England:

> The England of May Day stretched green under our prow; and we sailed past the little white watering-places of the Channel, and up the brown Thames to London town, where, for the time, our wanderings are at an end (*Star*, June 3, 1890).

Redney soon felt a renewed excitement to be, at long last, in London, to have a fresh bouquet of images to record. She and Lily found lodgings at Mrs Helen Hahn's boarding house at 99 Gower Street, near the British Museum, one of many in the area, all alike in their smell of cooking in the dark entry hall, their carpet on the first two flights of stairs, oilcloth on the third. Ninety-nine Gower, north of Bedford Square, built of yellow brick, had four shallow marble steps up to a Georgian doorway with simple pilasters and fanlight. Across the street and down a bit lived Dame Millicent Garrett Fawcett, staunch worker for woman's suffrage, behind a double door of Chinese blue. The girls settled in at Mrs Hahn's and began their eager exploration of London. Redney was already mentally gathering copy for her next book, *An American Girl in London*, which would repeat the formula of *A Social Departure*: a single girl leaves her home and her roots to travel in search of new adventures and fresh growth.

As with her first view of Washington, Redney was prepared to like everything she saw. Washington had been one mecca: the citadel of all that American business bustle which had been half of her Brantford heritage. Now, in Britain, Redney was at last able to see for herself that other half: the fountainhead of Brantford's social and cultural ideals and, as always, with fresh sights to record, she was enthusiastic. She liked the general griminess of London's buildings, North American brick being "so clean and neat and sanitary", and particularly "the well-settled, well-founded look of everything, as if it had all come ages ago, and meant to stay for ever" (*An American Girl*, p. 31). After the predictable grid-pattern of North American streets, she loved the "gratifying" complexity of London ones that "turn and twist and jostle each other, and lead up into nothing, and turn round and come back again, and assume *aliases*, and break out into circuses and stray into queer, dark courts" (*An American Girl*, pp. 30-31), a pattern as complex and surprising as her own life. London's colours, silvered by the misty air, seemed quietly decorous compared to India's vibrant tones. It was all very understated and refined. Unlike American street crowds, the English people showed "no eagerness and no enthusiasm. Neither was there any hustling" (*An American Girl*, p. 27). They looked remarkably staid, and queued meekly everywhere.

One morning shortly after her arrival, Redney primped longer than usual at the mirror, and went round to see Mr Alfred Gibbons, editor of *The Lady's Pictorial*, a popular magazine of the day. She showed him the *Star* articles of her world tour, offering to convert them into a serial for his magazine entitled "A Social Departure". To her delight, Mr Gibbons agreed, but suggested that for contrast and added interest Lily should be metamorphosed into an English girl. He would also engage an artist to illustrate the text. Redney sailed out of the office into the hum and roar of London with singing heart. She was one step closer to her goal, and as she walked down the street she could see her first published book, there beyond the glass of every bookseller's window.

At the end of May, 1889, Redney and Lily parted company; Lily went to Paris and Redney moved down to

Wallingford, near Oxford, to meet Everard's family and stay the summer. She felt some trepidation and nervousness as the train neared; she was, after all, a colonial and a career-woman, probably not what his family expected Everard to marry. His father sounded formidable; Evey had told her how, when he brought some rather racy books home from Oxford once, Septimus had burned them, in a pile, at the bottom of the garden.

The Reverend Septimus Cotes, then sixty-seven, in charge of three rural parishes, proved indeed to be a little intimidating, but Evey's mother Redney loved on sight, and they formed a firm friendship. Like Redney's own mother, Ellen Cotes was Irish, warmly loving, with a wonderful, quirky sense of humour. May, Everard's eldest sister, had married a Mr Masterman and so was no longer part of the household. Bobby, then nineteen, was the only other boy in the family. Still at home were Rosemary (Sissie), age twenty-nine, and Florence (Florrie) then twenty-six, who were talented but angular, a little eccentric, not at all like their mother, whereas Rhoda, Redney's favourite among the sisters, a pretty, lively sixteen-year-old, had all her mother's gentle wit.

As soon as she had settled in, Redney sent a chiding note to S.S. McClure in New York, to whom she had sent her world tour manuscript, hoping he would syndicate it for American magazines.

Newington Rectory
Wallingford
Berks
June 1st

Dear Mr. McClure,

In London a week ago I got your letter saying that you had sent my mss and Miss Lewis's to 99 Gower St. by same mail. So far they haven't turned up, and as I have made an arrangement to publish them in London which will probably turn out well I am rather anxious about them. Did you mail them and when? If so I can enquire at the General Post Office here. If not please send them on at once to me at the address at the head of my letter where I will be for the summer. A number of letters have been forwarded to

me from Gower St. but not the articles so far, and another
mail has come in since. Regretting to trouble you I am
                                        Yours very sincerely
                                        Sara J. Duncan[20]

Her handwriting in this letter is bigger, bolder than it was
later in her life. One can see Redney's hand racing across the
page, never hesitating, flowing, forthright, demanding
McClure's notice. S.S. McClure had emigrated to the United
States with his widowed mother from a stone cottage in
Ireland when he was nine, and was now another of the
Gilded Age's self-made men. He was a little man of tremen-
dous energy who had had the brilliant idea that he could sell
articles by the day's popular authors to newspapers, by
paying the author, say, $150 for a story, then selling it to a
hundred newspapers at five dollars each. In short, he
launched the first American newspaper syndicate. By the
time Redney wrote to him five years later he was raking in
the profits, selling stories by Conan Doyle, O. Henry,
Damon Runyon, Booth Tarkington, and, in 1888, one by
Joaquin's *inamorata* Miriam Leslie on the wiles and pitfalls of
society. Just at the time Redney wrote to him, McClure was
busy introducing America to Rudyard Kipling, who had just
left India for good to live in England.[21] Redney must have
been crestfallen that McClure didn't want to launch her as
well, but, comforted by Gibbons' enthusiasm, she set to
work on her revisions.

Newington Rectory was a quiet, idyllic place in which
to work, a rambling hundred-year-old house with a large
garden, and a stream at its bottom. Looking out the windows
at the damp greenery and perennial borders showing the
usual happenstance huddle of an English garden, Redney
began to prune her manuscript. She changed Lily into
Orthodocia Love, of Love Lodge, St.-Eve's-in-the-Garden,
Wigginton, Devon, a young person thoroughly English,
fresh from school, innocent, clinging as ivy: in short, an
excellent foil to the New Woman and front runner who is
Redney herself. Orthodocia is also typically English in her
ignorance of Canada, quite as galling as the American kind.
Redney writes of Orthodocia planning to look up her cousin

"ranching in Winnipeg, until we got to Winnipeg and she discovered that people didn't ranch there to any extent, on account of the price of city lots for pasture" (*SD*, p. 25). Redney also honed and polished her style until the quick, descriptive flow, the slightly bemused tone, the colloquial clip of her sentences was uniform and engaging.

During the long, sun-dappled afternoons in the garden, when not working on her book, Redney began her writer's *cachepot*: a black-bound notebook with "Dots and Dashes— Private Scribbles" written in her hand inside its cover. In it she jotted down quotations from her reading and a few original aphorisms. A perusal of this common-place book shows how eclectic were her reading tastes. There are references to Schopenhauer, John Stuart Mill, Kant, Montaigne, Mallarmé, Diderot, Flaubert, and Swift. On the cover of the book is a quotation that was a favourite of Everard's, from Longfellow's "A Psalm of Life":

> Trust no future however pleasant
> Let the dead past bury its dead,
> Act, act in the living present,
> Heart within and God o'erhead.

The book, however, which seems to have made the deepest impression on Redney and which merits two whole pages of quotations is *The Love Letters of a Portuguese Nun*, five letters from Mariana Alcoforado, a Baja nun, to Noël Bouton de Chamilly, later Marquis de Chamilly, written in the year 1668. The first English translation of the letters appeared in 1678, and there were many subsequent ones, including an American one in 1890, which may have been the one Redney was reading. Among the passages which she records are: "I love you to distraction, and yet I would spare you so much that I would not even dare to wish you to be agitated by the same transport". Another one reads: "But above all, believe it, the sweetest canticle is 'Nunc Dimittus'." It seems curious that, on the eve of her marriage, Redney was drawn to the theme of passion denied, of that emotional withdrawal from the world which she had witnessed in the Montreal nuns. Her preoccupation may have stemmed from a subconscious maidenly reluctance to contemplate the fearful, uncharted terrain of sexual union. Redney was still a virgin, and, like most girls born in Victorian times, had little idea what to expect. Then too, she may have already realized that she was bringing very little genuine passion to her marriage. Already, at the age of twenty-seven, Redney was moving towards the nun's narrow bed, towards ritual and discipline.

When she wasn't writing or reading, Redney explored the English countryside with Evey's sisters. It looked as if "it had all been carefully and beautifully made, and was usually kept under cotton-wool" (*An American Girl*, p. 271). The English woods were so different from North American ones; these were neat, smug, smiling woods, tamed and trimmed. Redney saw in them the orderly patterns of life at Newington Rectory, felt the pruning-shears of English convention, and longed suddenly for North American freedoms:

> The American woods are as different from English ones as the American temperament is . . . . They have all the sweetness of freedom, no hint of subdual anywhere . . . . Things come up there exactly as they like, just as things rise to the American tongue. There is untamed sunlight and unchecked shade . . . . A great green profusion, with wanton curves and whimsical outflingings as if a splendid, lavish joy in life exclaimed everywhere (*Those Delightful Americans*, p. 124).

There was no great green profusion in English society. Already Redney's initial enthusiasm for all things English had waned a little and as the idyllic mists lifted, the real thistles scratched her sensibility. There was, for example, the ridiculously rigid adherence to social forms which she would soon satirize in the Bangley-Coffin family:

> The Bangley Coffins were all form. Form, for them, regulated existence. It was the all-compelling law of the spheres, the test of all human action and desire. 'Good form' was the ultimate expression of their respect, 'bad form' their final declaration of contempt (*An American Girl*, pp. 226-7).

It was hard to imagine English girls riding cow-catchers. They preferred to trail languid hands in brackish water while their men punted them gently downstream in life. "I do not believe punting would ever become popular in America. We are a light-minded people; we like an element of joyous risk", Redney was to observe (*An American Girl*, p. 250). "Joyous risk" was definitely missing in British life, and Redney was still young enough to feel its lack.

Redney did manage, however, even in England, to take a trip that summer as unconventional as her world tour, if less protracted. Once again, taking the image as it came, she travelled to get copy for her book. Redney, another young lady and two young men, probably Cotes connections, hired a barge from Messrs Corbett of the London Salt Works in which they could float down the Grand Junction Canal. They got a carpenter to build two tiny cabins on it to accomodate them, "like Cherubs' packing cases" (*Two Girls on a Barge*, p. 12). It is precisely at this point in her life that one detects a change in Redney's attitude to her environment. Thus far she had lived happily in rooms furnished by someone else, a great many furnished rooms: in New Orleans, Washington, Toronto, Montreal, Ottawa, Tokyo, Calcutta, Bombay, London. From now on, she felt the need to create her own immediate setting. This was the first sign suggesting that her creativity couldn't bloom, orchid-like, without familiar soil. Redney's homeland was thousands of miles away; she was living in a new country, about to spend the rest of her life in another, even farther removed from her Canadian origins. She needed the comfort of her own context, self-created to surround her with beauty mirroring her past. "For my part I grow foolishly fond of the objects that help one through life the way furniture does", she was to write (*Two in a Flat*, p. 21). Accordingly, she decorated the barge with fairy lamps, a large Japanese umbrella and Liberty curtains "draped artistically everywhere" (*Two Girls on a Barge*, p. 10). Thus accoutred, Redney could enjoy her "happy gipsy life" (*Two Girls on a Barge*, p. 163). Her interior decorating was her compromise between the two opposing pulls in her life: to be restlessly on the move, searching for new sensations, or to be rooted, safe in familiar surroundings. Beginning in the summer of 1889, these conflicting needs tightened into an unresolved tension, and remained.

With the four young people aboard, the barge moved slowly down the Grand Junction Canal, then meandered into a branching "baby canal". "Mr. and Mrs. Bargee" and son Eccles were there to oversee its locomotion, while Dob, the horse, plodded placidly along the tow-path pulling the barge along by a rope attached to his halter. It was a pastoral interlude in Redney's life, making her aware how very deep the stream-bed of tradition lay in England's green and pleasant land. The barge glided through Coventry, for example, "where the old order scarcely changes, and the new has never begun" (p. 148), so that "only the cut of the farthingales and the patter of the clogs . . . have altered in these streets of a thousand summers" (*Two Girls on a Barge*, p. 146).

After her barge holiday, Redney returned to Newington Rectory, remaining for fall and early winter. In October of 1889, while "A Social Departure" was appearing in *The Lady's Pictorial*, with charming illustrations by F. H. Townsend, Redney received an exciting letter from Andrew Chatto, of the English publishing firm, Chatto and Windus:

Oct. 1889

Dear Madam,

We return our best thanks for the promise of the right of the chapters of your contribution to the "Lady's Pictorial" entitled "A Social Departure". We think we might be disposed to undertake the publication of it in book form with the greater number of illustrations. Would you be willing to accept a very moderate sum for the rights of reproduction? We should like to know the number of chapters in which it will be completed.[22]

Redney could feel the exhilarating wind in her face, as she rushed forward, down the easy grade towards her first published book.

Spring comes early in England; by February, 1890, there were yellow primroses opening everywhere and Redney was back in London, staying with Everard's Uncle, Charles Cotes, a lawyer, and his wife Lady Edith, at their elegant residence at 87 Gloucester Place, Portman Square. Redney was enough of a snob to preen in this patrician setting. She had visited Andrew Chatto on January 29th and negotiated her first contract for *A Social Departure*. On February 4th she received an advance on royalties of thirty pounds, and on March 18th, the first forty-eight pages of proofs. Chatto had secured the original blocks of Townsend's illustrations from *The Lady's Pictorial* for the book.

In London, Redney revelled in the city's rich variety and recorded its sights for *An American Girl*. London was just then beginning one of its most carefree decades, the Gay Nineties, and it was a good world in which to find oneself: solid, safe, orderly, but exuberant. It was a time of material plenty for all except those at the very bottom of the class structure. Everyone knew their station, and kept it, their appropriate dress clearly defining exactly what that was. Clerks wore pin-striped trousers and silk hats. Skilled craftsmen wore white aprons, engineers blue overalls, coalmen had leather hats with flaps behind to protect the neck, stout coats with leather patches, corduroy trousers. The draymen who delivered beer, immense fellows, wore white baize coats and red flannel caps.[23] Living in Portman Square, and chaperoned around town by Lady Edith, Redney could look down on them all, not only metaphorically, but also in fact, by riding on the top of the bus: "I must say I like it—looking down upon people who were travelling in the same direction as I was, only on a level below", she writes. "I began to understand the agreeableness of class distinctions", continues Redney, with her usual acumen for linking local customs to character, and "wondered whether the arrangement of seats on the tops of the buses was not probably a material result of aristocratic prejudices" (*An American Girl*, p. 29).

Redney had time now to get acquainted with London, to form more detailed impressions than were possible in May of 1889, and because she was riding the crest of excitement of her first book, she was mostly favourable. One memorable moment comes, "moving through the lovely, thronged, wet, lamplit London streets" in a brougham, when Redney feels very much as her Canadian heroine, Mary Trent would feel. Redney knew that London would mould and mellow her as her previous environments had; she would be "realised" by London:

> Not a bit for what I was . . . nor exactly for what I represented, but for something else, for what I might, under favourable circumstances, be made to represent. . . . It was even part of

the thrill to know that one would be obliged, in a way, to hand oneself over .... I was only a possibility, a raw product, to be melted or hammered or woven into London, by my leave. And that was superb to experience, the solicitation, even tacit and involved, of London, the knowledge that one was taken as important enough, one was coloured by what one had or what one's father had, as being important enough, to make suggestions to (*Cousin Cinderella*, pp. 126-27).

It was all there for Redney in that spring of 1890: the delicious new sense of her own importance, of her potential, of the new shining threads weaving themselves day after day into her sensibility.

Japan had been a red camellia, just the aesthetic essence of itself, and nothing more. India had been a lotus, silken, seductive, mysterious. Britain was an ancient oak; its branches had sheltered Redney since childhood, offering her the comfortable shade of familiar moral and literary traditions. "We're all right out here", says Lorne Murchison, referring to Canada, "but we're young and thin and weedy. They didn't grow so fast in England, to begin with, and now they're rich with character and strong with conduct and hoary with ideals" (*The Imperialist*, p. 98). Redney had pursued the American Dream of material success and found it wanting; now she would embrace the British one of cultural eminence. She therefore made her pilgrimage to the Poet's Corner of Westminster Abbey to pay homage to Chaucer, Ben Jonson, Milton, Browning; she visited Dr Johnson's house in Gough Square and Goldsmith's grave. She, too, would write books fine enough to merit the approval of the British reading public, not lightly given by readers raised on a diet of literary Greats, and possessing those "delicate appreciations that seem to flower where life has gone on longer" (*The Imperialist*, p. 109). Redney immersed herself in English newspapers and periodicals, and attended the London theatre, for she was now in the "very citadel of the imagination" (*Cousin Cinderella*, p. 33) and meant to profit from this new Mecca.

As well as literary ambitions, Redney had social ones, and was pleased that Lady Edith could assure her *entrée* to all the best places. Everard's charming Canadian fiancée, insisted Lady Edith, must sample all the delights of a London Season. Redney visited the House of Lords, noted the absence of cuspidors so conspicuous in Washington's Capitol, and was gratified to glimpse Prince Edward in the gallery. She went to Aldershot for an impressive parade of martial strength, to Ascot for Gold Cup Day, to the "Private View" opening of the Royal Academy Show in Burlington House, where Redney's own smart frock made her feel superior to the English maidens in colours "unattainable out of a London fog" with uneven hemlines and indeterminate hairdos (*An American Girl*, p. 167). But the central jewel in her social crown was added on Friday, March 14th, 1890, when she was presented to Queen Victoria at St James' Palace.

Redney's description of her presentation in *An American Girl in London* is the best thing in the book, faithful in fact and feeling to the ritual of that memorable day. Redney was awakened early at Portman Square to breakfast in her room and to have her hair done amid a jumble of white boxes and tissue containing her gown, headdress and bouquet, the latter "a gracious wonder of white roses and grasses" (*An American Girl*, pp. 293-4). This event would be a fine dress rehearsal for a prospective bride. When she was quite ready, in her white dress with sweeping train, her requisite head-dress of three white feathers, her long tulle lappets, "it seemed to me that I was a different person, very pretty, very tall . . . too much fascinated with my outward self" (p. 293). Too much fascinated with her outward self . . . and with the outward world: it was perhaps Redney's tragic flaw.

As she gazed into the mirror, a clear-cut self confronted her there, as it had five years before in the crystal depths of the Fountain of Youth: Sara Jeannette Duncan of Brantford, Ontario, about to meet her Queen, about to have her rarity confirmed. Redney's Brantford upbringing had made her a Monarchist and social élitist, so that she was excited at the prospect of seeing Queen Victoria, but even more excited that "Queen Victoria should see me, for an instant and as an individual" (p. 292). A little clutch of admiring people gathered outside the Portman Square house to see her and

Lady Edith depart. Then came the long wait, from noon until three, in the line of carriages stretching to the Palace, eating tiny sandwiches wrapped in tissue, careful of the crumbs, conscious of the people lining the Mall to see the Privileged pass: "We sat in state amongst them in the rain, being observed, and liking it. I heard my roses approved, and the nape of my neck" (p. 296). It was at this moment, sitting in the carriage, that Redney had an epiphany, inhaling the perfume of her own importance:

> I think there came to me then, sitting in the carriage in the warmth and pride and fragrance and luxuriance of it all, one supreme moment of experience, when I bent my head over my roses and looked out into the rain—one throb of exulting pleasure that seemed to hold the whole meaning of the thing I was doing, and to make its covetable nature plain. I find my thoughts centre, looking back, upon that one moment (p. 296).

At last came the actual presentation, Redney proud rather than intimidated to be "in the same room with so many jewels, and brocades, and rare orchids, and drooping feathers, and patrician features" (p. 311), walking forward towards the small enthroned figure in black satin with coronet of pearls and diamonds. Suddenly, Redney found roses in her path: "Somebody's roses had dropped; I was walking on pink petals" (pp. 305-6). She curtsied to the Queen, curtsied to the other nine royals present, the Princess of Wales in brown velvet, Princess Beatrice in yellow satin, backed carefully towards the door, and it was over.[24]

Three weeks later, on April 8th, Chatto and Windus wrote to tell Redney that they had had an American offer of sixty pounds for an edition of *A Social Departure*, thirty-five pounds of which would go towards making the plates for the illustrations, leaving twenty-five to divide between Miss Duncan and themselves. On April 23rd, they informed her that Messrs Gage and Company in Toronto had ordered 78 copies of the book, for which, since it was registered under English copyright, they would pay a royalty of 12½ per cent. On May 2nd, Redney's hands trembled with excitement as she tore off the brown paper wrappings on her six author's copies of *A Social Departure*, just arrived in the mail from Chatto, and held them in both hands. This was the pot of gold at the end of her world tour: her first book! The accompanying letter informed her that Chatto and Windus had been unable to sell the rights to a Canadian edition, but that the American one would be published by D. Appleton simultaneously with theirs, on the following day, May 3rd, 1890.

With *A Social Departure*, Redney's dreams of fame came true; it was an instant success with both critics and public. The London reviews in the spring of 1890 were raves, the only small shadow cast by the *Illustrated London News* who called the author "American".[25] The *Pall Mall Budget* referred to *A Social Departure* as "the most charming book of travels it has been our good fortune to come across", and the *Daily Telegraph* declared that there wasn't a dull page in the whole book. Now there was a new star, of medium magnitude, on the London literary horizon, joining that brightly shining group of best-selling authors: Marie Corelli, Conan Doyle, Rider Haggard, and the only Canadian to precede Redney, Gilbert Parker.

In Canada the summer reviews were, understandably, just as ecstatic. "We defy anyone not to giggle a score of times, or not to laugh outright" wrote the Montreal *Star* critic (Aug. 2, 1890). *The Week* called the book "healthy, breezy, amusing" with "the touch always light, descriptions never tedious" (July 25, 1890) and Toronto's *Grip*, as anxious as the other journals to claim Redney as one of its own, announcing that "Miss Duncan has occasionally written for GRIP in days gone by", pronounced the book "fresh, chirpy, witty, deucedly clever" (October, 1890, p. 252). Redney became even more certain that her formula of travel-and-record was, for her, the right one.

The popularity of *A Social Departure* continued down through the years. "It probably sold better than anything else Sara Jeannette Duncan wrote", concludes Professor Tausky in his study of her work. By 1893, Chatto and Windus had printed three English editions. By 1903, 16,000 copies had been sold in the United States alone.[26] In 1910,

Nelson would publish it in their shilling library. As late as
1914, Toronto's *Saturday Night* printed one of its chapters
(Aug. 1, 1914). In 1915, a Canadian journalist called it "one
of the best contemporary books of travel",[27] and in 1922 *The
Times* mentioned that "it has gone through edition after
edition . . . and still finds demand in the libraries" (July 24,
1922).

Redney warmed herself in the sunlight of all this
praise, but the patrician in her, she who had met her Queen,
wanted to be recognized in high places, too. She therefore
despatched a letter and copy of the book to Lord Lansdowne
in India:

> *Newington Rectory*
> *Wallingford, Berks.*
> *June 4th.*

Dear Lord Lansdowne,

I think you were kind enough to say
before I left Calcutta last year, that you would like to see my
"impressions du voyage". Now that they have reached at least
the outer dignity of a book I have much pleasure in sending
them to you with this. I need not say how gratified I shall be if
my little volume affords you any amusement—but I must
take the opportunity of thanking you again for the kindness
which made it possible for me to give its Indian chapters their
chief interest.

> I have the honor to be,
> Faithfully yours,
> Sara Jeannette Duncan.[28]

In mid-summer, 1890, after an absence of almost two
years, Redney returned, triumphant, to Canada. The press
was now eagerly following her movements, and she loved
the notoriety. *The Week* informs its readers on June 13th that
"Miss Duncan will be in Canada sometime during the
summer" and *Saturday Night* notes that "Miss Sara Jeannette
Duncan was in the city for a few days this week, having
completed her journey round the world. She went from here
to visit her old home in Brantford" (Aug. 30, 1890). Later
comes the announcement: "Miss Sara Jeannette Duncan,
first known as Garth Grafton, is to be married to Mr. E.C.
Cotes, of the Bengal Civil Service. She will leave Canada
early in October and expects to reach Calcutta about December" (*Saturday Night*, Sept. 27, 1890).

There were Brantford parties for the bride-to-be, meetings with old friends, and long sessions with the dressmaker
sewing Redney's trousseau from the very best fabrics in her
father's store. But these happy distractions didn't keep
Redney from her writing. With fresh confidence she was
gathering her other travel impressions into two more books:
An American Girl in London and *Two Girls on a Barge*, for both
of which Chatto and Windus were waiting, hopeful of
repeating the financial success of *A Social Departure*.

In *An American Girl*, the heroine's sensibility is Redney's,
but her name is Mamie Wick and she hails from Chicago,
where her father has made a fortune in baking-powder. The
romantic plot has Mamie courted by a young Englishman,
Charles Mafferton, whom she rejects at the end, going home
to marry a Yale professor. Considering that Redney herself
had chosen a foreign husband and a foreign land, this choice
of home and home-grown mate on the part of her fictional
alter ego is intriguing. Mamie Wick is a clever topical choice
on Redney's part, for rich, young American girls in the '90's
were prominent and popular on the London social scene.
The Queen, the weekly society journal, had a column headed
"Americans in London", with a photo of the reigning American beauty, and accompanying account of her social
triumphs. The germ of Mamie's character Redney had
discovered as far back as 1886:

> We mean clearly American women when we talk of Ameri-
> cans in London society, and it seems to me that those of us
> who know them need hardly marvel much over their success
> in English upper circles .... A young lady, fresh from her
> native Illinois, need not be a Daisy Miller, however, to
> inspire curiosity, interest, admiration, even affection in the
> insular breast. She is wholly a novel being—in her uncon-
> scious criticism, in her untrammelled ways of looking at
> things, in the width of her intellectual range, in her quick
> appreciation and adaptability. Her reading has been wide,
> and she has learned to discriminate ... and her independ-
> ence is just pronounced enough to be pleasant. Then she talks
> well, and dresses well, and looks well, and the average
> Englishman adds up the list of her virtues and pronounces
> their sum-total, "quaint". Different from his sisters, "brought
> up differently, you know", but so charming in her difference

that quite frequently she merges her American patronymic in the peerage now (*Week*, Sept. 23, 1886).

Daisy Miller is an obvious model for Mamie Wick, but there is another one who preceded her by two years, and whom Henry James himself, borrowing her creator's surname, may have had in mind: the heroine of Joaquin Miller's *The One Fair Woman* (1876) is a bright, ingenuous young American girl in Rome who attracts a number of Italian suitors. Her name is Mollie Wopsous. Did Redney deliberately give her heroine the same initials? Certainly Joaquin was still in her mind, for when Mamie sees William the Conqueror in Madame Tussaud's Wax Museum, she comments that if his crown "were only a wide-brimmed, soft felt hat—he reminds me *very much* of those Californian ranchers and miners Bret Harte and Joaquin Miller write about" (p. 110).

Once more, as October haze settled over violet woods, Redney prepared to leave Canada, but this time for good. She caught her father looking sad and pensive, watching her over his newspaper, as he sat round the dining-room fire, lit to banish the chill of the first frosts. Her mother was busy working "SJC" into the corners of table napkins and the centres of pillow shams, refusing to get alarmed at the prospect of a daughter going to live among cobras and cholera, declaring that the hot climate would do wonders for Redney's weak chest and winter cough. The rest of Brantford felt cheated at not getting a look at Redney's intended or their share of nuptial champagne and cake, but sent its wedding gifts round to West Street anyway. At last, everything was packed, the tearful farewells said, and Redney sailed for England. She spent a few days at Newington Rectory, gathering contradictory bits of advice from Wallingford neighbours who had either lived in India, or had relatives there, which was practically the entire parish.

Then, in the last week of October, she boarded yet another "P and O" ship for the two-week voyage to India. As she stood on the deck, slim and solitary, watching the gangway being withdrawn and the other passengers waving to friends gathered in little knots below under umbrellas, a gentle rain was falling. The ropes were cast off; the English coast soon became a silver smudge on the horizon as the ship moved slowly out to sea.

Japan . . . Ceylon . . . India . . . Egypt . . . England. Redney had gone round the world. She had had one brief moment of glory in the bright border of literary London. Now she had turned her back on familiar fields, on her Canadian home and her independent, single life. As the ship carried her towards an alien soil, the long drought began.

5
India

"A Shadow with a Pair of Eyes"

> One sees oneself projected like a
> shadow against the strenuous
> mass of the real people, a shadow
> with a pair of eyes. There is such
> intensity and colour and mystery
> to see, that life is hardly more
> than looking on.
>
> *Sara Jeannette Duncan in an interview
> with G.B. Burgin.*

What an expense of courage and care it took, thought Redney, standing in her garden, to make familiar flowers bloom in India. Certainly, her garden didn't look like her mother's, or her mother-in-law's. All of Anglo-India had English gardens—no one cultivated native plants—but the hollyhocks and foxgloves were withered by the hot sun as soon as they bloomed, their stalks grew long and leggy, their leaves bleached. Every morning the mallie hauled water in buckets from the tank, but the earth was still caked hard, full of little snaking cracks. These drooping flowers were mocking reminders of those in former greener fields. There were pinks, recalling those spicy little bouquets which Redney had given her aunt, and violets, but not like the tender ones of New Orleans. These were "violets in exile, violets in pots, with the peculiar property that violets sometimes have in India, of bringing tears to the eyes if one bends over them".[1]

Sometimes Redney felt ready to give up the struggle, to let
the spiky, lush growth crowding the fence take over, as it
would if one turned one's back even for a moment, but she
had need of "this friendly solace of the flowers of home", of
this looking-glass into her past. In those early days of
marriage, Redney's hope and trust focused on her flowers:
"The first pansy-bud was an event" and she and Everard
"chronicled daily at breakfast: 'Two nasturtiums and a
pink', 'two pinks, three nasturtiums, and the monthly rose' "
(*Memsahib, p. 205*).

Her flowers and her fireplace; necessary domestic idols
in a foreign land. It wasn't a real fireplace, of course, only a
kerosene stove, with two mocking eyes in its doors. After
dances at Government House, enjoyable because Evey was
such a capital dancer, Redney sat, holding his hand, in front
of the silly stove, needing "the warm glow of home love
caught and held" (*Memsahib*, p. 191), recalling the beautiful
fires at West Street, crackling maple logs crowned by marble
mantels, white marble in the drawing-room, pink in the
study and her favourite in the dining-room: brown marble
with roundels of brightly-coloured flowers. Redney made
toffee a few times on the stove, but it just wasn't right: not
like those toffee-making larks in the big West Street kitchen.
By mutual consent, Redney and Everard soon packed their
stove's "self-contained moroseness" out of sight. Her flowers
and her fireplace: both failures.

Like her imported garden, Redney's idealism couldn't
thrive in India. The moonlight-and-roses of the Taj Mahal
garden and the shining vision of "palms and pomegranates"
which had prompted her marriage faded fast under India's
relentless sun. On her world tour, she had been charmed by
the East as she strolled its streets a cool spectator, confident
that exotic colour could inspire her indefinitely. Now India
was too much, too close, like the snakes continually slither-
ing into the house, try as one might to keep them out. The
romance of the East had fled in the night. The grim realities
of Indian life struck Redney suddenly, brutally, full in the
face, on the day of her wedding. It was not at all like her
dream of a wedding. She and Everard had been married on
Saturday, December 6th, 1890, a week after her arrival—a

sad little affair, with none of her own family present. The ceremony wasn't held in either of Calcutta's fashionable churches, St Paul's Cathedral, full of Gothic traceries, or St John's, with a Zoffany altar-piece, but rather in St Thomas' church, attached to the Free School, a modest structure whose foundation stone had been laid by Lady William Bentinck in 1830. St. Thomas' was on Free School Street, a short walk from Sudder; being the closest Anglican church, it was the one which Everard regularly attended. The service had been conducted by Rev S.B. Taylor, M.A., a chaplain who had been in India since 1872. The wedding announcement had duly appeared in *The Englishman*, Calcutta's leading newspaper, in two lines of copy,[2] being overshadowed three days later by Calcutta's most fashionable wedding of the year: that of Alicia Sydney Bayley, daughter of the Lieutenant-Governor of Bengal. Alicia was married in St Paul's with full panoply, and *The Englishman* listed all the wedding gifts, and their donors, including a pair of "silver mounted boar tusk boot hooks" from Mr Alston and "ivory whist markers" from Mrs Bob Henderson.[3] Redney read all about it over her morning tea and toast, and made bitter comparisons.

She and Everard had no honeymoon. As soon as they were married, they moved into quarters at 1 Sudder Street, round the corner from the Museum. Built in 1790, the building belonged to the Museum and housed several staff members, including Everard, who had lived there since coming out in '84. It was known as "Sudder Dewanny Court", made of pink stucco with a matching wall around it marbled with cracks. The Sudder Street house was another shock to Redney's sensibility. The rafters curved erratically, the doors sloped in various directions and there were trailing decorations in mud arranged by white ants. The drawing-room had plenty of French windows, but the room behind it had no windows at all. Upstairs the bathrooms had holes in the walls into which one emptied the bath water from portable tubs. Most of the windows had glass in them, but not all, and some were protected by iron bars.[4]

Redney busied herself at once creating a setting as comfortable and congenial as possible, the first of many such frantic attempts in India to make her own beautiful environment to counteract the disturbing one beyond the windows. She hung her drawing-room windows with Indian saris, pale yellow and white, spread blue-and-white dhurries on the floor, placed a big Japanese vase in one corner holding a graceful palm. There were cherished pieces of old china here and there—she always had to have those—and wicker chairs with Liberty cushions. She fortified herself with its beauty, sitting quietly as sunlight striped the floor and sparked Benares brass, listening to "the cooing of the doves in the verandah" (*Memsahib*, p. 134). Redney sometimes felt like a dove herself now, one of those dove orchids in Kandy's Botanical Gardens "with wings half furled sitting upon her nest". For a while she enjoyed the novelty of her new role. She had servants to supervise, meals to plan, Everard's clothes to see to—they hadn't been mended since he came to India. Redney tried to remember some of her mother's housewifely hints, but she had never really listened to them, and most of them, in any case, wouldn't apply to domestic life in India.

Her kitchen certainly didn't look like West Street's capacious one. Redney's was about seven feet square, with shelf, table and charcoal stove coloured pink like the walls. But then, Redney didn't spend any time there; the bawarchi, Kali Bagh, was in charge of the cooking. In the beginning, her servants were also a trial to Redney. She was learning Hindustani as fast as she could so that she could talk to them; the language was easier to master than the servants. There were so many of them. There was Kasti, the bearer, in charge of all the others. He looked after Sahib Cotes' clothes and money and gave him a daily massage. Redney's ayah did the same for her. Then there was Kali Bagh, who did the marketing as well as the cooking, and who was most skilled at lining his pockets as he did so. The kitmutgar waited on table, the mussalchi brought hot water, squatted to wash the dishes in an earthenware bowl, cleaned the silver, carried home the market basket, the cook not deigning to do so. The mallie saw to the garden, scratching and scraping with his trowel early every morning before the heat got unbearable. The syce looked after the pony, lived in a space much smaller than his charge's. The dhoby took the dirty laundry away on a donkey, beat it between two large stones, brought it back. The bheesty brought water every day in a goatskin. The sweeper took away all refuse, carefully preserving the table scraps which formed his diet. One never saw the sweeper or spoke to him; he was one of India's shadows. In the beginning, her servants were one of the battering realities which hit Redney head on. They squabbled and fought loudly among themselves; they tried to deceive their greenhorn *memsahib*; they spoiled her privacy. They brought the strange, disturbing world that was India into her house, buzzing round her like hornets, and it was a permanent invasion.

Outside her house, India's jarring contrasts bombarded Redney's genteel Canadian soul, nurtured on a middle ground, on continual compromise. There was no *via media* in India; even the climate and geography were violently dual. In the dry season it never rained. The relentless sun turned the ground to concrete and pounded into Redney's head; her clothes were always inelegantly soaked in sweat. Duststorms blew into her pretty drawing-room, reducing everything to a common greyness. When the rains began, they fell torrentially for three months. In the northern plains there were no hills, not even the smallest mound; in the hills there were never ten yards of level ground.

Every time Redney looked out the windows of "Sudder Dewanny Court" the contrasts were there. Across the weedy road lived a "riotous Rajah" in a weird, castellated old place, with a slouching guard at the gate. When the Rajah went abroad of an evening, perfumed and oiled and turbaned, four badly-uniformed horsemen pranced behind his carriage, while the cooking-fires of his retainers formed a starry constellation on his extensive grounds. To the north of Redney's house there was a bustee, where the family lived almost exclusively in the yard, and the acrid smell of cow-dung fires stained the air all day. There seemed to be three old women, five babies, a cock and goat. Redney sat by a window, watching, as they cooked in their mud fire-place, served the food onto plaintain leaves in lieu of plates. The Rajah and the bustee; India's incredible contrasts, always there, beyond the windows with no glass. Always the splendour and the squalor together; incense and garbage; the opulent and the grotesque.

Redney soon realized that there was no way to reconcile the one with the other. India's world, she was beginning to discover, underneath the mystery and colour which had seduced her on her world tour, was a dark pit of horror and existential chaos, without reason or logic or consistency. Where could a writer find pattern and form in all that welter? Always, that amoral jungle tangle, just beyond the neat British compound, lay ready to invade the Western mind, like the snakes curled up on the bathroom's cool, right-angled tiles in the hot weather. Redney feared that primitive, violent world which she had first encountered in the vultures of the Towers of Silence. No one in India, not even the Viceroy, could escape it. Even at Government House jackals howled each night in the shrubberies, stinking civet cats climbed in through the windows. Once Lady Curzon, Redney's future friend, woke to find one, five feet long, drinking the glass of milk by her bedside.[5]

In addition to the homesickness, the inside domestic problems, the outside chaos and evil, the heat, the rains, there were, for Redney, every day, hundreds of little unexpected annoyances to sting and fester. "The really trying things—the things one hadn't reckoned with beforehand— were that one's envelope flaps should all stick down;" that book pages should curl up, or, occasionally, be eaten by fish insects, "that the towel should sting one's face; that the punkah should stop in the night" (*Memsahib*, p. 308).

Then there was her new social world. The Anglo-Indian social scene was stuffy, stale, rigid with absurd conventions and formality. It made her feel cornered, almost comatose. From Government House affairs on down to small dinner-parties, the formality was always there. Redney found herself thinking nostalgically of the freedom and originality of Washington parties. On Thursday, December 18th, just after her wedding, Redney had been presented to the

Lansdownes at a Drawing-Room, a typical affair of moth-
balled propriety:

> The Drawing Room at Government House on Thursday
> night was largely attended and was a very brilliant and
> successful function. Lord William Beresford first, in a few
> words, addressed the ladies in the ante-chambers and reques-
> ted them not to hurry, but allow each lady to take time to pass
> before their Excellencies individually. There was far less
> crushing this year. With some exceptions the dresses were not
> so artistic or so striking as they have been seen on other
> occasions. Most noticeable was a rich white satin court train,
> with seed pearl garniture, and Swiss bodice of perfect cut
> (*The Englishman's Overland Mail*, Dec. 24, 1890).

The names of Mr. and Mrs. Everard Cotes occurred in the
Public Entrée list; the Private Entrée was reserved for the
highest-ranking officials and their wives. Surely the "rich
white satin" was the dress in which Redney had met her
Queen. Redney gives a full account of this second presentation in *The Simple Adventures of a Memsahib*, her autobiographical novel giving her first impressions of India, but
after St James, it was anti-climatic and a pale imitation. As
her card was passed from one ADC to the next, then "Mrs
Everard Cotes" — that still sounded strange — was read out by
the military secretary as she curtseyed to the Lansdownes,
Redney remembered that she had already curtseyed to them
in Toronto and had seen them many times in Ottawa. After
being presented, one wrote one's name in the Government
House book and thereafter got invited to various social
functions there. The Viceroy was only in Calcutta from
December to February; he spent six or seven months in
Simla escaping the heat and two or three on tour. In those
three winter months, however, there were evening parties,
garden parties, dances, official dinners for up to one hundred and twenty every Thursday, and smaller lunches and
dinners. At these Government House parties, Redney met
the British bureaucratic presence in India.

Redney soon perceived that the British in India lived
on the edge of a volcano and they knew it. They ruled with
an iron hand, not allowing natives to sit in their presence,
shouting out their orders, using their red-tape — rule-books,

minutes, lists, copies in triplicate—as reason's whip, to keep
irrational, primitive India at bay, that world of banditry,
massacre, flood, drought, famine, plague. Since the Mutiny
of 1857, the iron hand had trembled, the grip had tightened,
the whole system grown more rigid, less humane. The
British answer to India's mystery and tangle was a right-
angled, Western logos: supervision, regulations, correspondence, clerks by the thousands, writing by the ream. Redney
observed it all, and made mental notes for future political
novels.

She cast an equally satiric eye at the rigid Calcutta
social scene. Everard belonged to the Bengal Club, to the
Golf Club, to the Tollygunge Club, where there was horse-
racing every Saturday afternoon, and he was part of a social
circle of middle-rank civil servants. Anglo-Indian society
was divided into castes quite as precise as Hindu ones, and
one's status was determined by the size of one's paycheque.
"It's rather an uninteresting social bias— . . . but it has the
advantage of simplicity. You have a solemn official right to
expect exactly what you can pay for" (*Memsahib*, p. 133).
Civil servants and administrators were Brahmins, subdivided
into the Covenanted Ones, the Judges, Commissioners,
Collectors, who got "three hundred a year dead or alive", for
their salary was paid to their widows, and the Uncovenanted
Ones, whose business was with education, science, engineering,
and whose pension ceased when they died. The British Army
came next, corresponding to the Hindu warrior caste. The
merchant caste included plantation owners, businessmen and
European workmen. The lowest caste of Anglo-Indian society
were the Eurasians. The status symbols, as Redney was quick
to note, were not Sèvres china or Chippendale furniture, but
"the locality of your residence . . . the size of your compound" and the number of horses you owned, preferably
Australian Walers (*Memsahib*, p. 78).

In Brantford, British social forms had been tempered
by American democratic ideals. In Britain, they were rigid,
as Redney had recognized in *An American Girl*, but in India
they were positively ridiculous.

Calcutta, in social matters, is a law unto herself—inscrutable, unevadeable. She asks no opinion and permits no suggestion. She proclaims that it shall be thus . . . . Calcutta decrees, for example, that from twelve to two, what time the sun strikes straightest and strongest on the carriage-tops, what time all brown Bengal with sweet reasonableness takes its siesta, in the very heat and burden of the day—from twelve to two is the proper hour forsooth for the memsahib to visit and be visited (*Memsahib*, p. 130).

There was a book on every civil officials' desk called The Warrant of Precedence ranking everyone in order, so that a hostess could find out if an Inspector of Smoke Nuisances should precede a Junior Settlement Officer in to dinner.[6] The Anglo-Indians lived like an army of occupation; they were inside the garrison, and they made no social concessions to the jungle beyond. When Lord Baden-Powell went on a tiger-shoot, he used India's symbol of splendour, the elephant, to carry his claret, soda-water, table silver and ice.[7] Since civil servants all came from exactly the same middle-class British background, there was a bland, utterly boring homogeneity to the social group in which Redney found herself. She stifled many a yawn at "the tedium of Calcutta small-talk" (*The Path of a Star*, p. 43) as she sat through dinner-parties like the one described in *The Path of a Star* (pp. 193-7) where the food was so much more exciting than the guests. The men always wore white tie and tails, the women décolleté dresses and long, white kid gloves, impossibly hot and hard to clean. Every house, every table, every conversation was the same. They ran together in Redney's mind into one large brown blob, the way her favourite water colour had run in the rains. Guests were asked at "eight for half-past", and proceeded into the dining-room in strict order of rank. On the dining-room walls were polo teams in blackwood frames; on the sideboard, silver egg-sets and golf trophies. The table was always decorated with a large bowl of roses, place-cards, fretwork silver dishes of Marzipan and toffee fudge, individual finger bowls with sprigs of verbena. There would be five or six courses, and champagne, always champagne, and it all took a very long time. After dinner there might be music, a piano solo by one of the ladies who had brought her music, just in case, or a comic song by one of the gentlemen from the last Saturday Club skit. An hour after dinner, the butler brought round whiskey and soda; then everyone kept one eye on the Senior Lady, since no one could leave until she had "made a move".[8] Redney would take her revenge in her Indian novels, aiming some of her best satiric barbs at the Anglo-Indian dinner party.

The memsahib's life had few domestic chores, for "all its material cares devolve into a hundred brown hands, and leave us free for our exalted occupations or our noble pleasures" (*Memsahib*, p. 261). After she had made her consultation with the cook on marketing and menus, refilled the decanters and cigarette boxes, issued clean dusters and arranged the flowers, the typical memsahib turned to such "exalted occupations" as charity bazaars and endless rounds of visiting and gossip. Redney turned her back on all of this and devoted her energies to her writing. More and more, the discipline and ritual of her writing would signal the nun's retreat from the pain of the real world. She quickly established her daily routine. She rose early to tea and toast, then rode or bicycled, ate breakfast, did her minimal domestic duties, then got down to her writing, usually from ten o'clock to two or three in the afternoon. She was satisfied with only three or four hundred words a day, "but they are carefully thought out and she seldom makes any further correction when the day's work is done".[9] Since her arrival in India, Redney had been spending her daily writing sessions revising proofs of *An American Girl in London*, in response to a November 21st letter from Chatto and Windus, enclosing the numbers of *The Lady's Pictorial* (September to November, 1890) in which it had been serialized. She worked straight through without a break for lunch, or tiffin as it was called, but stopped in time for tea. After tea, when the air had begun to cool off, she might play a game of tennis, or drive along the Maidan, where masts of ships anchored in the Hooghly river pierced the rose-red sky, and pained her. Similar ships tied to the New Orleans levee had beckoned her to that wider world, and she had chosen it. Now, displaced and disenchanted, she was condemned forever to all its disadvantages and drawbacks.

The Maidan was, like the rest of Calcutta, terribly British. It was Hyde Park in India, the exercise ground for dogs, horses and British humans, with an expanse of burnt grass, bicycle tracks, tennis courts, cricket-pitches, golf links. A band played in Eden Gardens and all Calcutta took the air there until it was time to dress for dinner. The Maidan, according to Lord Frederic Hamilton, "has been admirably planted and laid out, with every palm or tree of aggressively Indian appearance carefully excluded from its green expanse, so it wears a curiously home-like appearance".[10]

In fact, Redney soon realized that a great deal of Calcutta was eminently British. As the winter seat of government, it had the largest British population in India, boasted the best shopping for British goods. Its buildings were in the classical eighteenth-century style of British architecture, with Doric or Ionic columns, porticos, balustraded roofs: symmetrical, restrained, dignified, strangely at odds with their flame-and-flash setting.[11]

The Museum building, where Everard spent his days and where Redney sometimes came to wander through cool marble rooms, was typical. The original building, completed in 1877, extended along Chowringhee facing the Maidan for over three hundred feet, its Greek facade, brick overlaid with plaster, quite as solid and dignified as Government House. The main building was only two stories; there had been plans for a third, but when alarming cracks had appeared near the foundation, officials decided not to risk a higher structure. The most popular exhibit in the Museum was a taxidermist's triumph in the gallery of large mammals, a simulated fight between a lion and tiger, both of them stuffed and stationary, with plenty of red sealing-wax blood.[12] Behind the Museum were extensive gardens and a large tank, the delight of the staff, for it contained more species of fresh-water sponges "than any body of water of similar area that has ever been investigated".[13] Everard spent much time thumbing through the 12,000 volumes in the zoological library; at the moment he was writing a pamphlet on the silkworms of India.[14] After six years on staff, his enthusiasm was beginning to pall; much of his work was routine; then, too, he had not yet had a promotion. The first superintendent, Dr J Anderson, an Edinburgh zoologist, had retired in 1886, two years after Everard came out, and been replaced by Wood-Mason, an Oxford graduate of forty-five who had moved up from assistant-curator, a quiet, kindly man who also had rooms at 1 Sudder Street.[15] Bent over his microscope, with the stale air smelling of formaldehyde and dust, Everard more and more was relying on Redney's fey imagination to colour his life.

Sometimes, to be sure, Redney felt as if her imagination were stuck in formaldehyde too. The impact of British India was, in one sense, as negative as England's had been positive. England had been imagination's citadel, towards which all literary roads led; Calcutta was not only a fossil-bed of social customs, it was a cultural desert as well. Redney had always found her friends among painters and writers. In Calcutta, painting was in the hands of "Mrs. Cubblewell and Colonel Lamb, and Mrs. Tommy Jackson" who "paints roses beautifully" (*Memsahib*, p. 181). In India, alas, "the arts conspire to be absent" (*The Path of a Star*, p. 20). Redney had complained of the philistinism of Canada's cultural scene, but it was a rich feast compared to India. Culturally, she had condemned herself to an extremely narrow cell.

Behind its sterile, British façade lurked another, very different Calcutta. Redney only had to stand on the Hooghly Bridge at sunset to see it: an endless belt-on-a-wheel of moving people, never varying in thickness, never stopping, never accelerating, inching slowly forward at the same slow, resigned pace. Calcutta was stuffed with people, Indian people, overflowing with them, breeding like rats. They lived crowded into fetid passages hardly wide enough to walk in, twisting, turning, miles of them with drains and compounds of festering filth. Rubbish decayed in the streets, drinking wells filled up with sewage. There were annual outbreaks of cholera and plague and the death-rate was thirty-six in the thousand.[16] Rudyard Kipling gives a short history lesson on Calcutta:

> Thus the mid-day halt of Charnock—more's the pity!
> Grew a City.

As the fungus sprouts chaotic from its bed,
So it spread—
Chance-directed, chance-erected, laid and built
On the silt—
Palace, byre, hovel—poverty and pride—
Side by side.
And, above the packed and pestilential town,
Death looked down.[17]

Death did, indeed, look down. That was another of the shocks of Indian life for Redney: that dark vulture's wing, always above one's head. "In a climate like this it was a popular opinion", Redney was to write, "that a man must either enjoy himself or commit suicide" (*The Path of a Star*, p. 62). Every newspaper told of suicides among the white community:

A European, named I. Ollyet, employed on the Hooghly Bridge, committed suicide by taking opium on Saturday night.... It appears he was dismissed from his employment, which preyed on his mind (*Indian Daily News*, Feb. 18, 1897).

—Mabel Davidson, aged 19½, assistant mistress of the Byculla Schools, Bombay, committed suicide after the G.I.P. Volunteers' ball at Igatpuri on Wednesday by throwing herself into a well (*Indian Daily News*, Jan. 8, 1896).

There were bizarre murders, and accidents:

It appears that Mr. Lillywhite, Telegraph Master, his two sons, two daughters, a boarder and two servants, were poisoned at dinner on Good Friday.... The cook, who was arrested on suspicion, confessed that he had been bribed by six durwans and another to poison the whole family, for which they paid him 100 rupees and a bottle of brandy (*Indian Daily News*, April 6, 1896).

A Mr. Scott, who hails from Calcutta, and is employed with Messrs. John and Co. of Agra, has, says a correspondent, been bitten by a mad dog, and is under the Civil Surgeon's treatment (*Indian Daily News*, July 15, 1896).

The body of a European, probably that of Mr. Low who was drowned on Sunday at Titaghur, was found floating in the river yesterday morning. The flesh was eaten away from the face and parts of the body, rendering identification difficult (*Indian Daily News*, Sept. 25, 1896).

Illness took its appalling toll: "Uncovenanted people have a way of dying pretty freely, but that's out of sheer perverseness, to get more furlough", explains Mr Sayter with heavy irony to the visiting British M.P. "Most of them go for ever because they can't arrange it any other way. And as for cholera, I give you my word not one man in ten dies of cholera out here; they go off with typhoid and dysentery, or in some comfortable way like that, and probably have a punkah the whole time they're ill" (*Memsahib*, p. 251). Cholera was the quickest killer. A friend could be well in the morning and dead by nightfall. Kipling tells of a club scene where a "man asked a neighbour to pass him the newspaper. 'Get it yourself', was the hot-weather answer. The man rose but on his way to the table dropped and writhed in the first grip of cholera".[18] It was a shadowed world.

"Nobody goes to India to take root, as people come to Canada", Redney had written during her world tour (*Montreal Star*, Oct. 30, 1889); it was also an impermanent world. The belt of Anglo-Indian people never stopped moving either, but its pace was faster, more erratic: cool months on the plains; hot ones in the hill stations; leaves and furloughs in England; children packed off to school there; wives sometimes departing with them; engineers, soldiers, forestry inspectors, constantly on the move, living in tents. Anglo-Indians were a restless lot—if one moved perhaps one could escape the heat, death's shadow, the routine of red-tape, the tedious social round. Even the Viceroy, during his three months in Calcutta, sailed up river with all his servants and papers every Saturday afternoon for week-ends at Barrackpore, the closest possible copy of an English country estate.

In the midst of this chaos, Redney clung to her writing. On January 8th, 1891, she received a letter from Chatto and Windus, addressed to yet another name, Mrs Duncan Cotes, enclosing a royalty cheque for eighty-two pounds on *A Social Departure*.[19] The proofs for *An American Girl* had apparently been revised by "Miss Cotes", one of Everard's sisters at Newington—perhaps Rosemary who herself wrote books on wildflowers. Redney was now feeling the frustrations and inconvenience of being seven thousand miles distant from her publisher. Chatto also inform her that "we are now proceeding with a set of plates for America. We fully expect that Messrs. Williamson will take our edition for Canada . . . . We thank you", the letter continues politely, "for your hint of advertising in the Indian papers which we will bear in mind. We seldom advertise in other than the London papers which go all over the world". Obviously, Redney was realizing "how essential ambition was to bearableness of life in India" (*His Honour, and a Lady*, p. 161). A letter from Chatto of February 25th indicates that she had wanted her married name to appear on the title page of a new edition of *A Social Departure*: yet another name attached to her writing, sign of the splintering self, of the secure ego which was coming unstuck in the Indian sun. Chatto, however, demurred:

> Your letter unfortunately reached us after the new edition of *A Social Departure* was printed off and a portion of it in the printer's hand (this in anticipation of any demand that may arise after the publication of *An American Girl*): but, in any case, we think it would really be better to retain on the title page the name with which the book is identified, and under which it has met with so much success. To now give another name would, we fear, lead to confusion, the more especially as *An American Girl* has been so widely advertised as by Sara Jeannette Duncan.

On March 9th, *An American Girl in London* was published. It had been serialized not only in *The Lady's Pictorial* the previous autumn, but also in the American edition of the *Illustrated London News*. The reviews were all favourable, and the book sold well. Redney and Everard celebrated its success in the spring of 1891 with a trip to Europe, a delayed honeymoon. Redney was already collecting material for *An American Girl's* sequel, *A Voyage of Consolation*, which would repeat the pattern of *A Social Departure* and *An American Girl*: a single girl goes abroad in search of adventure. To get her heroine, Mamie Wick, to Europe for an extended tour, Redney has her break off her engagement to the American Arthur Page, although she will marry him at the book's end.

While Redney was in Paris, staying at a Luxembourg hotel, she received two letters from Chatto, the first on June 15th, informing her that they were preparing *Two Girls on a Barge* for publication following its serialization in *The Lady's Pictorial* with Townsend illustrations. For some reason Redney wanted this book to come out as anonymously as possible, with initials "V.C.C." only, but a Chatto letter of June 19th reveals that she reluctantly consented to have the full pseudonym "V. Cecil Cotes" appear on the title page. It seems a curious choice, for Violet Cecil Cotes was the name of a deceased sister of Everard's. All during her writing career, Redney had a strange habit, when casting about for characters' names, or pen names, of choosing familiar ones from her own world, as if identities, hers and others, were interchangeable.

By the end of June, Redney was back in Calcutta, correcting proofs of *Two Girls on a Barge*, and, at the end of July, writing a long, scolding letter to Chatto, in which the hard-edged Brantford Scot cum American go-getter is uppermost:

Calcutta,
July 30.

Dear Sirs,

I write to acknowledge your letter and cheque for £121.0.4 which reached me by last mail. I am gratified at the sales of the "American Girl", but disappointed in the great falling off of "A Social Departure", which I hoped to continue to do well for some time to come. May I ask if this book has had any sale in Australia, or if it would be possible to arrange for an Australian edition. I should like, if possible, to receive separate accounts for India and Australia, as it would assist me in regard to those markets in future. Do you consider the advisability of a somewhat cheaper edition of "A Social Departure" yet? I must protest with you one item in the account you send — the royalty of 3d on sales to Canada. My agreement with you tells me that my royalty is to be reduced *in proportion* to the reduction in the price at which you sell to the colonies, and you informed me that your best terms to Canadian publishers were *one half* the retail price, which Mr. Williamson of Toronto thought very advantageous to him when I mentioned it last summer. According to that my royalty ought to be rather more than 6¢ per copy. If you have found it necessary actually to sell 800 copies of the two books to Canada at a *quarter* of the wholesale price, which would make my royalty 3d I think the proposition should have had my approval as well before so great a reduction of profits was made. In which case I should certainly have preferred to arrange a Canadian edition printed in Canada and copyrighted there, which I should be inclined to do in bringing out any further books. That the author of a book which sells at $1.75 should receive upon each copy the sum of six cents seems to me an unnecessary hardship. I hope there has been some mistake which you will be willing to rectify as I think it makes a difference of quite ten pounds in the account. You will be sorry to hear that The American Girl has been stolen by no less than four firms in the U.S. The Appletons have brought out both books in paper at 75 cts.

Believe me
Sincerely yours
S.J. Cotes

Redney here was sharpening the tools of what would become one of her main defences against those numbing realities of Indian life which were leading her to restlessness and apathy. Redney would concentrate on making money; she would buy her way out with frequent trips to more congenial settings. If India's hot sun turned the ground to concrete, it also hardened Redney, making her an extremely shrewd, calculating business-woman, stubborn and tough. For the rest of her life, she drove a hard bargain, counted every penny of her profits. *Two Girls on a Barge* was published on August 14th, 1891 and on August 24th, Redney received a letter from Chatto reiterating that 3d. per copy for the 800 sent to Canada is all she is entitled to, and that Indian and Australian sales have been too low to warrant colonial editions.

The hot season of 1892, mid-March to mid-June, found Redney stuck in Calcutta. The previous year she had escaped with Everard by sailing away to Europe. In these early days of marriage, she was reluctant to leave her husband and join the wives migrating to Simla's cool heights. In May of '92, Everard would have a promotion, becoming Deputy

Superintendent of the Museum, replacing W.L. Sclater who resigned; it was impossible for Everard to leave Calcutta, so Redney stayed too.

Exactly on March 15th, the punkah wallah arrived with the hot weather, to pull the rope on the punkah, the large fan kept going day and night. The shops put up grass-tatties for the wind to blow through, while a coolie stood outside in the heat throwing water over them. The brain-fever bird shrilled "all day long in the thickest part of the banyan tree, where nobody can see or shoot him. He comes and stays with the hot weather, a feathered thing accursed" (*Memsahib*, p. 265). The hot air hung in the streets "with a kind of inertia, like a curtain that had to be parted to be penetrated" (*The Path of a Star*, p. 221). "Rather than saying the air was hot, one might say that the heat was aired; the heat was the thing you breathed and moved in" (*Set in Authority*, p. 293). Strong men fell over dead from heat apoplexy, and received a line in the newspapers.[20] By now, like all fledgling memsahibs, Redney had lost her fresh colour, acquired a shadowy ring under each eye. She was thinner, her nerves more on edge; she caught herself sounding petulant with the servants. It may have been now that she took up smoking, a habit which she maintained for the rest of her life. It was a double defence: a reminder that she was a front-runner and feminist (smoking was still considered shocking in a woman), and also a relaxant for her overwrought nerves. She did it with flair, using an elegant holder, stabbing the air at parties to emphasize a witty point, her long legs crossed at the knee in the daring new fashion.

The heat made it difficult to write. It was too hot to make the barest physical movement, the smallest mental leap. It was no accident that the natives called the supreme being "the immovable one". Redney fought against the weight of burning air, tried to feel in her mind those cold Scots winds which had spurred her ambitious father to upholster his life. She wrote every day, even when the thermometer soared to 100 degrees or higher, while the punkah creaked overhead and the brain-fever bird screamed outside the window. If the external world was dusty and dry, her English flowers drooping in the heat, Redney fought to keep the cool spring of her own creativity spilling out onto the page. The rewards of writing, both pecuniary and personal, became her only resource.

She was working on *The Simple Adventures of a Memsahib*, one of her finest creations. At last, on June 15th, as Redney wiped her sweating palms once more and took up her pen, the rains began. The rainy season lasted until mid-September, and was even more trying in some ways than the heat. It was a time of universal illness, both those that killed and those that annoyed: eczema, impetigo, boils. Insects multiplied. For a month there might be a plague of large, repulsive greenflies, then one of stinkbugs, stinkbugs in the soup at dinner, stinkbugs in the ink bottle on Redney's desk. It was during the rainy season that snakes slithered into the house, naturally preferring a dry place to a wet one. Sometimes a krait, a thin, little poisonous devil, stretched out straight along the edge of a rug or lay along the top of a door, falling off on you when you opened it. Cobras often sought shelter on the porch. The furniture perspired, the roof leaked, the matting rotted. Green mould grew in Redney's shoes, her evening dresses turned all sorts of strange colours, centipedes zig-zagged across the floor. Redney felt as if "all her relations with the world were being submerged" that "the very fabric of her existence was dissolving" (*Memsahib*, pp. 311-12). Birds flew about with torn pieces of paper in their mouths, trying to make their nests, but the wind blew the paper round their heads like bandages, and they grew alarmed and dropped it. Redney clung, drowning, to her pieces of paper, and the irony of *Memsahib* bit deeper. A welcome letter of July 1st, 1892, from Chatto confirmed arrangements for its publication in London; Appleton's would publish it in New York.

At this point in her life, the impact of India on Redney's talent, if not on her temperament, was all to the good. India's contrasts and chaos and confusion had forced her into her first stage of detachment, given her a new tool of irony and satire. Under *Memsahib*'s realistic fabric of Indian life, those strong threads of documentary detail which had already run through all her journalism, *A Social Departure*, and *An American Girl*, is a sharp criticism of the hypocrisy, snobbery, parochialism, and dullness of Anglo-Indian society. It is shown to be a social organism forced to turn in on itself, becoming disenchanted and diseased at the core, concerned with money and status, blind to everything else. This was Redney's first expression of what would become a dominant theme in her fiction: the sterility of imperialism. The ideal of Empire inspires and uplifts: Britain as all-powerful and all-wise father, with dutiful daughters growing and learning under that benevolent arm. It was an ideal which also appealed to Redney because of the importance in her own life of the father-daughter relationship. But the reality was far different. Redney was now seeing at close range the waste of lives in an Empire which England didn't understand: all those bored, isolated, frustrated people, people of talent like herself, condemned to pass their lives in a cultural desert, forever cut off from the wellspring. Redney expressed the ironies of it in *Memsahib* with Jane Austen's tone: the same ironic stance, the moral firmness, the acerbic wit, the crisp, epigrammatic narrative voice. One is aware throughout of a writer possessing that easy familiarity with Austen's novels which only comes from many re-readings.[21]

Part of *Memsahib's* irony comes from its dual point of view. We see India through two pairs of eyes, as Redney looks back to her younger self. There is Helen Browne, the young English bride, the new memsahib of the title: the Redney who arrived in India, eager, optimistic, and in love with her new husband and with the exotic India which she had glimpsed on her world tour. Then there is the narrator, Mrs Perth Macintyre: Redney, the established memsahib, older, wiser, more cynical, more detached. Mrs Perth Macintyre, after twenty-two years spent in India married to a tea merchant, is about to return to England, and her ironic point of view shows what an astounding change Redney's sensibility had undergone in her first two years in India. Mrs Macintyre looks back along the dusty road she has travelled:

> For I also have seen a day when the spell of India was strong
> upon my youth; when I saw romance under a turban and soft
> magic behind a palm, and found the most fascinating occupa-

tion in life to be the wasting of my husband's substance among the gabbling thieves of the China Bazar (p. 376).

Memsahib mirrors Redney's own life. She had married Everard because of the lure of the East with all its "romance under a turban". She had married him, as Judith Church would marry in *His Honour, and a Lady*, to escape life's dull alleys, to feel forever the pomegranate breezes of the wider world. But the irony for Redney was that the wider world had, paradoxically, turned out to be the biggest blind alley of them all. In *Memsahib* she vented her spleen, spat it out in her satire of Anglo-Indian society, but underneath, Redney's anger was really directed at herself, for she it was who chose. She had accepted her husband and her Indian life freely, with her eyes open. She had locked herself in. She was like the Carmelite nuns "who have imposed a life sentence on themselves" (*Week*, Nov. 10, 1887).

Redney realized two years into marriage that it was a mistake. Mrs Perth Macintyre's disillusion with matrimony is Redney's:

> "Liver", however, very seldom ensures in the early days of matrimony, and Helen, unacquainted with this domestic bane, laughed it to scorn. It was her unconscious belief that the idylls of the Brownes could not suffer from such a commonplace (p. 171).

Between the ideal and the real, in life, in marriage, falls the shadow, and one defence against the pain of that knowledge is detachment. Evey was easy to live with, considerate, devoted to Redney. He was the perfect husband. And since he was hers forever, he unwittingly left her nothing new to dream about and scheme for and work towards. It was the same old pattern repeating yet again: the shining ideal became tarnished by familiarity, then boredom spread. The idylls of the Cotes' marriage, like the Brownes', were soon spotted with "liver"; Redney could feel the abscesses of tedium. She realized now that she should have stayed single, stayed the scintillating, sought-after Garth Grafton, flirting with literary greats. She should have stayed in London to savour the fruits of her literary success at their source. With the publication of *A Social Departure* she had stood poised on the very lip of literary London and all its delights, and she had walked away.

Most of all, she feared apathy. At the end of *Memsahib*, Helen Browne is "growing dull to India, too, which is about as sad a thing as any. She sees no more the supple savagery of the Pathan in the marketplace ... the early morning mists lifting among the domes and palms of the city" (p. 379). The New Orleans sun had nurtured. But the Indian sun was too relentless, too revealing; the emotional self was forced to shut its eyes, to step back into the shadows. And, with one notable exception, to stay there. Mrs Perth Macintyre is at one remove as she sits on the sidelines of a Government House party:

> The old, old ambitions, the stereotyped, political aims, the worn competitions, the social appraisements — how they have repeated themselves through what illustrations of the great British average, even in my time! How little more than illustrations the men and women have been as one looks back — pictures in a magic lantern, shadows on a wall! ... solemn warning to those that are so eager to come after, if only the glamour of India left people with eyes to see. How gay they were and how luxurious, and how important in their little day! ... And now — let me think! — some of them in Circular Road Cemetery — cholera, fever, heat apoplexy; some of them under the Christian daisies of England — probably abscess of the liver; the rest gray-faced Cheltenham pensioners, dull and obscure, with uncertain tempers and an acquired detestation of the climate of Great Britain (p. 162).

"If only the glamour of India left people with eyes to see". These are heartfelt words on Redney's part. If only she herself had truly seen when she was on her world tour, before she made her irrevocable choice. "Shadows on a wall": all those loyal servants of Empire narrowed and negated by imperialist realities. There is a profound feeling of distance, of physical and psychological exile in *Memsahib*. Already Redney had begun to step back into the shadows, but she still had her weapons. Pinned to the wall with wonderful satiric accuracy are the British Parliamentarian who arrives in India every cold weather to get at the "truth", the frivolous, flirtatious English memsahibs, the ever-so-charming bachelors encroaching on marital preserves, the slothful, worldly Anglican clergymen who care more for their claret than their parishioners' souls, the snobbery and insensitivity of Anglo-India as a whole:

> The cholera arrived punctually, and increased the native death-rate with its customary industry. The Lovitts lost a bearer from this cause, and a valuable polo pony from heat apoplexy. The latter bereavement was in the paper (p. 266).

In the furnace heat of India, Sara Jeannette Duncan's style had been refined into new terseness. "Without being actually slangy", she says of the typical memsahib, "she takes the easiest word and the shortest cut; in India we know only the necessities of speech — we do not really talk, even in the cold weather" (p. 378). Under India's hot sun, Redney's maturity had come quickly. The last paragraph of the book shows how far she was from youthful optimism, as Mrs. Perth Macintyre prepares to leave India:

> I hope she [Helen Browne] may not stay twenty-two years. Anglo-Indian tissues, material and spiritual, are apt to turn in twenty-two years to a substance somewhat resembling cork. And I hope she will not remember so many dead faces as I do when she goes away — dead faces and palm fronds gray with the powder of the wayside .... So let us go our several ways. This is a dusty world. We drop down the river with the tide tonight. We shall not see the red tulip blossoms of the silk cottons fall again (p. 379).

The final irony, the paradox, is that as Redney's actual world grew dustier, her art, for a time, grew greener. *The Simple Adventures of A Memsahib* reveals on every page the great curves and dips of a broad-leaved, full-grown talent.

By August, 1892, Redney had finished *Memsahib* and had bought her way to Britain. She was ensconced at 24 Upper Addison Gardens, Kensington, in a furnished flat, enjoying London's fresh pace. What a safe, comfortable, ordinary world it seemed! No vultures, no scorching suns, no ash-covered figures with burning, fanatical eyes. Everything softened, muted ... kind English voices, silver teapots, week-ends at Newington with watercress sandwiches under

the sheltering elms. For the rest of her life, Redney would
have her middling Canadian soul trying to find its ease
somewhere between the two extremes. She went frequently
to England, usually without Everard, because she wanted to
taste as many crumbs as possible of that gay, literary life
which could have been hers forever had she chosen differen-
tly. A first-class ticket from Bombay to London cost fifty-two
pounds, a second-class one, thirty-two to thirty-eight pounds;
from Calcutta it was more. No one but a fool, said Samuel
Johnson, ever wrote except for money. Everard's salary was
not large; Redney wrote now to keep herself in steamship
tickets. From now on she had the two very different worlds
of India and England, and a blissful third one: the two-week
interval between, the blessed relaxation of the sea voyage,
where she could lie back in a deck chair and let her mind
circle as aimlessly as the gulls. The royalty cheques from
Chatto kept coming, but Redney cast her net now in new
waters, and began turning out articles for American and
British magazines. Her first effort, entitled "Eurasia" by
"Sara Jeannette Duncan", appeared in *Popular Science Monthly* in November, 1892. It is a sympathetic sociological study
of the plight of the 20,000 Eurasians living in Calcutta,
showing how they are passed over for jobs, socially ostra-
cized, forced to live in "crooked little streets" where "the
pleasant south wind does not always blow through to sweet-
en them, and they bear much need of sweetening". It was a
large sea into which Redney had cast her net, for the
magazine was then in its hey-day. It formed the chief
entertainment for Americans with money in their pocket
and no movies, radio or television in existence. By 1885
there were already over three thousand weekly and monthly
journals in the United States.[22] The Big Three were the
Century, *Atlantic* and *Harper's Monthly*, all of which paid
roughly one hundred and fifty dollars per article. From now
on, Redney kept up a steady production of magazine articles
as well as novels, and in the romance-realism seesaw of her
writing, they firmly weighted down the realistic end.

  At the end of 1892, back in Calcutta as the cold weather
began, Redney wrote a children's book called *The Story of*

Sonny Sahib, entering it in a competition sponsored by the *Youth's Companion*, a Boston magazine which would also publish four of her articles between 1893 and 1904. She didn't win the competition, but the story was accepted for publication.[23] The germ of the story came from an old ayah, who had been through the Mutiny of 1857, and weepingly described to Redney how children had been killed before her eyes in that terrible time. *The Story of Sonny Sahib* by Mrs Everard Cotes—Redney's first use of her married name—would be published by Chatto and Windus in 1894, and by Appleton's in New York in 1895. Its hero is an English boy who, on his mother's death and father's disappearance, is raised by his ayah, and finally reunited with his father. Perhaps Sonny is a metaphor for Redney's sudden gush of feelings of displacement; it was written at white heat, in only three weeks. It is charming—the whimsy and childlike wonder which had made Redney so happy in Japan are well suited to juvenile stories. This particular one sold well for many years to come.

Redney spent the whole year in Calcutta in 1893, suffering through the hot weather, the rains, the return of more hot weather in August before the temperature became bearable again in November. By the beginning of March, Redney was correcting proofs of the first thirty-two pages of *Memsahib*, just received from Chatto.[24] *Memsahib* was then appearing serially in *The Lady's Pictorial*, and the Townsend illustrations, as usual, were being passed on to Chatto by Mr Gibbons.

The vulture's wing brushed Redney closely when she opened a letter from her family in Canada telling her of brother Charles' death on April 2, from tuberculosis. Since leaving school he had been working in the Duncan store. He was only twenty-six, and was buried in Greenwood cemetery on April 4th, next his brother Henry. The family had the words "Their sun is gone down while it was yet day" carved on their tombstone. For Redney, the shadows grew darker. There was, however, some pale Canadian sunshine too: her fame in Canada was growing. Archibald Lampman in his "Mermaid Inn" column for the *Globe* on March 4th, 1893, wrote: "We have all heard of Miss Sara Jeanette [sic] Duncan, now Mrs. Cotes, and have read more or less of her entertaining and popular work. Her success has been phenomenal, and her name meets the eye in almost every newspaper".[25] Hector Charlesworth, describing "The Canadian Girl", commented:

> The Canadian girl who has carried the fame of Canada's self-reliant girlhood into all countries is Mrs. Sarah Jeannette Duncan Coates [sic]. . . . Mrs. Coates, or it is more natural to call her Miss Duncan, with her crisp force is another of those striking girl-individualists that have sprung up during the recent period of rapid development.[26]

There was more fame to come. On May 18th, 1893, *The Simple Adventures of a Memsahib* by "Sara Jeannette Duncan" was published and heralded with glowing reviews. Redney was heartened, re-energized, threw herself even more completely into the discipline of her work. Before a year had passed, she would have finished two more books, *Vernon's Aunt* and *A Daughter of Today*. Both of them show her leaving the straight road of autobiographical fiction which she had trod thus far to wander in more fanciful fields, with much less satisfactory results.

Vernon's Aunt was written first—written off the top of her head to make money. It tells the story of Miss Lavinia Moffat, English spinster of forty-two, who comes to India to visit a nephew in a remote forestry encampment, learns to cope with elephants running loose, scorpions in her bonnet. It is Redney on her favourite theme of a single woman going in search of adventure, but it is also Redney on her worst behaviour, trying very hard to be funny, and not succeeding. There is no irony to leaven the lump; nor any of her fine natural descriptions, and her major failing as a novelist is starkly revealed: her inability to weave plot and character together so that they are mutually dependent. The plot of *Vernon's Aunt* is contrived and implausible, a silly superstructure of unlikely coincidences. Redney has chosen to distance herself not through irony, but through farce, and the result is lamentable. *Vernon's Aunt* was serialized in *The Idler*, a British magazine edited by Jerome K. Jerome, with the final installment in July, 1894. Chatto then brought it out in a 3/6 volume, with the *Idler* illustrations, proposing to pay Redney a royalty of six per cent. She asked for more. Chatto replied: "We could not afford a royalty of 8% for every copy sold, and [trust] that you will accept our proposal of 6d. per copy which is the utmost which the market will allow".[27] *Vernon's Aunt* was published in mid-October, 1894, and Appleton's did an American edition. One feels that six pence a copy was all that Redney deserved.

A Daughter of Today is a more significant work, revealing further Redney's splintering of the self. Its heroine is a New Woman and single adventuress called Elfrida Bell — another case of Redney needing an amulet of reality, for Bell was her mother's maiden name. Elfrida grows up in Sparta, Illinois, then heads for Europe to live the Bohemian life, painting and writing in Paris and London. She is fiercely egotistical, wildly unconventional, and shocks her staid English friends by becoming a chorus-girl. Failing miserably as both painter and writer, she finally commits suicide. Is this Redney, married to a very conventional Englishman, living in a very conventional social community, letting her confined ego out to play in Bohemian fields? Was Redney, through Elfrida's suicide, perhaps acknowledging the death of her impulsive, intrepid younger self? "Those that write", says one of her characters, "transcribe themselves in spite of themselves" (*The Imperialist*, p. 68). *A Daughter of Today*, like *Memsahib*, is a mirror-image of the younger self. In *Memsahib*, Redney looks back at that eager bride who arrived in India in December, 1890; in *A Daughter of Today* she looks back at her Brantford and New Orleans self, so sure, so vibrant, so ambitious. Elfrida is very like that Redney, for she has Redney's fierce little flame of ego, Redney's ambition "to do *good* things . . . and to have them appreciated and paid for in the admiration of people who feel and see and know" (p. 125), Redney's keenly appreciative aesthetic eye — "the joy in art" is the "key to her soul" (p. 228) — Redney's thirst for a wider world of colour and passion, Redney's creed, embracing Arnold and Aristotle and Whistler, Redney's sympathy with the cause of liberated

women. Like Redney, Elfrida lets her writer's needs deter-
mine her life choices; she becomes a chorus-girl to get
material for a book just as Redney opted for exotic scenes
which she could describe in print. For Elfrida, as for
Redney, it proves to be an unwise choice.

Redney also introduced a motif in *A Daughter of Today*
which she would use in two more novels: the single career
woman who refuses marriage. In *A Daughter of Today*,
Elfrida refuses the hand of Laurence Cardiff, even though
she is poor and lonely and he offers status and security. In
creating Elfrida, Redney sought to define herself, including
her limitations as a writer. Elfrida has "a curious prismatic
kind of mind" which "reflects quite wonderfully, the angles
at which it finds itself with the world ... But I doubt her
power", says her friend Janet Cardiff, "of construction, or
cohesion or anything of that kind" (p. 174). Elfrida herself
comments that, in order to write a novel, "one wants a
leading idea ... and I have none" (p. 258). This would
prove to be a more prophetic statement about her own
talents than Redney knew. Like *Vernon's Aunt*, the plot of *A
Daughter of Today* is hackneyed and arbitrarily imposed. Its
texture, like all Redney's books, shows that her mind was a
prism, a fine reflecting instrument, but that is all. Without a
firm, autobiographical base, she founders. *Memsahib* has a
fixed, ironic point of view; *A Daughter of Today* suffers from
the lack of one. There is no ethical norm in the novel; the
authorial voice wavers between admiration of Elfrida, and
condemnation. *A Daughter of Today* was published by Chatto
and Windus in a one-guinea, two-volume library set in June,
1894. Redney received a royalty of 15 per cent and an
advance of thirty pounds.[28] In November, 1894, Chatto
brought out a 3/6 edition, paying Redney a royalty of 6 per
cent. It is a curious coda to the splintering self that in both
volumes given to her mother-in-law, Redney has written:
"Mrs. Cotes. With love from her daughter, Dorothy. Oxford,
June, 1894." From then on, as her sense of self weakened,
new names sprang up constantly in an attempt to fill the
vacuum.

Redney was able to hand the volumes so oddly inscribed to her mother-in-law in person, for she had been in

Oxford since May, where Ellen Cotes, now a widow, had moved into a house at 201 Iffley Road. The spring had been full of fresh plans and new goals for Redney and Everard. They had said a permanent good-bye, so they thought, to Calcutta: a reluctant good-bye on Evey's part, a rejoicing one on Redney's, since she wanted very much to leave India for good. At her urging—she was always the dominant member of their marriage—Evey had resigned from the Indian Museum in April. Redney had convinced him to abandon entomology in favour of journalism, brushing aside the fact that his talents and experience all lay with science.[30]

Using Redney's royalty income, she and Evey had a fling in Paris before going to stay with Mrs. Cotes in Oxford. In Paris, Redney probably renewed her friendship and reminisced with Lily Lewis. Lily was writing for English and French periodicals. (She would later marry an American, Roland Rood, son of Professor Ogden Rood of Columbia University, spend her married life in Paris, have a baby who died, get a divorce and pass a rather sad old age in England.[31]) Paris on the whole appealed to Redney much less than London: "There isn't a street, or a public building, or a statue, or a fountain, or a thing that doesn't shout at you, 'Look at me! Think about me! Your admiration or your life!'" (*Voyage of Consolation*, p. 98). The Eiffel Tower has "the familiarity of a demonstration of Euclid, and to the non-engineering mind was about as interesting" (*Ibid.*, p. 83). She and Everard had stayed first at the "London and New York" hotel, but found it too noisy and moved to the Hotel Dominici, Rue Castiglione. William Dean Howells was then in Paris, and spent an evening with Redney.[32] When Redney and Everard arrived in England in May, feeling refreshed and hopeful, Everard began casting about for a journalist's job while Redney did her best to keep some income coming in. As soon as she was settled at Oxford, on May 16th, she sent off to Jerome K. Jerome, editor of *To-Day*, an article which she had written just before leaving India, advising him that "I do not, of course, want my name to appear as it is a news article".[33] "The Mission to the Harem", signed

"G.G.", appeared on September 20, 1894, and described an interview with Miss Lilias Hamilton, a New Woman physician and single adventuress, who was about to visit the Amir and his harem of wives in Cabul, Afghanistan, "a country of blood and stones", which was then dangerous territory for any English person, let alone a pretty, thirty-year-old single woman. For Redney, Lilias, whom she calls "a remarkable illustration of modern feminine development", represented the freedom and determination of her own younger, daring self.

Redney's old friend Pauline Johnson was just such another; she had been daring enough to go on the stage, not quite, however, in Elfrida Bell's capacity. Pauline, in that spring of 1894, was taking London by storm, giving recitals in full Indian costume of buckskin, dangling scalps and bear's-claw necklace. In a rich, dramatic voice, the beautiful Pauline, an eagle feather in her dark hair, recited her poems and the English took her to their hearts. Her first platform reading had been in 1892 at the Toronto Young Liberal Club, along with other Canadian authors. Two weeks later, emboldened by her success, she had given an entire program in Toronto's Association Hall, reciting "The Song My Paddle Sings", written for the occasion. After a cross-Canada tour, she had come to England to perform and to see to the publication of her first book of poems. Later, she would tour America, sometimes sharing the program with Joaquin Miller, who, at afternoon "drawing-rooms", would fling a bearskin on the floor and gracefully recline on it while he recited his romantic poems.[34]

In September, 1894, Redney had a holiday in Braemar, Scotland, enjoying its misty glens. By November, she and Everard had taken a furnished flat in London at 34 Wanrest Gardens, Kensington, and were looking forward to a winter season of cultural delights. Then Everard was offered the editorship of the *Indian Daily News* in Calcutta. They deliberated, weighing the pros and cons. Since nothing of a journalistic nature had turned up for him in England, Everard decided to accept. By January, 1895, an unhappy Redney, propelled by her Calvinist sense of wifely duty, found herself back in the smells and heat of Calcutta, more than ever determined to buy her freedom through her writing.

Some of her creative energies, however, were put at her husband's service. Everard was a novice in newspaper work; he needed Redney's help. Together they plunged into the challenging new currents of editorship of the *Indian Daily News*. The *News* office was situated at 19 British Indian Street, and was probably very much like the one of ink-stained walls and high ceilings described in *The Path of a Star* (p. 124). There were dusty files of old newspapers ranged round the walls, along with three or four messengers who habitually squatted there, half asleep, waiting to run errands. The paper was an unpretentious one, much less prestigious than *The Englishman*, with a four-page format whose front page, in the British tradition, was made up of advertisements, for Pears soap, Egyptian cigarettes, French champagnes. There was a column of miscellaneous items headed "By the Way", "Home News Notes", giving events of the Empire, and, of course, local items, both political and social, with detailed reports of the ladies' bazaars, the tennis tournaments, the Hunt Club paper chases, the Saturday Club dances. Much of the copy was gleaned from British or Indian papers. Redney did the sort of editorial work she had done in Washington: occasional editorials, book reviews, drama criticism. She was quite as determined as she had been in Toronto to raise the Philistines to a higher cultural level. "That amusing play, 'Charley's Aunt', is likely to be given at the Saturday Club towards the end of next month", she writes. "It is to be hoped that something will be done beforehand to improve the acoustic properties of the auditorium, as it will be a thousand pities if such an excellent play fails to be heard, and becomes, as far as the audience is concerned, merely a dumb-show. This has been the fate of all previous theatrical performances at the Saturday Club" (*Indian Daily News*, Jan. 27, 1896).

Everard crusaded in his editorials for better hygiene, better sewage. Beginning in May, 1896, Everard served on the Municipal Commission, and gave detailed reports in the paper of their deliberations on such matters as the overworking of Calcutta's tram horses, and how unwise it would be to move the site of the Municipal office "with all its unsavoury appliances" nearer to Government House (*Indian Daily News*, May 1, 1896). Everard hammered out editorials condemning the sale of milk diluted with tank water full of cholera germs (*Indian Daily News*, May 13, 1896), commending the Municipality of Calcutta for hauling away cart after cart of refuse from one of the bazaars just as the Plague "which battens on filth" is about to take its yearly toll (*Indian Daily News*, Oct. 12, 1896). Seeing him in his new crusader's role, Redney was forcibly struck by his sterling moral worth, his high standards, his keen sense of civic duty. On the surface, Evey had a school-boy's love of pranks and practical jokes which appealed to the fey young Redney, the "Helen Browne" one, but not to the older, sardonic "Mrs Perth Macintyre" side of herself.

"We are but children of a larger growth and happy are the traditions that keep us so", Evey was to write.[35] Once he dressed as a straw-chewing shepherd at a Government House fancy-dress ball, teasing the great ones there in a broad Oxfordshire dialect. Underneath this boyish banter, however, Everard had his own strength, and at this time in their lives together, Redney was continually conscious of it. There is a great deal of Everard in John Church, a main character in *His Honour, and a Lady*, the new novel which Redney was working on in addition to her editorial duties. "Life with John Church could be measured simply as an area of effort" she writes (p. 150), and demonstrates his factual, scientific mind, his devotion to duty, his moral integrity.

His Honour, and a Lady is Redney's first novel of the Indian political scene. Like the exotic backgrounds of her "single-adventuress" novels, politics would become for Redney another leading idea. *His Honour* tells the story of two Lieutenant-Governors of Bengal: the first, John Church, moral and upright, is a burnt offering to the ideals of imperialism while the second, Lewis Ancram, substitutes hypocrisy and deceit to gain the governorship. Technically, the book shows some gain for Redney, with more dramatic action and less authorial analysis, more "showing" than "telling", as Henry James would say. There is some of the same acrid irony and satire as in *Memsahib*:

> Gentlemen native to Bengal are not usually invited to balls at Government House.... The reason is popularly supposed to be the inability of gentlemen native to Bengal to understand the waltz, except by Aryan analysis ... they are asked instead to evening parties which offer nothing more stimulating to the imagination than conversation and champagne—of neither of which they partake (p. 200).

There is also much of *Memsahib's* terse style. Many ironists might envy the following description of Bhugsi, a village in Eastern Bengal: "The town squatted round a tank, very old, very slimy, very sacred. Bhugsi bathed in the tank and so secured eternal happiness, drank from the tank and so secured it quickly" (p. 234).

His Honour, and a Lady is most interesting, however, for its exploration of the thwarted love theme, one which would obsess Redney for the rest of her writing career. In this novel she introduces a love pattern which she would repeat in three later novels: a woman falls in love with a man who, for one reason or another, is unattainable. She yearns for him, sees him as the ideal mate. Later, his behaviour tarnishes the ideal, so that when he is free to marry her, she refuses and is left without love, living a lonely, disciplined life. The parallels with Redney's own life are obvious: she too had fallen in love with an ideal, but her heroines see the realities while there is still time to say no, to refuse marriage, whereas Redney was already trapped. Her ultimate choice, however, was the same as her heroines': she settled for heroic isolation and the discipline of hard work.

Redney packed the completed manuscript of *His Honour, and a Lady* in her suitcase as March's heavy heat hit Calcutta, and sailed away to London. She took a flat at 24 Sussex Villas, Kensington,[36] delivering her novel to her new literary agent, A.P. Watt, who, until his death in 1914, would see to all publishing arrangements for her. Alexander Pollock Watt, born in Glasgow and educated in Edinburgh, was London's very first literary agent, having set up his office in Paternoster Row in 1876. He was "a most agreeable man"[37] who served as agent for Henry James at one time, and for such best-selling authors as Wilkie Collins, Bret Harte and Rider Haggard. Redney was hopeful that financially he would work similar miracles for her. She was pleased when he sold the serial rights for *His Honour, and a Lady* to the posh *Pall Mall Magazine*, where it would appear in the fall of 1895, the publication rights to Macmillan's of London, Appleton's of New York, with publication in 1896.[38]

Sometime during her summer in Kensington, Redney was interviewed by G.B. Burgin, novelist and journalist, who, between 1894 and 1938, would churn out some ninety novels, two of them with Canadian settings. This interview shows just how far Redney has withdrawn emotionally after five years in India. She tells Burgin that life there

> slips away easily in a succession of dramatic days, and one sees one's self projected like a shadow against the strenuous mass of the real people, a shadow with a pair of eyes. There is such intensity and colour and mystery to see, that life is hardly more than looking on.[39]

A shadow with a pair of eyes. Like Judith Church, Redney was now aware that "India had become a resource . . . a place in which she felt that she had no part, could never have any part, but that of a spectator" (*His Honour, and a Lady*, p. 15). In India, "society has no fringe, no border-land, no mystery", Redney complains to Mr. Burgin. The mystery of Indian life was forever impenetrable, and stuffy Anglo-Indian society offered none. "The eternal novelty of the river and the eternal sameness of the people" (*His Honour, and a Lady*, p. 100) struck an eternally discordant and, for an artist, frustrating note. "Roses", Redney tells Burgin, "cannot be induced to flourish in Calcutta".[40]

1896 began with a small honour for Redney, then back in Calcutta. The *Indian Daily News* reported on January 4th that "Mrs. Cotes" had won the medal at the Ladies' Golf Club for highest score. February's tedium was tempered by Mark Twain's visit to Calcutta, for he gave three readings at the Theatre Royal. The account of his opening night must surely be Redney's writing:

Mark Twain made his first appearance before a Calcutta audience yesterday evening at the Theatre Royal.... His appearance, with his thick, waving grey hair, grizzled moustache, square jaw, deep-set twinkling eyes and bushy eyebrows has been the same for years. It is a typically American face, full of shrewdness, and logic, and fair-mindedness. Mark Twain talks as he writes. The same ordinary prelude leads up to the same unexpected flash, with all sorts of odds and outs of humour by the way, things he didn't particularly set out to say (*Indian Daily News*, Feb. 11, 1896).

Listening to him, Redney must have recalled her happy Washington days, and her first sight of Mark Twain in his pepper-and-salt tweeds, sprinkling his wit over the heads of Congressmen. Twain tells a reporter that he would like to stay longer in India, but that the heat is driving him out, as well it might, for on February 29th, the temperature in Calcutta was 100.6 fahrenheit. When, on April 14th, the temperature rose to 109.2 the *News* reported:

The exceptional heat which prevailed in Calcutta on Tuesday, was accountable for seven deaths from heat apoplexy and sunstroke amongst Europeans and Eurasians, and thirteen deaths among natives. Ten horses and three bullocks fell down dead in the streets on the same day (*Indian Daily News*, April 16, 1896).

Redney fled to Simla at the end of April, retreating to nostalgia, for spring in Simla was almost like a Canadian one, with "young grass" and "small pushing buds, and stray dandelions", and a blossoming cherry tree in a little garden just above the Tonga office (*Indian Daily News*, April 24, 1896). Her mind also drifted back to her happy Japanese days, as she compared Simla rickshaws to Tokyo ones:

Tenderly, under these grievous circumstances, does one muse upon the slight poetic rickshaw of the streets of fantastic Tokio, with one inodorous runner between the shafts, and not attached to a handle in this cumbrous fashion, who swings you along through miles of fairy-land with his hat bobbing up and down like an excited mushroom, and a paper globe with a verse on it dancing like an illuminated idyll under his elbow! The first *khud* rebukes the comparison, of course, for Tokio is as flat as Calcutta (*Indian Daily News*, April 24, 1896).

This is yet another of Redney's distancing mechanisms. More and more she looked backward to happier times. She had always found her greenest fields in the past, or the future, rather than the present. Now she turned her eyes more and more frequently over her shoulder, along the path she had taken. Eventually, this backward gazing would remain intensely focused for many months on her early Brantford years, and her finest novel would be the result.

Redney returned to Calcutta in mid-May, just as *His Honour, and a Lady* arrived in the mail from Macmillan's[41] and evidence in *News* editorials suggests that she spent the remainder of the year in Calcutta's inhospitable environment.[42] As she sweltered in the stuffy *News* office, a note of homesickness for Canada's cold, invigorating spaces crept more and more often into her editorials. In June, 1896, when Sir Wilfrid Laurier and the Liberals "for the first time in almost twenty years" ousted the Conservatives from power in Ottawa, she wrote:

> The land of the beaver and the maple leaf sends few of her sons to this country. Three or four cadets every year from the Engineering College at Kingston . . . form the most regular contingent, and now and again a pioneer for oil or gold or coal betrays to Anglo-Indians by an unfamiliar twist in his speech and an American crispness in his capacity for business, the fact that he is a British subject from far North and further West, but that is practically all. Canada has room at home and a climate fit to live in; Canadians take root beside their tamaracks and their children after them (*Indian Daily News*, June 27, 1896).

She also noted in this column how the Toronto *Globe* to which she still subscribed, is "a cruel month in coming". Seen from India's desert wastes, Canada's green fields, particularly her cultural ones, looked more and more attractive:

> A whole band of poets and one or two novelists have arisen in Canada . . . . The necessary condition of life without anxiety and without penury have been established; and out of the tranquillity that ensures art buds timidly, like a flower newly acclimatised (*Indian Daily News*, Oct. 12, 1896).

From now on, Redney's backward glances at her past focused most often on her native land.

In October, the Plague was spreading so fast that hundreds of Hindus were jamming the railway stations and leaving the city. India was also suffering a severe drought, with terrible famine in the North-West, and dwindling water supplies everywhere else. Christmas was a particularly homesick time for Redney. "The frosty chime is not in the church-bells, nor the accustomed flavour in the plum-pudding. More than all, the children are not here", she wrote (*Indian Daily News*, Dec. 25, 1896).

Through the spring heat and cholera epidemic of 1896, the fall heat and plague, the continuing homesickness, Redney had been escaping mentally to Europe. She had been writing *A Voyage of Consolation*, most aptly titled, the European adventures of Miss Mamie Wick. The London *Bookman* reported in September, 1896, that

> the author of that extremely clever story "His Honour and a Woman" [sic] has just completed a sequel to "An American Girl in London." "The new story is entitled "An American Girl Abroad" and has already been secured for early serial publication by a well-known lady's weekly newspaper. It may not be generally known that Mrs. Cotes (Sara Jeanette Duncan) is a prominent member of the staff of the *Indian Daily News*, Calcutta.[43]

Under its first title, "An American Girl Abroad", *A Voyage of Consolation* was serialized in *The Queen*, beginning in April, 1897.[44]

Redney was covering familiar ground in *A Voyage of Consolation*, trying to repeat the successful formula of *A Social Departure* and *An American Girl in London*: the single North-American girl who wants to see the wider world. The detailed descriptions of France, Italy, Switzerland and Germany are based on her European jaunts of '91 and '94. Taken as a whole, the book is, like *Vernon's Aunt*, another steamship ticket to England, not another literary masterpiece. The scene where Mamie, Mrs Portheris and Dickie Dod spend seven hours lost in the Catacombs, and Mrs. Portheris eats her kid boots from hunger, shows Redney at a new low: its humour fails dismally. The basic plot of *A Voyage of Consolation* re-uses that of *An American Girl*: Mamie turns down her English suitor, Charles Mafferton, and goes home to the States to marry her American one, Arthur Page. The fact that Redney repeats for the second time this pattern of a heroine declining the wider world in favour of home roots in North America is, in view of her own irrevocable choice, significant and revealing. *A Voyage of Consolation* was published by Methuen's in London, Appleton's in New York, in the spring of 1898.

By mid-March, 1897, Redney had written its last page and as the punkah-wallahs and brain-fever birds began their several callings, she left Calcutta for the cool hills of Simla. Evey would follow later, for Redney had persuaded him to resign his editorship of the *Indian Daily News* in favour of a job as government press correspondent in Simla. Calcutta had vanquished them; Redney, particularly, was thrilled to be leaving, to be heading for a new setting, to be trading the parched plains for the green freshness of the mountains, like the dog which she had once met going to Chakrata for his diseased liver, "one more homesick alien" going "to look for his lost well-being in the Hills" (*Memsahib*, p. 365). As Redney travelled by train the nine hundred miles from Calcutta into the hills that March, her mind veered backward to her first ascension, though that time she had not gone as far as Simla. She had transcribed it all in *Memsahib*, which she had written shortly after. She and Evey had been still in the first bliss of marriage as they journeyed upwards, ever upwards, from the sweltering plain. First had come Dehra Doon "where all the hedges drop pink rose petals, and the bulbul sings love songs in Persian (*Memsahib*, p. 33), then hills and more hills, "insisting always upwards round the nearer masses to hills that were greater, further, bluer" (p. 346). She felt suddenly hopeful again, suddenly eager, as she sat back in the tonga, being carried up the last few miles from the railway station to Simla, to her new home, the only place in India where roses do well. The ones at Annandale, where the ladies practised their archery, were particularly fine.

In many ways, Simla was a strange hot-house in which to try to take root. Seven thousand feet above sea level, the lack of oxygen made Redney's heart race, her head feel light. Simla had a nostalgic Mardi-Gras feeling: everyone escaping from duty and drudgery on the hot plains below, so very far below, with nothing to do but amuse themselves, all those young wives without spouses, all those young bachelors without scruples. It was a gay, mad, carnival scene of endless tennis parties, dinner parties, garden parties, sketching parties, private dances, balls at Viceregal Lodge, drinks at the club, tea on the Mall, tiffin at Peliti's.[45]

Redney was gratified to discover that India's sharp contrasts were in the background in Simla—there were, to be sure, ragged hill tribesmen in the Mall as well as red-coated Government orderlies carrying despatch boxes or invitations to tea. There were Tibetan women with huge chunks of turquoise in their ears, as well as Englishwomen in pale, flowered hats. But Simla was the least Indian part of the country, the most English. It looked like Surrey with a slight Eastern flavour. At the top of the Mall rose the noble Gothic spire of Christchurch Cathedral where, after Sunday service, all Simla stood gossiping on the terrace, the ladies clutching their feather boas against the wind. On weekdays, Simla filled the café at Peliti's, the fashionable hotel, or did some desultory shopping at the jewellers', the saddlers', the wine merchants'.

In every direction, up and down the steep inclines, were tendrils of narrow roads, too narrow for buggies. Only the Viceroy had a carriage; ladies rode ponies or were pulled in rickshaws; gentlemen rode or walked. Along the twisting paths were glorious thirty-foot rhododendrons, tall deodars, swinging monkeys. Simla lived in cottages, with gates at the road, paths winding to the front door between pink cosmos growing everywhere like weeds, cottages with gabled roofs of corrugated iron, lace-curtained windows, fuchsias and ferns in hanging wire baskets on the porches. Inside, the bungalows were dark, with uneven floors and low ceilings, smelling of damp, just like English ones. Redney moved into one of these while she looked about for a house to buy, and began her writer's scrutiny of this strange community of 3,000 Anglo-Indians, enjoying "the most desirable things—roses, cool airs, far snowy ranges", finding "an ark of refuge from the horrible heat that surged below" (*The Pool in the Desert*, p. 135). Not that Simla's climate was ideal. From January to March, it was snowy, stormy, with fahrenheit temperatures in the low forties; April, May and June brought increasing heat and dryness; July, August, September brought the rains, when white monsoon clouds blanketed the mountains; October, November and December were cool, crisp, rather like a Canadian autumn, with temperatures in the fifties and sixties.[46] Still, it was much more tolerable than Calcutta's furnace heat. If the climate was an improvement, the inhabitants were the same, as Redney soon discovered to her disappointment. They were quite as rigid and narrow socially as their kind down below.

To be sure, Simla had cultural pretensions. There was, to begin with, the Simla Amateur Dramatic Club. During the previous summer they had done *Lady Windermere's Fan* and *Iolanthe*, keeping up with London, where Wilde and Gilbert and Sullivan kept audiences amused all through the Gay Nineties.[47] Then too, there was the annual exhibition, in August, of the Fine Arts Society held in the Town Hall, opened by the Viceroy, displaying the usual amateur daubs of flowers and sunsets. Down in the plains, "the arts conspire to be absent", but Simla's poor, straggling specimens, Redney decided, were almost worse than nothing. For the most part, she turned her back on Simla society, feeling the ladies' whispers and disapproval; she wouldn't get involved in Good Works, or Gossip, of which there was a bigger crop in Simla than anything else. She dressed in odd, original ways, smoked openly at parties, insisted on riding astride when every other female rode side-saddle, even had a Western saddle sent to her from Canada.[48] Eventually, Redney would find a few kindred souls, even in Simla, and would cast an exploitative eye on the Amateur Dramatic Club, but for the moment she concentrated on her writing, and on the beautiful views.

Redney scribbled a Simla column for the *Indian Daily News* and sent it down to Everard. "The oldest inhabitants still find Simla cold, and the visitors pronounce it perishing", she wrote during a cold snap (*Indian Daily News*, April 25, 1897). By the end of April, "Simla is practically full. The Club has all its rooms occupied, and the eleven o'clock service at Christ Church exhibits crowded pews" (*Indian Daily News*, April 28, 1897). More than a hundred ladies had decided together to send cards announcing their arrival through the post rather than delivering them in person, which was the way Simla had always done it. The Simla correspondent, sounding remarkably like the old "Garth Grafton" of "Women's World", remarks that for years the men have been grumbling at the penance of paying calls in "the hottest part of the day", but that it was left to the women to do something about it (*Indian Daily News*, April 28, 1897). Redney worried about Everard on Saturday, June 12th, when Calcutta had an earthquake. She later learned that he had been working at his desk in the *News* office, where he kept a pair of scissors stuck in a jam jar. When they flew out, he decided it was time to vacate.[49] "We were compelled to stop all work, and seek another press, in order to bring out even a four-page paper . . . the rain added to our difficulties, which were already sufficiently great. . . . We can assure our readers", apologizes Everard on the following Tuesday, "that every effort is being made to secure a new habitation" (*Indian Daily News*, June 15, 1897). June 22nd was the day decreed in England for the official celebration of Queen Victoria's Diamond Jubilee, but in India the usual tangle of red-tape was complicating the matter:

> The Government of India has addressed local Governments with a view to ascertain the opinions of the commercial and other communities whether that date [June 22], or the 21st, or both days, should be observed in India and granted as public holidays under the Negotiable Instruments Act (*Indian Daily News*, April 12, 1897).

Sometime after June, 1897, Everard joined Redney at Simla and they settled into their new life. He became secretary of the Golf Club; they bought two ponies, Arabi and Pat, so that they could ride together in the surrounding hills. Redney was now busy writing *The Path of a Star*, which would be finished by June of 1898, published in 1899 by Methuen in London and (under the title *Hilda*) by Frederick Stokes in New York. In Simla, Redney's four hours of writing were spent in her bedroom, propped among the pillows, where "she would work with pencil and paper, and one just did not venture to disturb her during that time", according to a niece who later came to visit.[50]

Simla didn't rejuvenate Redney's art. *The Path of a Star* finds her still detached, playing with themes of thwarted love, heroic self-sacrifice and isolation. There are three love stories in *Path*: Alicia Livingstone nurses a secret love for Duff Lindsay, who in turn harbours an unrequited passion for the Salvation Army lass Laura Philbert. The heroine Hilda Howe is also thwarted in love. She is a single adventuress and career-woman, an actress, who comes to India vibrantly alive, poised, sure of herself, entranced by its richly-coloured frieze. But Hilda, like Redney, is denied emotional fulfillment there, for she falls in love with an Anglican priest sworn to celibacy.

Realizing that this ideal man can never be hers, Hilda abandons her career and the attempt to find a life of love and artistic fulfillment; she enters a nunnery. Images of self-denial and isolation, of the consolation of ritual and discipline, crowd the novel as they crowded Redney's own life. She had now placed herself emotionally in the narrow bed of the fictional Portuguese Nun and the real-life Carmelites of Montreal. Redney describes Hilda's feelings during her last night on stage thus:

> She was living for the moment which should exhale itself somewhere about midnight after the lights had gone out on her last appearance — living for it as a Carmelite might live for the climax of her veil and her vows if it were conceivable that beyond the cell and the grating she saw the movement and the colour and the passion of a wider life (p. 253).

The love scenes between Stephen and Hilda are cloying and sentimental. The real India had made it impossible for Redney to go on finding "romance under a turban". She was Celtic enough to need some form of romance in her life;

from now on, and with greater frequency, she would spin
sentimental fantasies into her novels, cobweb creations of
hand-holding and fancy words. There is never any real
passion because that is something Redney herself had never
really experienced. Then too, as always, she was keeping a
sharp eye on the market-place, where Anglo-Indian writers
like Maud Diver, Alice Perrin, Ethel M. Dell were churning
out formula romances to enormous sales. Whatever the
cause of Redney's emotional retreat, it had a bad effect on
her art.

If *The Path of a Star* signals a loss of verisimilitude, it
also signals a stylistic decline. Redney is here following the
path of a literary star: Henry James. She begins in this novel
to desert her own crisp style in favour of James' subtle,
intricate analysis of character and setting. Unfortunately, in
her hands, it results only in obfuscation. The following
passage, where Alicia Livingstone sits in her drawing-room,
shows Redney on her disastrous Jamesian path:

> Things fell into their places, one could observe relative
> beauty, on the walls and on the floor, in Alicia's hair and in
> her skirt. Little meanings attached themselves—to oval por-
> traits of ladies, evidently ancestral, whose muslin sleeves
> were tied with blue ribbon . . . to odd brass bowls and faint-
> coloured embroideries. The air became full of agreeable
> exhalations traceable to inanimate objects, or to a rose in a
> vase of common country glass; and if one turned to Alicia one
> could almost observe the process by which they were absorbed
> in her and given forth again with a delicacy more vague (p. 17).

"Delicacy more vague" indeed. This is all very subtly done,
but what does it mean? Redney's vision of life had failed to
keep up with her clear vision of material objects. There is, to
borrow James' phrase, no figure in the carpet. Redney had
sent Henry James, whom she knew casually from London
literary circles, a copy of *His Honour, and a Lady*, and his
thank-you letter is itself a Jamesian triumph, full of what
Leon Edel sees as James' habitual epistolary mix of "accolades and muted strictures, a wrapping of sharp criticism in
the soft cushions of kindness":[51]

> I think your drama lacks a little *line*—bony structure and palpable, as it were, tense cord—on which to string the pearls of detail. It's the frequent fault of women's work—and *I* like a rope (the rope of *the direction and march of the subject*, the action) pulled, like a taut cable between a steamer and a tug, from beginning to end.[52]

The cable isn't taut because Redney wasn't sure any more where the steamer was headed. "Youth demands colour and blue sky", E.M. Forster wrote about one of his characters, "but Martin, turned thirty, longed for Form. Perhaps it is a cold desire, but it can save a man from cynicism".[53] In Canada, or even in England, Redney might have found the necessary Form. But, as another Canadian writer, George Woodcock, has pointed out:

> The temptations which India offers to the writer are not those of more self-consciously ordered and articulate countries— the temptation to the easy generalisation, to the rash abstraction; they are rather the temptations of the idiosyncratic and the particular, the temptations of a land that woos one with a deceptive appearance of everlasting eccentricity and contradiction. Where facts are so novel and experience so varied, the writer must seek, like the painter of a jungle landscape, for the particulars which establish a pattern the mind can comprehend and which also make that pattern true.[54]

Redney got lost in the jungle tangle; she couldn't find a path. Emotional detachment came first, then moral. Redney began to hear the meaningless echo which Forster's Mrs Moore heard in the Marabar caves: "Pathos, piety, courage— they exist, but are identical, and so is filth".[55] "People are born and burned and born and burned and nothing in the world matters", says one of Redney's characters (*His Honour, and a Lady*, p. 97).

By choosing India as her permanent setting, Redney had unwittingly arrested her own growth towards wisdom and that unique vision of the world which every great novelist must have. She had condemned herself to be forever a competent journalist, nothing more, with a journalist's skills of accurately reporting scene and dialogue, but with no taut line. Speeding through the Canadian Rockies in the cow-catcher, the mountains had seemed incredibly close.

The Himalayas mocked Redney because they were "prodigiously far off", so that they looked like "the country of a dream just hanging above the world" (*Memsahib*, p. 356). Every time she looked out the windows of her Simla house they imaged her art, and her failure. "It is their remoteness, their unapproachableness, that make these Himalayan Snows a sanctuary", she had written (*Memsahib*, p. 356), a sanctuary from the world, like a Carmelite nunnery, a sanctuary from the quandaries of moral and artistic meaning.

Redney turned her back on the snows in March of 1898, and made another trip to England, so that she was there when *A Voyage of Consolation* was published. She was interviewed by Florence Donaldson for an article in *The Bookman*. Redney was now thirty-seven and Miss Donaldson gives a fine view of the brave, bright face which was Redney's public mask:

> In person Mrs. Cotes is tall and slight, with dark hair and grey eyes. The prevailing expression of her mobile face betrays the dominant sense of humour which is the key to her literary success. The observant eye, quick repartee, and often racy speech are equally characteristic. The frequent amused smile seems to show a kindly indulgence for, and pleasure in, the trivialities of life, while a general carelessness in dress betrays the Bohemian temperament.[56]

In July Redney was in Brantford, visiting her family. Her brothers had not yet married and were still living at West Street. Blake was twenty-five now, charming, handsome, working in the store, doing a fine job of decorating the windows and clients' homes; he, too, had the Duncan aesthetic sense. Gordon, much more dour and serious, had been in the family business for ten years now, while Leslie worked at the Brantford Bank of Commerce. The boys had nicknamed Ruby "Duchess" because she held her head so high, was always so impeccably groomed. Ruby had become a talented, if desultory, pianist and painter; somehow she lacked the drive to channel her energies in one forward direction. Redney's father looked older, thinner, his aquiline nose, so like her own, beak-like. He was serving as City Alderman and chairman of the finance committee and when

Lord and Lady Aberdeen had visited Brantford in September of '96, Charles Duncan had, in the Mayor's absence, read the civic address.[57] Her mother disapproved of Redney's smoking, particularly since her daughter's health was obviously so poor, her bronchitis chronic now, her face thin and pale. A letter to John Willison, her friend from Ottawa days, now editor of the *Globe*, reveals how her physical health had deteriorated as her mental unhappiness grew:

> *Brantford*
> *July 4th*
>
> Dear Mr. Willison,
>
> I find I shall be here until the end of the week. After that I think of going to Dansville [in New York State] to try the hydropathic treatment there but my permanent address is c/o Charles Duncan, P.O. Box 165, Brantford. I am sending you "A Voyage of Consolation". It has pages at which I hope you will endeavor to smile, for the encouragement of Canadian literature!
>
> I forgot to tell you that Miss Ousaud was kind enough to call, as you proposed. We nearly came to blows over the Saturday Review and she had too much the best of it for I was a weary wreck but I enjoyed meeting her very much. She has a particular definiteness of mind which is rare and stimulating in a woman. If I can find them I will also send the last Indian mail's batch of papers which may interest you for their local comments on the plague and the people. The blue pencillings are not pertinent, being my husband's, to keep me in touch with what he is doing. Perhaps they will give you the idea though, that the daily task of a Simla correspondent is sufficiently varied.
>
> Believe me
> Dear Mr. Willison
> Yours very sincerely
> S.J. Cotes.[58]

As autumn came, Redney felt an elegiac weight of nostalgia, remembering how high the flames had once leapt on the West Street hearth, dancing off the walls in delightful dream-shadows of things to come. She went, one sad September afternoon into the Brantford fields, to gather golden-rod seeds to take back to Simla:

A friend of my youth lent herself to the project; she took me in her father's buggy, and as we went along the country roads I saw again, in the light of a long absence, the quiet of the fields and the broad, pebbled stretches of the river, and the bronze and purple of the untrimmed woods that had always been for me the margin of the thought of home. The quiet of after-harvest held it all . . . it was time to talk and to remember. And so, not by anything unusual that we did or said, but by the rare and beautiful correspondence that is sometimes to be felt between the sentiment of the hour and the hour itself, this afternoon took its place in the dateless calendar of the heart which is so much more valuable a reference than any other (*On the Other Side of the Latch,* pp. 153-54).

Another letter to Willison, written from New York in October, where she may have been visiting the Wimans, reveals Redney's longing to re-root herself in North America:

> Town and Country Club
> 12 East 22nd Street
> New York
> Oct. 10th

Dear Mr. Willison,

Many thanks for your kind telegram which my father has sent on to me here by post. A day or two before I left home Mr. Cotes started for Louisville Ky. on the chance, which seemed a good one, of getting an appointment on the Louisville and Nashville Ry. Your message however, suggests a welcome alternative in case he is disappointed and I have forwarded it to him, asking him to write you immediately. I am so very sorry that I missed you when I was last in Toronto, and shall grieve particularly if this opportunity has come too late as it would have been a great pleasure to have a "family tie" to the Globe since I have to live so far away from it myself.

Some day however, when my bronchitis has finally fled, you will have to make room for me again there, for I have quite succumbed to the charms of our own Toronto as a haven for my old age.

I sail on Saturday by the Cunard "Campania", after a week's end in Boston. I am irritated in advance by the Declaration of Independence and I know the beans won't agree with me, but I must go in order to be able to say so truthfully in print.

With many cordial thanks for your kind thought of my
petition, and hoping that Imperial tour of the East may soon
be imminent.

Ever yours sincerely
Sara Jeannette Cotes
P.S. My very kind regards
please, to Mr. Acland.[59]

The "Mr. Cotes" referred to is not Everard; it may have been
his younger brother Bobby, or some more distant relative.

Back in Simla, Redney made an influential new friend
in April of 1899: Mary Curzon, wife of Lord Curzon, the new
Viceroy who had arrived in January to succeed that dour
Scot, Lord Elgin. Mary was nine years younger than Redney,
and extraordinarily beautiful. She had been a Gibson girl,
one of the models for Dana Gibson, the New York artist. She
was tall with a tiny waist, masses of dark hair, and remarkable blue eyes. Arthur Balfour called her "intoxicating,
delicious and clever". She had been born Mary Leiter,
daughter of a self-made American millionaire who owned
the Chicago department store which later became Marshall
Field's. Her father had retired from active business in 1881,
and moved into a huge turreted castle of a home on Dupont
Circle in Washington. Redney may well have met Mary in
Washington; Mary, too, was a friend of Frances Hodgson
Burnett. Like Redney, Mary had been in London for the
1890 Season; she had charmed Gladstone, the Prince of
Wales, and Lord Curzon, who had quickly fallen in love with
her. They didn't marry, however, until April, 1895. "Your
wife", wrote Queen Alexandra to Curzon in her congratula-
tory letter, "is both beautiful and wise".[60]

Redney and Mary had much in common, besides their
Washington background and a shared London season. They
had both married Englishmen; they both felt immensely
alien in India and homesick for North American culture;
they were both bright, witty women who expressed themselves best in words; Mary's diaries reveal a piquant prose
and visual acuity very like Redney's. In 1903, Redney would
capitalize on her friendship by writing "The Home Life of
Lady Curzon", by "Sara Jeannette Duncan" for the March
issue of *Harper's Bazar*. The Curzons lived in Simla in

Viceregal Lodge, built by Lord Dufferin in 1888: "Not at all a 'lodge'," writes Redney, "but a castle, imposing and beautiful, with a banqueting-hall, a ball-room, and suites of apartments for guests and for the household, composed of four hundred servants". During early morning pony rides, Redney often met the Curzons' two little girls, Cynthia and Irene, taking the air with their nurses, their white donkey, and their shaggy Irish terrier. The Curzons hated Simla. "One of its loathsome features", wrote Lord Curzon in a private letter, "is its sinister novelty, always having to begin again with each year a new set of idlers, gossips and liars. I do not think there is a more pitiable position in the world than that of the Viceroy and his wife set down for 7 months amid that howling gang of jackals".[61] "No one knows how I loathe Simla and its cruel climate. I never feel well here", complained Mary.[62] It must have alleviated the gloom to find such a kindred spirit as Redney, fellow victim to the imperialist ideal, always ready to talk wittily of books and the lost charms of North American life.

Perhaps Mary passed on helpful hints about motherhood to Redney, for at the age of thirty-seven a surprised Redney found herself pregnant. Unfortunately, few details are known of this momentous event in her life, beyond the fact that her continued ill-health would complicate the pregnancy. The baby was born in 1900, probably at the beginning of the year, and only lived a few days.[63] Redney had never really liked children or had strong maternal feelings. She makes not the slightest reference to her pregnancy in her writings. One suspects that it may have been, at that late stage in her life, an unplanned one, and that she was secretly relieved to have escaped having motherhood thrust upon her. At the same time, Evey's disappointment and her own sense of failure made the shadows lengthen yet again.

She must have noted the fine irony of a new century of hope and promise beginning just as her own life reached an all-time low. Her pregnancy had strained her physically. Her cough, like that of one of her characters, had "always been an old, habitual possession, a thing other people watched and worried over, a bore and a bogey" (*His Royal*

Happiness, p. 97). Now, suddenly, she was spitting blood; there was a shadow on her lung; it was tuberculosis, from which her brother Charles had died. The doctor ordered her to spend the entire summer on a chaise in her garden. She was only allowed inside for meals and at night. Redney was ill and depressed, but the habit of many years helped: she wrote every day, sitting on her cane chaise, and by summer's end had finished *On the Other Side of the Latch*, to be published in 1901 by Methuen in London, and under the title *The Crow's Nest*, by Dodd Mead in New York.

The garden where Redney spent the summer writing was at Holcombe, bought with book royalties, a fine house on Simla's Choura Maidan just opposite the large Cecil Hotel. For many years Holcombe had been the home of J.E. O'Conor, C.I.E., the Director-General of Statistics to the Government of India.[64] Redney had had a short spurt of enthusiasm in supervising its redecoration to suit her. There was a beautiful drawing-room, and a music room where steps — Redney's idea — holding pots of flowers, led up to the window. The drawing-room was like "a room in some old country-house, with latticed windows and a carved bookcase above the carved mantelpiece".[65] Redney had filled the house with books, old china, chintzes, tried to make it as English as possible. This wasn't safe, snug England, however; there was wire netting on the stairs to keep the rats from going up. Holcombe was the first of the four houses which Redney would buy in Simla, enthusiastically redecorate and sell for a profit. She always insisted on a beautiful view; Everard, on proper drains. Her house-buying became her final frantic effort to create an environment that would inspire her writing and mirror a clear-cut self. However, typically, selling the house for a financial profit became as important to her as the initial search and subsequent refurbishing.

Helping Redney during her invalid summer at Holcombe was Rhoda Cotes, Evey's youngest sister, who had "come out" that spring. She was loving, light-hearted, a fine pianist, and she and Redney formed a close, life-long friendship. Redney never suffered fools or bores gladly; she didn't need a large circle of acquaintances; in public, particularly as she got older, she was a little too dignified and distant to win friends easily. She allowed very few people inside her private garden and Rhoda was one of them. Later Rhoda would be married from Redney's house; Rhoda had met Reginald Hailey, whose brother would become Lord Hailey, at Oxford, and while they were not yet formally engaged, they wrote to each other regularly. During their weeks together Redney tried to prepare her young sister-in-law for Indian life.

Redney sat, that summer of 1900, day after day outdoors, casting a sad, nostalgic eye back over her life's garden, conscious of its dry patches, its inhospitable soils, writing *On the Other Side of the Latch*. Its title captures her sense of being now forever exiled. She had married Evey with high hopes for her marriage and her art, but her imagination had bruised itself against India and her husband's limitations. If the portrait of Everard given in *Latch* is an accurate one, then, as a soul-mate Redney found him wanting. She refers to him as "Tiglath-Pileser", borrowing the name of an Assyrian King of Biblical fame.

> With Tiglath-Pileser everything is secondary at present to the state of the drains and the kitchen floor. When, between showers, we walk abroad upon the shelf my footsteps naturally tend to the border where the wild puce-coloured Michaelmas daisies are thickening among the golden-rod, and the master's would take the straightest direction to the plumber and the coolies who are making another stone ditch for him . . . . So we have agreed upon the principle of a fair partition of interest. He comes and assumes moderate enthusiasm before my hedge of purple and yellow; I go and pronounce finally that nothing could be uglier than either paint or tar for the kitchen roof. By such small compromises as these people may hold each other in the highest estimation for years (pp. 201-2).

In the Holcombe garden are Japanese plum trees. Redney loved their pink-and-white blossoms; Everard wanted plums as well, and pruned them so that 'where there should be masses of delicate bloom there are stumps, bare attenuated stumps tied up in poultices" (p. 44).

Perhaps it is significant that *On the Other Side of the Latch* (so states its title page), is by Sara Jeannette Duncan (Mrs. Everard Cotes), not, as was more usual, the other way round. More and more, as time passed, Redney wished she had stayed single. "The common-placeness, the eternal routine, the being tied together" of marriage, says one of Redney's heroines, "must be death, absolute death, to any fineness of nature" (*A Daughter of Today*, p. 158). Redney needed constant stimulation, new enthusiasms; one man, however fine, couldn't hold her interest for long. In the middle of her commonplace book, the adjoining pages blank, is the cryptic comment that marriage is "no more than a sort of friendship recognized by the police".

Everard loved Redney with all the fine sincerity of his nature, with unfailing gentleness and sympathy, and she took advantage of his love to dominate and manipulate him, then despised him for letting her do so. In his later life, he had something of the manner of the cowed school-boy. One feels sure that Redney put it there. For her he had left his scientific career to share her world of writing; for her he had moved from Calcutta, his home for thirteen years, to a new venture in Simla. Everard, unlike Redney, was fond of children, one of those adults whose playful charm children adore; he was always patient with them, a fine story-teller.[66] It must have come as a severe blow to him that now Redney would never give him a child. Disappointment in their marriage was mutual. "There is no charm like spontaneity, in idea, behaviour, or looks" decided Redney (*On the Other Side of the Latch*, p. 56). Everard was conventional, conservative; his own writing reveals a factual attitude to life, needing only its clichés, not its odd colours. Of all flowers, Redney hated only geraniums—"aren't you tired of the stiff little exotics!" (*Globe*, July 1, 1885) she once wrote; they were Everard's favourite flower. Their basic differences of personality, in spite of their genuine fondness for each other, grated, stone against stone. "We are round pebbles on this coral strand, worn smooth by rubbing against nothing but each other", wrote Redney (*On the Other Side of the Latch*, p. 105), perhaps thinking of her marriage.

Through her Holcombe garden that summer of 1900 blew chill winds. "We are far withdrawn and very high up", observed Redney. She had, in her garden, as in her house, done her best to create beauty within a narrow space, to plant her memories on the hillside. In front of the house was a patch of Canadian goldenrod. Outside the dining-room windows, a bed of roses (not as splendid as her mother's). On the khud-side, English foxgloves and wallflowers. There were the poulticed Japanese plum trees which didn't bear fruit, and a "spare bedroom", an empty space for blooms which needed to expand. There were tubs of lilies and fuchsias in pots. There were no orchids.

On the Other Side of the Latch is a charming work, one of her best, a fine bouquet of memory's blooms, even though, at the time of its publication, reviews were not enthusiastic. By her own admission, Redney was influenced by the enormous success of *Elizabeth and Her German Garden* (1898), a similar flower-treatise written by the English wife of a German Count at her country *schloss*. Redney had another model in her old friend Charles Dudley Warner's *My Summer in a Garden*. She would learn of his death that October, just as she was moving back into the house to escape the garden's chill. Warner, too, had seen his garden in a moral context:

> The principal value of a private garden is not understood. It is not to give the possessor vegetables and fruit . . . but to teach him patience and philosophy, and the higher virtues, — hope deferred, and expectations blighted, leading directly to resignation, and sometimes to alienation.[67]

Redney also borrowed Warner's trick of anthropomorphising flowers. In spite of these influences, however, *On the Other Side of the Latch* is very much on her own terrain, working in those familiar furrows where her best skills lay: her finely-etched descriptive prose, her rapport with the reader: courteous, conspiratorial, sometimes, in this book, a little too coy. Redney is not troubled here with plot and character development, always her weak points. In her garden, she sees the pattern of her life:

> Here, in the garden, a wall of mist will often surround me, with the sun shining brightly inside; it turns the shelf into a

room, and makes one think of the impalpable barrier of one's environment, possible to break in any direction but never broken, always there, the bound of one's horizon and the limit of one's activities (pp. 216-17).

It is hard to flower in a narrow environment:

We might do better, all of us, under more favourable conditions. We complain unanimously, for one thing, of the lack of room. Cramped we are to such an extent that I often feel thankful for the paling that runs along the edge and keeps us all in. I suppose nobody ever believed that his lot gave him proper scope for his activities (pp. 16-17).

There are several telling images which reveal Redney's mood. The most revealing is that of a spider Redney encounters in her bathroom which

drew its legs a little closer under it, as you or I would do if we absolutely didn't care what happened so long as we were left in peace—that it had come there on purpose, being aware of its approaching end. I decided that the last moments of even a spider should be respected, but every day I shook the curtain, and he drew his legs together a little more feebly than the day before.... I admired his expiring, it was business-like and methodical, the thing he had next to do; and he was so intent upon it, not in any way to be disturbed and distracted, asking no questions of the purposes of Nature, simply carrying them out. One might moralise (p. 158).

"Our love of flowers is impregnated with our love of life", says Redney, perhaps thinking of New Orleans' magnolias and roses, feeling the blighted hopes and gathering shadows ... a shadow on her lung, the vulture's wing. "One questions, on such a day, whether it is quite worthwhile", writes Redney, permitting the reader a glimpse of her inmost self, "this attempt by the assistance of nature to live a little longer. I myself am almost convinced that persons afflicted with the gift of sympathy would be wise to perish easily and soon" (pp. 67-68), persons, like herself, who belong to "the unhappy minority, who have two sets of nerves, one for our own use and one at the disposal of every human failure by the wayside". "For us", decides Redney, "the world is not likely to become a pleasanter place the longer one stays in it" (p. 70).

In this despondent mood, Redney's thoughts wound backward to her bright Brantford days:

> I am homesick for a certain very sweet, very yellow, rather small and not very double briar rose that belongs to other years when it was much presented to "the teacher", also for a modest little fringed pink with a dark line on its petals which made the kind of posy one offered to one's grandmother. But I fear the other years are a country one cannot rediscover in every part (p. 261).

She felt very far from familiar fields, from life-restoring rains. No green freedoms, no green vistas . . . only the grim struggle to survive. Life's summer is over:

> There is a rustling among the roses when the wind comes this way . . . . Belated butterflies bask on the warm gravel with wings expanded and closed down. Wooing is dangerous now, shadows overtake you, and a shadow kills. The zinnias are all old soldiers, the snows have come nearer in the night . . . . The vicissitudes of some lives! (p. 266).

So ends *On the Other Side of the Latch*. Later, Redney would have one brief, brave flourish in "that country one cannot rediscover in every part", the country of her growing-up years. After that, the snow would settle, and remain.

6
Final Years
"The Humble Heart"

> It would go cowled like a monk
> among the ways of the world if it
> could, the heart of middle age; so
> wise it has grown, and so humble.

> Sara Jeannette Duncan,
> *Set in Authority*.

The long, thin shadows of Simla's deodars, fingers pointing towards death—her own, her child's, her bright hopes'—slanted across Redney's mind as she journeyed down to the dusty plain. She and Evey had returned to Calcutta at the beginning of 1901 because Everard, always full of duty and devotion to the Empire, was actively recruiting for the Boer War from among the white community. The Cotes took one of the two flats at 10 Wood Street, three doors down from the Saturday Club's quarters. From its sparsely-furnished bleakness, Redney sent off a letter to John Willison:

Jan 10 [*1901*]

Dear Mr. Willison,

        Do you think your readers remember "Garth Grafton" well enough to care to hear about her present life and occupations and experiences and views done in twenty chapters in the old Garth Grafton style? I have asked Mr. Watt to send you with this proofs of a thing between fifty and sixty thousand words which is of this nature. [It] describes Simla life from the point of view of a Simla garden, and incidentally is very personal so much so that I venture to think my fellow Canadians might regard it with a special interest, particularly if you drew attention to it editorially. If you *don't* want it will you let Saturday Night consider it? [next part missing]... and I think you could make rather a feature of it in your Saturday supplement.

    Reply to Holcombe, Simla W. India as I shall be there in March.

                With kind regards,
                Yours sincerely,
                Sara Jeannette Cotes.[1]

"Do you think your readers remember Garth Grafton?" Certainly Redney remembers her, and mourns her passing, but the "very personal" manuscript, *On the Other Side of the Latch*, in no way recaptures the sparkling wit and assurance of "the old Garth Grafton style", nor did it appear in serial form in the Toronto *Globe*, of which Willison was then editor.

The whole Empire grew shadowed on January 22nd when Queen Victoria, after sixty-four years on England's throne, slipped quietly away towards her Maker's, and all Anglo-India, conventional unto death, put on black crepe armlets and black ties. Mary Curzon, then visiting in England, voiced the prevailing sentiment in a letter to her husband, observing that "reverence has gone out of people's lives" now that "Edward the Caresser" had ushered in a new frivolity.[2] Redney courted this new levity, fleeing her own dark shadows, by beginning work on another of her trans-Atlantic sugar confections: *Those Delightful Americans*, in which a well-born young English couple visit America, and Redney plumps for "the great green profusion" of American freedoms, both social and personal, in preference to British formality. There is no taut line of plot and character development, and Redney was writing for the lady's magazine audience who loved to read about American millionaires on their Hudson estates and young men who carried gold cigarette cases with diamond initials. The book was appropriately serialized in early spring of 1902 in *Ladies Field*, an Englishwomen's weekly of society and fashion news, and was published by Methuen and Appleton's in late spring.

In December, 1901, Redney was heartened to be invited, probably at Mary Curzon's suggestion, to accompany the Viceregal pair on their first state visit to Upper Burma, which had been annexed in 1886, when Lord Dufferin was Viceroy. As always, Redney's spirits lifted with the prospect of new scenes, and Burma proved enchanting, with its saffron-robed monks, pink-petticoated women, and golden-coned pagodas. In her usual vivid, descriptive vein, Redney wrote up her impressions in two articles, "The Little Widows of a Dynasty" (*Harper's Monthly Magazine*, December, 1902) and "In Burma with the Viceroy" (*Scribner's Magazine*, July, 1902).

Her spirits lifted again in April, 1901, when she arrived in Edwardian London, the city sparkling with that easy gaiety and affluence which the first Great War would extinguish forever. The West End streets were full of suave, top-hatted gentlemen and perfumed ladies in bountiful flower hats; even the horses were wearing straw hats trimmed with flowers. Horse-drawn buses, painted in the distinguishing bright colours of the rival bus companies, picked up passengers outside the pubs, or wherever someone waved an arm. Society whispered the details of Edward's affair with Mrs Keppel, and all of London danced and pranced and preened itself and laughed immoderately.

Yellow broom flamed in the fields as Redney went down to Hertfordshire to spend some time with Everard's sister May Masterman and her little girls, Stella and Nellie. Nellie was later to recall a "clear picture" of her Aunt Redney:

> It was on a country walk in our village .... There was a little shop that sold fish and on the marble slab was a heap of

winkles. Aunt Redney asked me what they were and she said
she had never seen them before. I had to confess that I had
never tasted one, but that our nursemaid said they were
"lovely" and you got them out of their shells with a pin. My
Aunt said at once that she must try one in spite of my saying
that they were horrid little sea snails. The shopman was very
much amused at being asked for one winkle! However a pin
was found and rather to my surprise the winkle did come out
on the end of the pin and Aunt Redney popped it into her
mouth. She chewed it and chewed it as we walked on, but at
last she threw it out and said it was a tough proposition. At
that moment a small dog came in sight, and seeing something
being thrown out he thought it worth while investigating and
he also started to chew: however he very soon gave up and
spat it out, which tickled Aunt Redney who said—"There—
you see he agrees with me, so I don't want any more
winkles".[3]

The shadows, however, were still pursuing Redney. She
opened a letter from Canada with news of brother Leslie's
death, three days before his twenty-eighth birthday, on June
20th. Were *all* her brothers, one by one, to be taken from her?

Memories of happy times with her brothers began to
crowd her mind; more and more her thoughts circled
round her Brantford childhood, until Redney felt the com-
pelling urge to write it all down, to crystallize forever the
sweetness of those growing-up years. Day after day, she
scribbled furiously; the words came almost too quickly as
one remembered scene after another reeled through her
mind, bringing her the very taste and texture of her home:

> Mrs. Murchison and Abby sat on the verandah enjoying the
> Indian summer afternoon; the horse chestnuts dropped crash-
> ing among the fallen leaves, the roadside maples blazed, the
> quiet streets ran into smoky purple, and one belated robin
> hopped about the lawn (*The Imperialist*, p. 49).

By September, 1902, as Redney sat at her desk, writing, the
taunting Himalayan snows, so inaccessible, had disappeared. When she looked out the window she saw her West Street
home, her family and neighbours, Brantford's familiar tree-
lined streets. Redney was now many thousands of miles away
from alien Simla, many years back in time, writing what

would be her finest book: *The Imperialist*. Through an imaginative leap, she had again achieved the necessary consonance of self and setting: she was back in her beloved West Street home, a young Redney, alive, vibrant, idealistic. "That cynicism which, moral and immoral, is the real hoar of age" (*The Imperialist*, p. 268), which had held her in its icy grip ever since she had gone to live in India, suddenly melted away, and she flew straight up, on happy pinions, taking the image as it came, splendidly free and splendidly creative. "I fear the other years are a country one cannot rediscover in every part", she had written in a despondent mood (*On the Other Side of the Latch*, p. 261), but as her pen raced over the sheets, Redney was rediscovering virtually every part, recreating those Brantford years with richness and resonance and the perfectly reproduced rhythms of her native colloquial speech. "The ordinary detail of humdrum life and circumstance, pen-painted by an artist with sympathies keen enough to detect the mysterious throbbing of life that is inner and under", Redney had written, "fascinate us like our own photographs" (*Globe*, June 17, 1885). Documentary detail abounds in all her novels, but only in *The Imperialist* does she consistently catch the mysterious throbbing underneath, a persistent pulsing, a passionate beat, reverberating from her own partisan heart. This is what makes *The Imperialist* the superb book it is, a first-rate novel, not second-rate, like almost all her others. *The Imperialist* was written with passion, with love. Redney was no longer "a shadow with a pair of eyes", detached to the point of irony or fantasy or both. This is *her* life; she stands in the thick of it, intensely engaged, intensely exhilarated, intensely committed to her subject. There is irony here, of course, and even some sentimental rhapsodizing, but to a pair of eyes Redney has added a feeling heart. It is the emotion behind it which pushes *The Imperialist* forward to great art. The novel is a long, lyrical love letter, addressed to Redney's family, to her home town, to her country.

With great care and affection, Redney draws the full-length portraits of her family. Stella and Abby Murchison, full of humour and impetuosity, are Ruby and Grace Duncan. Lorne Murchison with his "gravity, his sympathy, his young

angry irony" is her dead brother Charles, and Advena is
Redney herself. In John Murchison, Redney draws a most
loving portrait of her father:

> A great deal of John Murchison's character was there, in the
> way he held his pipe, his gentleness and patience, even the
> justice and repose and quiet strength of his nature" (p. 101).

Mrs Murchison, modelled on her mother, is viewed with an
affectionate but slightly satiric eye, for she is shown to be full
of common sense but totally without intellectual pretensions. Advena, "not much like" her mother (p. 203) is very
much her father's daughter, as Mrs Murchison points out (p.
105). There is no satire in Redney's portrait of her father,
only admiration and love, based on her realization of how
much her father's literary ideals and quiet encouragement
had contributed to her amazing early growth. She had spent
her life searching for another father-figure who could nour-
ish her art as he had—Joaquin Miller, William Dean Howells,
Charles Dudley Warner—but had never found an adequate
substitute any more than she had found another setting as
nurturing as Brantford's.

The intense feeling behind *The Imperialist* elevates the
style and form to impressive heights, showing Redney in her
finest vein, analysing the detail of the social cosmos with a
fine sense of scale, with irony and humour, with wisdom.
Like Jane Austen, Redney uses the smallest detail of character to represent the whole:

> It was a favourite word with Mrs. Milburn—*outré*. She
> used it like a lorgnette, and felt her familiarity with it a
> differentiating mark (p. 172).

> *   *   *

> In the profusion of the table it was little less than edifying
> to hear Mrs. Kilbannon, invited to preserves, say, "Thank
> you, I have butter" (p. 216).

There are still a few obscuring wisps of pseudo-Jamesian
mist in the prose here and there, but mostly it is sprightly
and precise, stuffed full of the same kind of aphoristic plums
with which Jane Austen delights the reader:

Adolescence was inarticulate in Elgin on occasions of ceremony (p. 41).

       *   *   *

No one could dream with impunity in Elgin, except in bed (p. 45).

As Redney worked on *The Imperialist,* turning her back on the snows, tumbling out her memories in her finest prose, she had a sudden and astounding revelation. In the book it is given to Lorne:

> The sense of kinship surged in his heart; these were his people, this his lot as well as theirs. For the first time he saw it in detachment. At that moment his country came subjectively into his possession; great and helpless it came into his inheritance as it comes into the inheritance of every man who can take it, by deed of imagination and energy and love (p. 74).

Across the oceans, across the years, Redney had at last found her perfect setting, found it "by deed of imagination and energy and love", found it through the act of writing about it. She had spent her life searching the world for the ideal self, the ideal setting, the ideal work of art. It had been a restless, relentless quest: New Orleans, Washington, Toronto, Montreal, Ottawa, Japan, Ceylon, India, England. Now, at last, she had found the setting in which the creative self can flower into art. She had embraced her true home—and lost it, all in the same moment.

"Every intelligent person's mind is supplied with infinite tiny feelers that stretch out in all directions, and instinctively grasp what is good and nutritious for the soul they belong to", Redney had written (*Week,* Nov. 24, 1887). She now realized that Brantford had given her more that was good and nutritious than any other setting, because only in Brantford were those feelers securely rooted in love and commitment. Brantford had formed her, moulded her, made her its own. Even in her early rebellion, she had belonged to Brantford; its narrow parochialism and prejudices had formed the wall over which she had leapt to freedom. Without the wall, she never would have learned to leap so high. "A man lives best where he's taken root", says

Mr Murchison (p. 154). All those other settings; all of them wrong, because all of them were marble friezes: static, cold, perceived with eyes only, not with the committed heart. Only a setting passionately loved, in which one is passionately rooted, Redney now realized, can inspire the highest flights of imaginative art. This is the irony, the paradox which lies at the heart of *The Imperialist*. It is superbly crafted because it is Redney working the only vein in which she can find gold, the only one — in spite of her life-long travels — which truly belonged to her.

"The human spirit, as it is set free in these wide unblemished spaces, may be something more pure and sensitive", says Hugh Finlay (*The Imperialist*, p. 111), referring to Canada. Everything Redney needed to develop the human spirit, to develop that inner vision so necessary to the novelist in his search for form, for the figure in the carpet, the taut line, had been right there in Brantford. Had she stayed, she might have made a permanent progression from first-rate journalist to first-rate novelist. Redney had chosen the world rather than her childhood town, the Empire rather than her own small corner of it, and her choice had been wrong. Now she saw that Brantford *was* the wider world, just as the wider world had proved to be a blind alley, a narrow cell; Brantford was the wider world in microcosm, just as Jane Austen's tiny English village had been for her. You can't go home again, but how passionately Redney wished now that she had never left!

Even as Redney perceived how right her native environment had been for her, she also saw how unsuitable, for any Canadian, are American and British ones. "It has become our business", says Lorne, "to keenly watch and actively resist American influence, as it already threatens us through the common channels of life and energy" (p. 232). Canada must not be imprinted with the "stamp and character" of the American republic, but with Canada's own peculiar stamp and character. Nor must Canada slavishly follow British patterns. England, as Redney paints it in *The Imperialist*, is too conservative, cautious, class-ridden. She channels her satire of England through her portrayal of Alfred Hesketh, the condescending young Englishman, and of Elgin's Milburn family, who reverence all things English, unaware that Britain's "cumbrous social machinery" is "a dull anachronism in a marching world" (p. 125). The Milburns are modelled on Brantford's first family among the manufacturing élite: the Waterous clan, owners of the Waterous Engine Works. This was odd on Redney's part, since sister Ruby had married Charles A. Waterous, son of the founder. Perhaps Redney wanted Ruby, who still lived in Brantford and therefore had a chance at full life and flowering, to see in the Milburns the dangers of becoming too terribly British. Ruby was smugly settled in a huge house on Dufferin Avenue with mahogany-panelled study and exquisite silver tea service; perhaps Redney wanted to ruffle her complacency, to make her as passionately patriotic for all things Canadian as Redney now felt herself to be.

Redney had once been eager to let her imagination shelter under England's hoary oak of literary and social traditions. Now, as she wrote *The Imperialist*, she saw that Canada was putting down its own tap-roots, its own cherished sense of continuity. Mr and Mrs Murchison perceive that their home "lay about them like a map of their lives; the big horse chestnut stood again in flower to lighten the spring dusk for them, as it had done faithfully for thirty years" (p. 101). Tradition, for Redney, must be Canadian, for only then is it alive, felt in the blood, pervasive, and precious.

It was in the act of writing *The Imperialist* that Redney became a Canadian nationalist, proudly heralding the unfurling leaves of a national culture and a national consciousness. This was *her* Canada with its "splendid, buoyant, unused air to breathe, and the simplicity of life, and the plenty of things!" (p. 110), holding "the promise of all": "In the scrolls of the future it is already written that the centre of the Empire must shift—and where, if not to Canada?" (p. 229) cries Lorne in an impassioned speech. In fact, her beloved country, young, hopeful, lively, confident was like Redney herself who once stood poised on the threshold of a bright future:

> Youth in a young country is a symbol wearing all its value. It stands not only for what it is. The trick of augury invests it at

a glance, with the sum of its possibilities, the augurs all sincere, confident, and exulting (p. 80).

"The augurs all sincere, confident, and exulting" . . . . and so they had been, in those early Brantford years when her own hopes and her country's were perfectly in tune.

Redney saw herself in all three of the passionate young idealists in the book, not just in Advena Murchison. Hugh Finlay, like the young Redney, is a "passionate romantic" (p. 68). He "had something, the subtle Celt; he had horizons, lifted lines beyond the common vision, and an eye rapt and a heart intrepid" (p. 69). Lorne Murchison also represents Redney's younger self. Lorne, it is true, is shown to be far too idealistic and uncompromising in his imperialist dreams. As Professor Tausky has rightly recognized, "Lorne's fatal error in tactics is his refusal to find any economic argument for imperialism that would make it attractive from the stand-point of individual and national self interest"[4], but Lorne's strength "as well as his political failing—is his ability to con-jure up an imaginative vision of Canada's future destiny".[5]

What is important in Lorne and in the other idealists in the book is exactly that: "imaginative vision" and it is the thrust, the energy, of that vision which counts, not the end on which it is focused. Mr Milburn is the foil for Lorne; he has never come within a hundred miles of an ideal: "The governing principle of his life was the terror of being converted to anything" (p. 206). Milburn is condemned by his creator because he has never seen farther than concrete economic goals. Redney was aware of her own growing mercenary propensities, quite as culpable as Milburn's, and in writing *The Imperialist* she tried to put them in perspec-tive. Milburn's goals are suspect because they are finite; the beauty of Lorne's idealism is that it remains partially unfoc-used. Without Lorne's kind of idealism, there is no real passion; without passion there is no real inspiration; and without inspiration there is no real art. Redney perceived that the well-spring of her own creativity, that same creativi-ty which was even then producing *The Imperialist*, had always been the power and the push behind her romantic idealism before it had faded in India.

This is the message of *The Imperialist*; long live idealism, the idealism of a youthful country, the idealism of
youth, the idealism of young Redney as she now stood
revealed to herself. The political theme of imperialism
which takes up the foreground of the book is, in its particularities, not at all important. In casting about for a theme, it
was natural for Redney to choose politics, which had already
provided the warp for *His Honour, and a Lady* (and which she
would use again for three more novels after *The Imperialist*).
Politics had always provided her with excitement and novelty: in Brantford, in Washington, in Ottawa and in India,
particularly after Evey turned to journalism and they both
became immersed in the current political scene. Redney was
very much a political animal, and as she began to write in
that autumn of 1902, imperialism was very much in the news.
In that year the first real Empire Conference was held in
London, instigated by the new Secretary of State for the
Colonies, Right Honourable Joseph Chamberlain (the Wallingham of *The Imperialist*), who preached imperialism with
fiery zeal, asking preferential treatment by Britain on her
colonial imports and high duties on foreign ones. The first
seeds of Imperialist policy had been sown at the Inter-
Colonial Conference hosted by Canada in 1894, and when
Sir Wilfrid Laurier and the Liberals had come to power two
years later, they had made it an important plank in their
platform.

Since all the rest of the documentary detail of *The
Imperialist* would be true-to-life, Redney wanted the Imperialist debate to be accurate as well. She therefore despatched
a letter to John Willison asking for help:

> *Holcombe, Simla.*
> *Sept. 18 [1902]*
>
> Dear Mr. Willison,
>   I have taken upon myself to write a
> Canadian novel, with a political *motif* and I am rather
> anxious that none of you shall be ashamed of it. I feel a little
> helpless so far from my material and I write to ask if you will
> very kindly send me a little. I want a week's issues of the
> *Globe*, preferably numbers dealing editorially with the ques
> tion of *Imperial federation*, and I want, if they are to be had in

pamphlet form, all *Sir. W. Laurier's speeches* on the subject, or any others that may be useful. It is asking a good deal of a busy man to look up this sort of thing, I know, but I trust to your interest in the result to excuse me. I am trying very hard to make it my best book, and the ground is practically unbroken. I have Holland's "Imperium et Libertas" which strikes me, admirable as it is, as a little like whipping a dead horse. If you know of anything more closely occupied with the practical intricacies of the question, will you send it to me, and I will pay up by return. I am sending per money order only one miserable dollar to pay for the papers etc but I should be only too glad to afford anything that would be helpful. I wonder if you have seen "Those Delightful Americans". I have given up as hopeless any attempt to get my books on the market of my own country. They always seem to fall between the two stools of the London & New York publishers. However, I have had the luck lately to place stories with Scribner & The Century, and a couple of Burmese sketches with Harpers, so should not complain. I am going to England after the big Durbar in January—anybody coming out to represent the *Globe?* All press correspondents to be taken care of by the hospitable Govt. of India. You ought to come. The *Times* is sending a man, also Daily Mail and Morning Post, and Reuter is to have 3,000 words a day!—and expect to be in Canada in June. It will be a pleasure to see you all again in Toronto.

> With kind regards
> & many apologies
> Yours very sincerely
> Sara Jeannette Cotes.[6]

Redney chose Imperialism as the main theme around which to weave her Brantford magic, but the reader never quite knows where she stands on the question. Is she for or against? Professor Tausky in his excellent study of *The Imperialist* writes:

There are whole pages on the social structure of Elgin, but nary a sentence of authorial opinion about imperialism. Instead, Sara offers one consistent and vital clue; the line dividing the proponents from the opponents of imperialism also divides the imaginative characters from the unimaginative.[7]

Other critics in discussing *The Imperialist*, tend to give us historical explanations of just what imperialism was all about, and argue exhaustively about where its author stands on the question.[8] Certainly, the book ends on an ambivalent note:

> Here, for Lorne and for his country, we lose the thread of destiny. The shuttles fly, weaving the will of the nations, with a skein for ever dipped again; and he goes forth to his share in the task among those by whose hand and direction the pattern and the colours will be made (p. 268).

This is Redney's final word on the matter. As Professor Tausky has noted, "Elgin is a community whose present life is energetic but not always wisely directed, and whose future development is uncertain".[9]

Precisely. Redney is consciously ambivalent about Imperialism; she consciously withholds authorial comment because Elgin's future direction, Canada's future direction, is not what matters most. What matters most is that "Elgin is a community whose present life is energetic"; what matters is the energy, the imaginative power to envision. Advena and Hugh hold a conversation which throws light on this point:

> "We're on the straight road as a nation" [says Advena] in most respects; we haven't any picturesque old prescribed lanes to travel. So you think that makes up?"
> "It's one thing. You might put down space—elbow-room".
> "An empty horizon", Advena murmured.
> "For faith and the future. An empty horizon is better than none. England has filled hers up" (p. 110).

As she wrote these words, Redney saw that her own mistake had always been to put a material goal on that horizon: a journalist's job on the Washington *Post*, the first woman to be hired by the *Globe* .... But always, as soon as she reached it, she didn't want it any more. By then the imaginative power had gone. Now she perceived that what counts—as she subconsciously realized when she painted her canvas of the boy in the cornfield—is an empty horizon, empty because the dream burns with its fiercest flame just before it becomes finite. After that, it is a fading coal. Wallingham may have a great vision of imperialism and even "creative imagina-

tion", but his vision is suspect, as Advena points out to
Hugh, because "even then your vision must be only political, economic, material. You can't conceive the—flowers—that
will come out of all that" (p. 110).

Redney falters a little, to be sure, when the idealistic
Hugh, engaged to Christie Cameron but in love with Advena,
trots out Redney's old "thwarted love" argument of self-denial
and sacrifice. Even Advena feels its attraction: "Isn't there
something that appeals to you", she asks Hugh, "in the
thought of just leaving it, all unsaid and all undone, a dear
and tender projection upon the future that faded—a lovely
thing we turned away from?" (p. 184). If the rose stays in the
imagination it will never become a briar. In Redney's earlier
novels, thwarted love stayed thwarted. But *The Imperialist* is
different; it is grounded in strong feeling. Abstract idealism
must therefore capitulate to emotion: "Before she [Advena]
had preferred an ideal to the desire of her heart; now it lay
about her; her strenuous heart had pulled it down to foolish
ruin" (p. 250). Like Redney herself, Advena and Hugh are
both a little "too much encumbered with ideas to move
simply, quickly, on the impulse of passion" but they do,
given time, so move. Redney too, for the first and last time
in her writing, has moved on the impulse of passion. We can
disregard her ideas on the subject of Imperialism, now a
dead, desiccated issue, but the passion behind *The Imperialist*
is still throbbing on every page. "I am trying very hard to
make it my best book", Redney wrote to Willison. She
reached her goal, and in great jubilation, as she wrote the
final page, she knew that she had reached it. *The Imperialist* is
a fine novel, and, as Claude Bissell has recognized, one of
Canada's best.[10]

Redney's creative verve, in the final months of 1902,
sputtered out in a collection of four short stories entitled *The
Pool in the Desert*, published in the late summer of 1903 by
Methuen and Appleton. The title story appeared in New
York's *Century Magazine* in May, 1903, and is yet another tale
of thwarted love and romantic clichés in which a married
woman falls in love with a man young enough to be her son,
then turns him down when, widowed, she is free to marry.

The second story, "A Mother in India", may have been Redney thinking of her dead child, and questioning the whole matter of maternal instinct, for when Helena Farnham's daughter Cecily returns to India from England, having been raised by relatives there, Helena has no maternal feelings at all and "would like to break the relation into pieces . . . and throw it into the sea" (p. 70). The young Cecily is, like Redney herself, an example of an expatriate who left her place of birth to live in a stuffy, constricted environment which effectively killed her imagination. "The Hesitation of Miss Anderson" is another soap-opera story of thwarted love returning to the single-adventuress theme, for Madeline Anderson sails away from New York to see the world, goes to Japan, then India, and at last ends in Simla's stagnant backwater.

By far the most interesting story in the collection is "An Impossible Ideal", which is Redney's mature, sardonic view of Simla society, just as *Memsahib*'s was of Calcutta:

> a small colony of superior — very superior — officials, of British origin and traditions, set on the top of a hill, years and miles away from literature, music, pictures, politics, existing like a harem on the gossip of the Viceroy's intentions, and depending for amusement on tennis and bumble-puppy . . . consider, you yourself, whether you are the sort of person to be unquestionably happy there (p. 134).

Into this cultural wasteland comes a masculine counterpart of Elfrida Bell: Ingersoll Armour, a painter from Wisconsin, who tries to turn himself into a staid, conventional member of Simla's parochial society but who, at the last minute, flees for his life, leaving India's barren soil to look for one in which his art can flower. As Dora Harris, his former fiancée notes, "A human being isn't an orchid; he must draw something from the soil he grows in" (p. 194). This is the saddest sentence Sara Duncan ever wrote; it is the final cry of pain after writing *The Imperialist*, the bitter fruit of her own experience, and the death-knell of her own secret myth: the belief that being an orchid, beautiful and poised and rare, she and her art could flourish anywhere. The four stories of *The Pool in the Desert* suffer from great dollops of coincidence and romantic twaddle; following as they do on the heels of *The Imperialist*, they amply demonstrate how much harder it was for Redney to create so far from the soil in which she had grown most, and how the aridity of India's cultural desert could shrink the silver pool of her creativity.

By January, 1903, Redney was ready for a change and a frolic and went off with Evey to join the hundred and sixty aristocrats who had come from England for the Great Durbar in Delhi, celebrating King Edward's coronation of the year before. King Edward didn't come, having sent the Duke of Connaught in his place, but it was Mary Curzon who stole the show, looking incredibly lovely in a dazzling parade of gowns, climaxed by a peacock dress in cloth-of-gold. For two weeks Anglo-India danced, played hockey and polo and football, drank champagne, acted like children at a prolonged picnic. At the Ball where Mary wore her peacock dress, 4,000 guests ate their way through seven hundred chickens, four hundred quail and one thousand plates of sandwiches.[11] It was the greatest show there had ever been, but it was also a cloth-of-gold mantle hiding the wasted limbs of Empire, a duty-dance performed by disillusioned civil servants.

In May, 1903, Redney was back in England and that fall went home to Brantford, her first visit in five years, conscious of the empty spaces round the table where Henry, Charles and Leslie used to sit. She wrote to John Willison, sending him *The Imperialist* proofs for serialization in the Toronto News of which he had just become editor.

Nov. 20th [*1903*]

Dear Mr. Willison,

Herewith by registered parcel "The Imperialist". The proofs I send are in a rough state and want a lot of work, which I should like to give them before the story appears, if you care about having it. The law case especially wants attention, and the political situation. Please send me back the proofs as soon as you have looked them over, as they form my only complete set at present and I would like to work on them. The novel finishes in the *Queen* by the 1st of January and will be published as a book probably about the end of that month in England, though we could delay the

Canadian edition if it suited you better. If you care to make a feature of it in The News I will accept whatever you think it is worth to the paper, as I should be particularly gratified to have the story identified with a journal based on the higher polity—for which by the way, I hope you will find it not unsuited. With these lofty sentiments, and best wishes, and many thanks for your kindness in wanting to see the thing.

> Believe me
> Yours sincerely
> Sara Jeannette Cotes.[12]

Another letter to Willison four days later thanks him for sending her his new book, *Sir Wilfrid Laurier and the Liberal Party: A Political History*:

> *Nov. 24th [1903]*

Dear Mr. Willison,

The very attractive looking pair of volumes that form your "Laurier" reached me this afternoon. They will travel across the Atlantic with me, and I expect to know a good deal more about Canadian Liberalism—and Laurier— when I arrive at Liverpool than I did when I left that port. Please accept my very best thanks. I will take the books to Simla and teach the wider Imperialism out of them there. I am glad my story commends itself to you. Please let me know when you intend to begin and tell them to post the paper to me while it is running. If proofs arrive in time from New York I will send them on to you, if not I suppose the copy you have must do. I send you herewith a few slips containing important and necessary corrections. The case in court, as it appeared in the *Queen* is laughable. Please be sure to get these slips substituted for the corresponding matter you have in hand. I hope you found Chap. XXVII later. I am almost certain I sent a complete set. If it is still missing let me know and I will see that you get it in good time.

If you publish a chapter a day you will finish about co-terminously with the *Queen* which would be desirable. It appears that I am again to visit Toronto at the benevolent bidding of the Author's Society—when I come we will meet.

> With kind regards
> Yours very sincerely
> Sara Jeannette Cotes.[13]

Redney enjoyed her hour of fame, for the Canadian Society of Authors' reception was given in her honour, a gala affair, complete with orchestra, in the palm room of McConkey's on Saturday, December 5th, attended by such distinguished Torontonians as Goldwin Smith, Pelham Edgar of the University of Toronto, Byron Walker, the club president, Dr MacMurchy, principal of Jarvis Collegiate, and his journalist daughter Marjory, one of Redney's particular friends, then in charge of the book column of the *News*. According to the *News'* account, "Mrs. Cotes had a pleasant word" for each guest and "looked remarkably well in a clinging gown of primrose silk . . . and a pretty topaz necklet" (Toronto *News*, Dec. 7, 1903). Redney read Lorne Murchison's impassioned speech on Imperialism from *The Imperialist*, and its most fervid phrases portentously elicited "a gentle clapping of hands from several of the gentlemen" (*Ibid.*).

During this Canadian visit, Redney also made a quick trip to Ottawa, staying at the fashionable Russell Hotel, and conscientiously sending off a gracious reply to a fan letter:

Dec. 8th [1903]

Dear Miss Ridout,

Very much thanks indeed for your kind letter which has reached me here. I am delighted to know that my wanderings with Orthodocia fifteen years ago gave you pleasure. I hope that your own design of going may come to pass and I am sure that if it does you will enjoy the experience as much as I did. I saw Mrs. Wilkes shortly before leaving Brantford. I suppose you sometimes come to see her. I hope that some day our visits may be concurrent and that we may meet there. Again thanking you for your letter which gives me great pleasure.

Believe me
Yours sincerely
Sara Jeannette Cotes.[14]

Redney dashed off another letter to Willison, just before she left Canada, letting him know, among other things, that she was now famous enough to warrant a visit from Canada's courtly Prime Minister:

Dear Mr. Willison,
                              I was so sorry not to have a spare minute
as I rushed through Toronto last week to say a final goodbye
in. It would be difficult however, in view of my constant
conversations with you in the News, which now by the way
arrives in the mornings. Well, fight the good fight—there is
nobody but you. What Forster said was true you know, about
those silent ministers. I saw Sir Wilfrid. He paid me the
honour of a visit. He may be a politician and a Frenchman
but he is a nice thing.

I am off on Xmas Day. May I have my cheque from the
News in time to cash?

It is quite abominable to have to go. Is it any wonder that
my sentiments are Imperial, with a husband in India and a
family in Canada and everybody else in England!
Remember me cordially please to Mrs. Willison.

                              and believe me
                              Always yours sincerely
                              Sara Jeannette Cotes.[15]

Redney was back in England, when, on February 9th,
1904, she read in the London papers of Erastus Wiman's
death. Shadows overtake you, thought Redney, reading now
of Chaz Wiman's downfall, quite as dramatic as his rise from
paperboy to millionaire. He had gone bankrupt in May,
1893, and the following year been convicted of forgery by
R.G. Dun, the New York mercantile agency in which he was
a partner. Charged with embezzling $200,000, Chaz was
found guilty, sent to prison, and released when the Court of
Appeal reversed the verdict. After that he lived in retirement on Staten Island, a broken man. He had suffered a
paralysing stroke three years before his death, and just a
week before the end came all his household furniture had
been sold at auction.[16] Redney remembered his lavish hospitality of the '80's, and felt another twinge of loss.

Redney was now a proud member of London's Ladies
Empire Club, established in 1902, for which she paid annual
dues of eight guineas. She used it as a convenient place to
meet friends, read the latest magazines, or write her letters,
enjoying its quiet luxury, as uniformed maids carried tea
trays to little groups of chic women with here and there an

occasional man, looking "conscious and furtive, and assiduously ministered to" (*Set in Authority*, p. 62). Redney sat at
one of the leather-topped desks on February 24th, writing to
John Willison about *The Imperialist*, and name-dropping
again:

> Dear Mr. Willison,
>
> Your most kind letter has just reached
> me. I am sorry to say that it is too late now for any alterations
> in the first edition, which should be on the book-stalls in a few
> days; but I shall gladly keep your hints for reference, and if
> there is an opportunity later will see to the ballot announce-
> ment mistake. The Indian anachronism I considered upon,
> but it is only a matter of a few years, and I was in the difficulty
> of either having to sacrifice the whole Imperial situation — as
> it is now — or my "Indian interest" neither of which I could
> make up my mind to do. So I left it. If you like to make a little
> note of this explanation & publish it when the book appears,
> it would discount criticism of that point perhaps, and I hope
> the reviewers won't be as well up as you are in practical
> politics! I am *very* glad you like the story. I now think of a
> novel bringing Lorne Murchison over here & giving the
> critical colonial view of London society, marrying him even-
> tually. Would you like to have it for the News? I propose to
> do it this coming summer. Dear old Jimmy Johnson[17] lunched
> with me here yesterday, and Baroness Macdonald joined us
> afterward. It was quite an Ottawa reunion. I wish you could
> have made another. I am off to Holcombe, Simla, on the 17th
> of next month. My husband has not yet proceeded against me
> for desertion but I don't know what he may have in mind. By
> the way I particularly want you to read his article on "The
> Situation in the Persian Gulf" in the Contemporary probably
> for April.[18] Don't forget. Always cordially yours
>
> S.J. Cotes.[19]

Did Redney ask Willison to read Everard's article because
she was hoping that such an influential figure in Canadian
press circles could find Everard a job in Canada? Perhaps
she *could* go home again . . . . She had been away from her
husband for almost a year now, a woman on her own, a
celebrated authoress, friend of Prime Ministers and Prime
Ministers' widows. Since Sir John's death in 1891, Agnes
Macdonald had been as restless a wanderer as Redney:
winters on the Riviera, summers in London, autumns in

Scotland, her paid companion packing and unpacking for Agnes and her invalid daughter, Mary. Agnes was a tall, angular woman with a sprightly wit for whom Nicholas Flood Davin once wrote a sonnet. She and Redney must have enjoyed each other, for Agnes had ridden the CPR cow-catcher through the Rockies three years before Redney did, loving it just as much, and her diaries, like Mary Curzon's, reveal a writer's sensibility.[20]

Reluctantly, on March 17th, Redney left London for Simla, disappointed that *The Imperialist* had not yet appeared on the bookstalls. She knew how good it was, and was eagerly anticipating plenty of accolades. She was shocked and angry and incredulous when the book finally did appear in late spring and the reviews were uniformly bad, worse than for any of her other books.

The English reviewers were bored by such a detailed study of a Canadian small town. *The Outlook's* critic found that "there is comfortable middle-class prosperity in Elgin, the record of which makes very dull reading" and the *Academy* critic remarked that "*The Imperialist* is as dreary reading as the campaign documents of a contested election". The *New York Times* reviewer was more positive, but he commented that Mrs. Cotes "draws better women and parsons than she does men" and concluded that "her story for all that, is good reading, barring the politics" (March 5, 1904).

The knives that cut deepest for Redney, however, were the Canadian ones. This novel in which she had revealed her heart and unabashedly declared her love and admiration for her native land was the one Canadian critics vilified most. The reviewer in the *Canadian Magazine*, with a degree of male chauvinism and condescension which must have made Redney furious, commented that imperialism "is a huge undertaking for any author, especially a woman, and if the reader finds difficulty in seeing clearly what Mrs. Cotes is trying to say, he will kindly remember that a woman attempting politics must be judged leniently".[21] Another review which hurt was the one in her own former paper, the Toronto *Globe*. Its opening sentence stated:

A story with contemporary Canadian life for its materials by Mrs. Everard Cotes is something in which the Canadian reader will undisguisedly be interested. It was natural therefore, to turn to *The Imperialist* with expectations which, in most cases, it may be surmised, will be unrealized (Aug. 13, 1904).

The review goes on to state that "the political passages of *The Imperialist* . . . are not living and real, and as a picture of Canadian feeling they are not convincing."

Redney was crushed. She had knit her soul into every page of this book. When the Toronto *News* had serialized it from December, 1903 to February, 1904, the headline had blazoned: "A Fascinating Love Story of Ontario Town Life of the Present Day—Depicting with Humour and Fidelity the Social and Political Conditions of the Country". It was indeed, thought Redney, a love story, of her love for her country, but a love unrecognized and unrequited . . . thwarted love. She would never again attempt a novel with a Canadian setting. In disappointment and despair, she would deliberately exile her imagination forever from those familiar Canadian fields. Artistically, of course, this was a mistake. The best expatriate novelists have always continued to focus on their home environments, to re-create their roots from the new perspective of a distanced view, novelists such as Henry James, James Joyce and Ernest Hemingway.

Along with such heroines as Hilda Howe, Judith Church and Judy Harbottle, Redney from now on would live without love. She had cut herself off from patriotic love, paternal love, marital and maternal. She was permanently isolated, emotionally and geographically, in her cell, but she was a tough survivor. The granite strength of her Presbyterian background came to her aid: she still had the discipline and ritual of her work.

The most ironic coda to *The Imperialist* came with its serialization in *The Queen* in thirteen installments, from October 3 to December 26, 1903, with illustrations by Lewis Baumer. Behind the title, Baumer drew a *habitant* leaning on his snowshoes: the handiest cliché of Canada, to be sure, but one which has absolutely nothing to do with an Ontario manufacturing town. The British, Redney realized once again, knew nothing of Canada and were determined not to learn. Back in London, in January, 1905, however, she tried one final avenue of approval: she sent a copy of *The Imperialist* off to Lord Landsdowne:

> The Ladies' Empire Club
> 69 Grosvenor Street W.
> *Jan. 8th* [*1905*]

Dear Lord Lansdowne,

I wonder if I may count upon your affection for Canada and the kind interest you expressed in the beginnings of my literary work there, far enough to send you my Canadian novel "The Imperialist"? The book was published a few months ago, but I was in India at the time, and felt too far out upon the periphery of the Empire to take a very active share in its distribution from the centre.

It seemed to me that among the assumptions and disputes over here as to what the "colonial view" really is, it might be worth while to present the situation as it appears to the average Canadian of the average small town, inarticulate except at election times, but whose view in the end counts for more than that of those pictorial people whose speeches at Toronto banquets go so far to over-colour the British imagination about Canadian sentiment. I thought it might be useful to bring this practical person forward and let him be seen. I hope I have not made him too prominent, but he is there.

My book offers only a picture of life and opinion, and attempts no argument. I have on this account the better courage in sending it. I should be very happy indeed if it might claim some stray half hour of your leisure time.

> and I am
> dear Lord Lansdowne
> Yours sincerely
> Sara Jeannette Cotes[22]

Later in the year, when she had returned to Simla, living now in another of her decorated bungalows, "Red Roof", Redney drew some small measure of comfort from the knowledge that one perceptive Canadian critic, at least, had appreciated *The Imperialist:*

> *May 4th,* [*1905*]

Dear Dr. MacMechan,

Your two most kind letters and the delightful article in the Halifax Herald have at last found me here. I hope, if it has occurred to you to wonder at my tardy acknowledgement of them, that you have remembered how near I live to the Roof of the World, to which the mails climb slowly.

I need not say that I have taken the greatest pleasure in your generous expression of liking for "The Imperialist". I confess I *had* wondered, a little here on my remote hill top, whether anybody had listened to me in Canada and had come rather to the conclusion that I had been too far away to be well heard, or perhaps I had forgotten my country's note. But that anyone should write like this reassures me quite, and that you alone should feel the book as you do justifies me very happily in having written it. I share with you the conviction of the individuality of the Canadian type. The spirit of place always seems to me strong in the land. I want to come back and work at it from closer range, and soon I think this will be possible. I am especially curious about your Eastern past. My mother is a New Brunswicker— Shediac and all that country has the charm for me of nursery description. I am sure it is as different from Ontario as Massachusetts is from Illinois. We feel that we have been almost long enough in India and I hope to sail through the "Ditch" for the last time, westward bound, in November, and be in Canada next summer. The Empire is a big place and interesting everywhere, but ours is by far the best part of it, and the most full of the future. I rejoice that you enjoyed Dr. Drummond. The dear original was Dr. Wm. Cochrane of Brantford who christened most of the Presbyterians now there. He has been dead these five or six years—[23] or I would never have dared!

Please accept my best and warmest thanks
and believe me
Yours very sincerely
Sara Jeannette Cotes

The College Magazine has not reached me. If you have another copy might I receive it direct? I should like so much to keep it.

S.J.C.[24]

Archibald MacMechan, born in Kitchener, Ontario and educated at the University of Toronto and Johns Hopkins, had gone to Dalhousie University in 1889 as professor of English Literature. Later he was to note that "Duncan is a social satirist of the Jane Austen type" and to cite *The*

Imperialist as standing out "from the vast desert of well-intentioned mediocrity known as Canadian fiction. Its distinction lies in its choice of theme and its truth to observation."[25]

Perhaps it was MacMechan's praise which spurred Redney to take up her pen again. She began another Indian political novel, *Set in Authority*. It would be serialized in the London *Times* weekly edition at the beginning of 1906, and published by Constable in May of that year. Its success would pour some balm on the wounds left by *The Imperialist's* reception. Along with John Galsworthy's *Man of Property* and Winston Churchill's *Coniston* it would be one of the "new novels taken up well"[26] and *The Outlook* would pronounce it "the novel of the year".

In *Set in Authority*, Redney has retreated to the old, safe ground: political intrigue and thwarted love. From now on, she would trek no more into the jungle of deeply personal experience in her fiction; for the most part, she would stay inside the safe, impersonal palings of politics and sentimental romance, the one abstract and theoretical, the other, dreamspun and unreal. This time, she would stay in the shadows for good.

Set in Authority, like *Memsahib* and *His Honour, and a Lady*, continues to explore the underbelly of imperialism, life in an outpost of Empire and the ridiculous rigidity of those idealists fresh from the centre who choose to ignore them. The wide gap between ideal vision, whether political or personal, and the reality was something Redney understood very well indeed. In *The Imperialist* she had clearly shown that it is the imaginative thrust behind the imperialist ideal which energizes and inspires; in her Indian political novels she shows how the imperialist reality enervates and inhibits. There are three fanatic idealists in *Set in Authority*. Lord Thame, India's new Viceroy, is the major one: "The product of fine principle, almost unalloyed" (pp. 21-22), who "doesn't think of anything but the aims of civilisation" (p. 10). The book has a contemporary political setting, so that Thame finds himself in India at a time when Indian nationalist sentiment was growing, sanctioned by the British

government in England with its liberal ideology of freedom
for the individual, but not by the British government in
India, aware of the realities. Lord Thame represents Britain
at the top of the authority ladder, as young Charles Cox, an
assistant-magistrate fresh out from England, represents it at
the bottom. Both are anxious that a British soldier who has
been given a light sentence for shooting a native be sen-
tenced to death. Cox and Thame are inflexible, set in
authority, taking no account of the Indian reality, particularly the attitude which makes of justice a huge jest.

The hero of the book is Eliot Arden, Chief Commis-
sioner of Ghoom, who understands the Indian reality very
well, including the need for expedience and compromise.
Although many years married, he is loved by the third
uncompromising idealist, Dr Ruth Pearce, who had taken
Arden "all human as he was, and had enshrined him; she
knew him mortal, but she would not have him less divine"
(p. 202). Again, Redney repeats her favourite pattern of
thwarted love: a single woman loves a man not attainable,
and yet turns him down when he is free because his behaviour has tarnished the ideal. Ruth refuses to marry Arden
after his wife dies, opts instead for the single life without
love, and pursues an advanced medical degree in England.
Redney dedicates this novel "To My Husband": the only
one of all her novels that is.

Set in Authority is finely crafted, with the same satiric
skills which Redney first demonstrated in *Memsahib*. Redney's
depiction of the community of Pilaghur is almost as dense,
carefully stratified and cleverly satiric as that of Highbury as
Jane Austen describes it in *Emma*. Pilaghur, as Redney
paints it, is many kinds of desert with its "forty or fifty
human souls of the human average, remote and isolated
from the borrowed graces and interests of their own world,
planted where they can never take root, slowly withering to
the point of retirement" (p. 138). Sometimes, Redney etches
character with the same acid which cut so deep in *Memsahib*:

> Her mother was the widow of John Tring, than whom Oxford
> has not produced a more brilliant biologist, or apart from
> that a more futile individual. He had proved the first, and

was convincing his friends of the second when death cut short the less edifying demonstration (p. 18).

But this is also an older Redney, farther down the road to fatalism, more resigned to life's dusty realities.... more resigned to life's dusty realities.

Her treatment of Eliot Arden's thwarted love for Ruth Pearce suggests Redney's own autumnal mood, as Eliot comes "to the point in life when the eager heart has learned how much it must do without," and must go cowled like a monk: "the heart of middle age: so wise it has grown, and so humble" (p. 233).

In September, 1905, she scribbled her first play: *Brown with an E* (probably a dramatized version of *Memsahib*) for the Simla Amateur Dramatic Club. The A.D.C. had been in existence since 1836, and had had its own jewel of a small theatre, the Gaiety, since 1887. The audience always came in full evening dress; the Viceroy had a special box, and such notables as Rudyard Kipling and General Baden-Powell had trod the boards. Play productions had run a wide gamut from one in rhymed alexandrines written and produced by the Viceroy, Lord Lytton, to such classics as Sheridan's *The Critic*. Each year there was one rollicking musical with lavish costumes and the Viceroy's band. The record for the longest run was held by one of these, *Floradora*, which ran for eleven nights in 1902.[27] The A.D.C. was a small stage for Redney to begin with, but already she had her eye on bigger ones.

In November, Redney, as she had in 1894 and 1898, prepared to leave India for good. In a happy flurry, she and Evey packed and sorted, sub-let their house, sold their ponies, and left their saddles and rickshaws to be sold in the spring, since Simla's potential buyers had already trundled down to the plains. The simple matter of disposing of a house in India and the complexities of getting one in England are chronicled by Redney in an amusing article for the English newspaper *Outlook*, entitled "In All Parts of London":

> When I came away we sold the furniture one afternoon at tea-time, all but the Gulf rugs and the objects of sentiment. I was to decide next day what the objects of sentiment were.

The house went by telephone—from the Club. I remember we were at breakfast, and the *khansamah*, who adores answering the telephone, and always makes obeisance when it rings, came and said, "General Issmith sahib gives sala'ams, and inquires whether your honour's house is to be hired for next year, and if it be so, the General sahib wants the house". To which the master replied: "To the General sahib give sala'ams and say very good; he can have the house.[28]

Everard stayed in India, moving down to Calcutta and putting up at the Bengal Club House at 33 Chowringhee Road, once the residence of Thomas Babington Macaulay, Law Member of the Supreme Council in the 1830's.[29] The London *Bookman* in its "News Notes" reported in January, 1906, that "Mrs. Everard Cotes (Sara Jeannette Duncan) has returned home from Simla and is likely to remain in this country".[30] She took over the lease of a top-floor flat from Mrs Montagu Summers at 40 Iverna Court, Kensington, a five-storey apartment building newly built of red brick, facing a quiet square, not far from Kensington High Street, and settled down to a staid English existence.

On March 12th, Redney received a letter from James Louis Garvin, saying that he would be delighted to come to tea with her, and that he hoped to get "In all Parts of London" into *Outlook* that week.[31] James Louis Garvin was a rising star in London journalistic circles—a good person for Redney to know. He had begun his London career in 1899, as leader-writer for the *Daily Telegraph*, before coming to *Outlook* as editor. Known to everyone as "Garve", he was a magnetic personality, thirty-eight years old, with a massive torso, dark hair standing straight up in erratic tufts, great, staring grey-green eyes. His Irish wit poured forth in full flood-tide; once started there was no stopping him. Redney may well have met him in India; he had been there for three months attending the Great Durbar in 1903, and always declared that to visit the East was to change one's life forever after. He had a charming Celtic impulsiveness. He had proposed to his very beautiful wife Christina, whom Redney would later meet, the second time he had seen her by going down on his knees in the street.[32] Redney would assiduously cultivate "Garve", not just because he was a useful contact, but because of the attractiveness of the man himself.

During that spring of 1906, while Redney was caught up in London's whirl, Everard joined a group of journalists touring the Far East, gathering material in China, Manchuria, Korea and Japan for his book *Signs and Portents of the Far East*, dedicated "To my Wife" and published by Methuen in 1907. It is a factual book, analysing commercial and military strengths, rather plodding in its style. His Tokyo impressions are very different from Redney's; Everard describes the law courts, a prison, and a national wrestling competition.

It was while Everard was away, in July, that Redney learned of Mary Curzon's death and knew that India had killed her, that the imperialist ideal had claimed another victim. Mary was only thirty-six, and had suffered a heart attack after a long period of ill health. Curzon had ended his term as Viceroy, precipitately, under a cloud, in 1905, and always blamed the Indian climate for Mary's death. "India, I know, slowly but surely murders women", the vibrant Mary had prophetically written.[33]

Redney was savouring a welcome solitude that summer and fall, insulated in her flat at 40 Iverna Court, getting a taste of what life would have been like as a single career woman in literary London. She was working on *Two in a Flat*, the two being herself and her housekeeper, Hammersmith, a black-eyed little person with a tight twist of hair who received ten shillings a week for unstinting cleanliness and devotion. *Two in a Flat* is a light-hearted look at the daily fabric of Redney's Kensington life, an indoors silver lining to *On the Other Side of the Latch*.

The book was published under a pseudonym, "Jane Wintergreen", in 1908 by Hodder and Stoughton; Redney had as many publishers as she had names. Perhaps because she could hide behind a pseudonym, Redney was more open than usual in writing about her personal life; we learn that she liked a glass of hot water in the morning, rose late, wrote in her dressing-gown, never ate potatoes, was fussy about her tea. These are the self-absorptions of those who live alone. We also learn that she kept Hammersmith at a discreet distance, eating separately, summoning her with a bell, that she had no ear for music, bought her flowers from a special old woman in the street—"Roses and lilies are accepted miracles at any time of year" (p. 204)—spent hours every day arranging them. Redney also recognized the gipsy in herself. "My own dispositions", she confesses, "are not permanent. An impulse will visit me in the night, and in the morning I am obliged to take some kind of a ticket" (pp. 21-22).

As with *Latch*, she makes the still-life of a quiet, domestic canvas colourful and absorbing, and reveals how much she was enjoying her single life. The char came every Friday, and for two-and-six left the flat shining. For the same price, a dressmaker came from time to time to sew and mend. On Wednesdays, at 4.30, Redney was "At Home" to her friends, with Hammersmith in clean cap and apron, and the best lace tea-cloth spread with plates of watercress sandwiches, walnut cake and hot scones. Redney's "coronet complex" in *Two in a Flat* drags in a Marchioness and a Bishop at more than one tea-party.

From her fifth floor height, Redney enjoyed looking down on the world. She could see one gnarled old apple tree, the entrance to the underground, the strange new motor-cars, "violent, erratic things, that emit insane sounds and have no minds of their own, but run like galvanised, headless bodies about the streets below" (p. 69). Wonderful sounds would come floating up: the first cry of "*Straw*berries! Ripe *Straw*berries!", the plaintive sound of hand-organs, reminding her of the ones in New Orleans, the occasional "clang and clash" of a fire engine, and on any wet day the "inevitable, cheerful whistle of a boy somewhere out in the rainy street". Inside, there was only the clock's ticking, the purr of the tea-kettle. For the moment, Redney was cocooned in contentment, her sensitive antennae probing her environment, reflecting, recording, with no interfering static. What a relief, to be free of the mosquito-swarms of squabbling Indian servants, of Anglo-Indian neighbours fanatically social, of all those little marital stings and jabs!

Two in a Flat is a charming, low-key book, showing Redney in a mellow, middle-aged mood. There is one wonderfully ironic chapter, "The Note of Kensington", which exactly captures the thin, reedy note of its genteel inhabitants, who "cast upon you lilac glances, gentle and fragrant, from which you can easily guess the colour-note of their minds" (p. 185). They shrink from vulgar displays of wealth, from strenuous pursuit of art, or money: "To keep alive a laburnum in London, there, if you like, is distinction in purpose and achievement—that is the sort of thing we think worth doing in Kensington" (p. 191). The book well deserves the high praise which the London *Bookman*'s critic gave it: "You will discover", he wrote, "how delightful and entertaining a volume can be written by a dweller in Kensington who is shrewd and humorous".[34]

When Evey joined Redney in London in the early spring of 1907, *Two in a Flat* was being serialized in *The Queen* (from March to July), entitled "Letters from a London Flat" by "Jane Wintergreen". Redney wrote to Willison on April 4th, offering him the book for the Saturday *News*. "My husband has gone back to India," she concludes, "and I follow in July. Grass widow-hood is a miserable form of grass".[35]

When July came, Redney's heart sank like a stone, as once again she found herself sailing up the muddy Hooghly towards Calcutta's wall of heat, only her sense of duty propelling her. Was she never to be free of this alien dust? Work was her only hope so she began another "voyage of consolation", transporting a single North American to England as she had in *An American Girl in London*. This time it is a Canadian girl, Mary Trent, from Eastern Ontario, daughter of a lumber magnate and senator, who comes to London with her brother Graham, and sublets a fifth-floor flat in Kensington which bears a remarkable similarity to 40 Iverna Court. The seed for *Cousin Cinderella* had first sprouted in Redney's mind in 1904, when she had written to John Willison that she was thinking of "bringing Lorne Murchison" to London and giving "the critical colonial view of London society, marrying him eventually." Graham Trent is very like Lorne, and when he says "Now we with our empty country and our simple record, we've got a point of view, if you like. It's inestimable" (p. 149), one can hear Redney consoling herself for her long exile. A point of view . . . it was all she had, and in *Cousin Cinderella* it is still the passionately patriotic one of

The Imperialist. "Canada is different", Mary Trent explains, compared to India and other outposts of Empire whose colonials see England as their real "home", and gravitate towards it as often as possible. "Nobody prefers to leave Canada", proclaims Mary proudly (p. 171). As in *The Imperialist*, Canadian character and way of life are consistently praised, English and American consistently, and subtly, condemned. The English here, as in *The Imperialist*, are shown to be too insular, class conscious, hypocritical, and the Americans too brash and rough around the edges. "There was a time when I wanted enormously to be finished at New York, but father said no, I wasn't an American—and now I am just as glad", explains Mary. "It is simpler to be a natural product and to finish where you begin, I think" (pp. 2-3). How very much poor Redney longed to do just that: to finish where she began, to spend a contented old age in Canada! Although not set in Canada, *Cousin Cinderella* is Redney's second poignant love letter to her country. It was serialized in *The Queen* beginning in January, 1908, and published in the spring of that year.[36]

The work was still in progress in October, 1907, Redney's thoughts still fondly fixed on Canada, when, standing in her garden one night with Evey, she looked up at the sky, saw a bright light, and exclaimed: "My father has just died". It was at that moment that the news of his death did indeed reach Calcutta, a fact which Everard later confirmed, astonished at his wife's psychic powers. Charles Duncan, her dearly beloved father, always so proud of her, so encouraging in his quiet way, had died on October 7th, "after a brief illness".[37] Of his eleven children, only five were still alive, only four of them huddled at Greenwood Cemetery on October 9th to see him buried: Archie, home from North Battleford, Saskatchewan, where he was working in a bank, Ruby, Gordon and Blake. Thousands of miles distant, his eldest and favourite felt a lifeline snap.

Redney was back in London in the spring of 1908, living in a flat at 25 Bullingham Mansions, a rather ugly yellow-brick building on a quiet cul-de-sac near Kensington High Street. From there she wrote a supplicating letter on

Everard's behalf to James Garvin, recently made editor of
The Observer, a post he would hold for the next thirty-five
years.

May 19th [1908]

Dear Mr. Garvin,

           I should very much like to see you and
talk over a matter upon which Mr. Moore, of the Central
News, tells me he has approached your paper. I think my
husband could be of real use to you in Simla and Calcutta —
incidentally I too, possibly — and (this is for your private ear)
I am very angry with the Daily Mail whose special correspondent my husband now is, and who are not behaving by
any means well to us in the juncture that has arisen, believing
as they do that they have us in a cleft stick.

           By arrangement with the Central News we
could offer you a special service, both by wire and post, at a
price much less than the Daily Mail now pay — and if you
remember, Reuter is a dull dog in these parts. I have taken a
tiny flat here and am trying to overtake all literature and all
art and all the dear world in three months. Is there any use in
proposing that you should come and see me or that I should
be permitted to meet Mrs. Garvin? I know what your preoccupations are — or I mistily imagine.

Believe me,
Yours sincerely,
Sara Jeannette Cotes

Of course I will come to see you about this in your office if
you can spare me ten minutes. Friday would be best for
me — about three.

S.J.C.[38]

When not "trying to overtake all the dear world in three
months", Redney was working on *The Burnt Offering*, which
would be published in the early fall of 1909. Indian nationalist sentiment and accompanying acts of violence had escalated
since Redney wrote *Set in Authority*. In 1908, for example, the
wife and daughter of Pringle Kennedy were mistakenly
killed during an attempt to assassinate a district judge who
had punished a revolutionary.[39] India was not just an
infertile soil, now it was also a frightening one, red with
blood. Thwarted love here — in Janaki's yearning love for
John Game, John's for Joan Mills — gets pushed into the

background, so that political unrest can be centre stage, still viewed by Redney in an imperialist frame. There are three fanatic idealists in *The Burnt Offering*, cold, intellectual ones like Lord Thame in *Set in Authority*, "creatures of theory", blind to the complexities of the real situation, to everything but their own egotism. Two of them had real-life counterparts: Vulcan Mills is modelled on the British Socialist parliamentarian Keir Hardie, who had visited India in the fall of 1907; Ganendra Thakore is based on the rabid Indian nationalist Bal Gangadhar Tilak.[40] The third idealist is Joan Mills, Vulcan's daughter, whose feminist views are as radical as her nationalist ones. Contrasted to these fanatics are the British rulers, fine men like Michael Foley and John Game who take a practical view of Indian life. In this book, Redney's own rigidity begins to surface: she is reactionary, very hostile to any form of Indian independence, committed to the view that if the Indian Civil Service since the Mutiny has grown rigid and red-tape-riddled, it is still redeemed by individuals like Foley and Game, or like Eliot Arden in *Set in Authority*, John Church in *His Honour, and a Lady*, all of them men of principle and humanity, with the "justice and repose and quiet strength" of her own deeply mourned father.

In *The Burnt Offering*, Redney reaches a further stage of detachment in which Mrs Perth Macintyre's prediction in *Memsahib* has come true: India's existential chaos has indeed turned her sensibility to cork. People are born and burned and born and burned, and nothing in the world matters. The pink house with doves cooing in the porch in which Redney began her married life seems to have turned into Ganendra Thakore's house:

> The house itself had long consented to its own decay. Its walls were grey where the sun struck and livid where the rain had leaked from the eaves' trough. The plaster pillars that were once so like Corinth and so like Chowringhee, still dropped fragments of their capitals, and round most of them twisted the dry mud trail of the white ants (p. 65).

"The house itself had long consented to its own decay": this is Sara Jeannette Duncan's final word, not only on India, but on herself as well. "The Burnt Offering" of the title, the sacrifice on the altar of empire of such finely principled men as John Game, killed by an Indian assassin's bullet, is a metaphor for Redney's own burnt offering, the sacrifice of her talent in India's burning sands. She had tried, in six different novels, to present the Anglo-Indian realities, both political and social, to the English-speaking world, but had they really listened? Satire of British indifference and ignorance concerning Indian affairs is strong in both *Set in Authority* and *The Burnt Offering*. Did anybody in England care what happened? Did she care herself? *The Burnt Offering* is her final Indian novel. From now on, Redney would write no more of Anglo-Indian realities, nor very much of any other kind.

In *The Burnt Offering* we hear the death rattle of imperialist ideals, and the novel forms an interesting companion-piece to *The Imperialist*. Beginning with *Memsahib*, Redney had been growing more critical of imperialism with each Indian novel, more disdainful and despairing of the whole concept of Empire. It didn't work because of the distance in miles, in understanding, in point of view between the centre and the colony. Imperialism saps, exhausts, depletes its human component. Britain was "a great government... growing old" (*The Imperialist*, p. 268), a tired old, distracted lion whose attention was focused elsewhere, and the centres of power would shift, as *The Imperialist* predicts, to the grown-up colonial offspring. Redney was perhaps the first Canadian to realize that whereas imperialism saps, regionalism succours and inspires. *The Imperialist* paves the way for all those later Canadian novelists who, as Redney herself did so successfully in *The Imperialist*, mine the rich ore of their own particular region: Alice Munro, content to stay fictionally in Wingham, Margaret Laurence in Neepawa, Mordecai Richler on Montreal's St Urbain Street, Matt Cohen in the country north of Kingston.

Still restless, root-less, Redney in the spring of 1909 was back in London, sending a spate of letters off to James Garvin, wooing him in every line, wanting him to serialize *The Burnt Offering* in *The Observer*. From habit as much as anything, she was still bent on upholstering her life financially.

Feb. 7th [1909]

Dear Mr. Garvin,

I am just back from India—What wonderful days for India!—and want to see you on business early this week if possible (I am off again next month). When could you give me a few minutes at the office? or would it suit you better to dine with me here, any evening except Mon. Wed. and Thurs.—7.30. That would be delightful, and perhaps you will be able to explain to me why Percy Landon and Lovat Fraser[41] are leaving the field of battle before we have even heard the order to advance!

Yours v. sincerely
Sara Jeannette Cotes

P.S. Please send me your London address. I want to come and see Mrs. Garvin, as she so kindly asked me to do when last I was at home.[42]

"What wonderful days for India" no doubt refers to the Morly-Minto reforms of 1909 whereby Indian representation was increased on the Secretary of State's Council, and the Executive Councils of the Government and Viceroy. Given her disapproval of Indian nationalism in *The Burnt Offering*, one suspects that Redney here is voicing the view which she thinks Garvin will want to hear.

Redney sent another letter off to Garvin three days later, showing the cutting-edge of her displeasure at being crossed:

Feb. 10th [1909]

Dear Mr. Garvin,

By all means let us have our talk when the omens are most propitious—that is forever and forever worthwhile. But our brief discussion—may it be for any quarter of an hour before Monday afternoon? This I beg, not for pure importunity, but because after Monday afternoon I may not be in a position to discuss—and I want to.

Yours very sincerely,
S.J. Cotes

For me Thursday is free between 5 and 7, all of Fri. and Saturday morning—also Mon. morning. Mr. Landon was to have come home hot foot by last mail—*Why* "hot foot"? and Lovat Fraser, upon whom we all depend, was starting for Teheran![43]

In a further letter of Feb. 17th, Redney writes: "It is a great thing for me that you will read "The Burnt Offering", whatever comes of it, and I stipulate for a talk about it before I go. That will be wholly delightful if you do take it, and a considerable measure of compensation if you don't."[44] In spite of Redney's purring, Garvin didn't print *The Burnt Offering* in *The Observer*.

The spring of 1910 found Redney, for the fourth year in a row, again in London. As her book profits mounted, she bought her escape from India more and more frequently. On March 3rd, she dashed off a note to Christina Garvin from the Ladies Empire Club, inviting her and her husband to tea on Wednesday, March 9th, the day before Redney's precipitate return to Simla.[45] She and Evey were racing back to India because he had been offered the job of Managing Director of the Eastern News Agency, which included the Associated Press of India and the Indian News Agency, a position he would hold until 1919. It was a fine opportunity for him; he was excited; Redney less so. Only fatalism and wifely habit were now keeping her at her husband's side. From now on, Everard would be tied not only to India but for part of every year to hateful Calcutta, with an office at 1 Garstin Place, a cul-de-sac off Hare Street, named for the Major-General who had designed its buildings. Everard appointed as his assistant a young relative, Everard Digby, making him manager of the Associated Press of India. This junior Everard was a twenty-eight-year-old journalist who had been Assistant Editor of the *Indian Daily News* in 1904, Calcutta correspondent for London's *Daily Chronicle*. His father, William Digby, C.I.E., politician and journalist, former editor of the *Madras Times*, was a staunch supporter of Indian nationalism, author of *India for the Indians*.[46] Young Everard Digby became not just a working colleague, but one of those charming bachelors who were welcome additions to so many Anglo-Indian households. In the Cotes' marriage, where stone rubbed against stone, Everard Digby provided some cushioning.

Redney insisted on a Simla base; sometime after 1905 she and Everard had moved from "Red Roof" to another house painstakingly decorated to suit her, called "Westonbert". Now, in the summer of 1911, Redney moved again, this time to "Dormers", the oasis for her remaining years in India. In addition to beautifying "Dormers", she was working on a new venture: a novel wholly set in England, with English characters and English political background called *The Consort*, to be published in May, 1912. This time it is a woman who is set in authority, her husband who becomes the burnt offering. Mary Pargeter, modelled on Baroness Burdett-Coutts, the British philanthropist, is immensely wealthy, powerful, idealistic, coldly intellectual. She is a skilful manipulator of those around her, particularly of her husband Leland, a sensitive artist whose literary talent is shrivelling slowly in her cold, spreading shadow. It is tempting to see Mary and Leland as the two warring halves of Redney's own personality. For the first years of their marriage Leland has no choice but to follow the path of a star: "She swam on in her appointed path, and he with her, as unable to get away as any other attending planet" (p. 32). Ultimately, however, Leland makes his break for freedom, just as Ingersoll Armour did. Leland sails away to America with his true love, Lady Flora Bellamy, on a fine curtain speech:

> The convention of marriage, when it is only that, is the most refined cruelty civilisation has learned to impose, and a farce at which I feel I have assisted too long. There are those who can sustain it; but me it has crushed—finished. It has cost me my power to cope with life, or to be of use in the world.... This that I am doing is hardly more than a clutch at my identity (p. 314).

Sudden flight, a desperate dash for freedom, the shedding of an old skin: Redney was engrossed now in a new theme, reflecting her own psychic tensions, which would occupy her final years. She is still harping on old themes in *The Consort*: thwarted love is still with us in the unacknowledged passion of Pamela Pargeter and Percy Acourt. The political issues of *The Consort*, like those of *The Imperialist*, form the main theme, but here they are vague and ill-defined. Redney is using politics instead of passion to whip the muse, as in her Indian novels, although now she merely shuffles through the old ritual dance. As Professor Tausky has noted: "The conservatism of *The Consort* is embittered and defensive".[47] *The Imperialist* glows with the fire of youth; *The Consort* is gritty with the ash of resigned middle-age.

Redney had now permanently turned her back on the real world. It had been a see-saw progression, that journey from burdocks to roses. She began her writing career firmly grounded in her own life experiences in Canadian, American, British and Indian milieus, mining her particular talent for defining national types as moulded by environment. She focused on autobiography with a fictional veneer in *A Social Departure, An American Girl, The Simple Adventures of a Memsahib, Two Girls on a Barge, On The Other Side of the Latch, Two in a Flat, The Imperialist*. This is the form in which she achieved her finest writing. The fictional component grows in *A Daughter of Today, Vernon's Aunt, A Voyage of Consolation, Cousin Cinderella, Those Delightful Americans*, but underneath is still a firm base of documentary detail. Anglo-Indian novels which tread the ideal-real tightrope in both theme and technique include *His Honour, and a Lady, The Pool in the Desert, Set in Authority, The Burnt Offering. The Path of a Star* and *The Consort* also blend realism and romance, but with a strong predilection for the latter. Her last three novels, however, would show Sara Jeannette Duncan far gone in fantasy, with depressing results for her novelist's art. The tragic irony of Redney's life is that, because of her journalist's skills, her visual bias, and her lack of philosophical depth, she needed to stay firmly rooted in reality to write with distinction. Yet her life choices of foreign land and husband condemned her to a reality too difficult, or too depressing to deal with creatively. She condemned her character and her craft together.

In December 1911, Anglo-India celebrated the Coronation of George V at the great Coronation Durbar in Delhi, and Redney celebrated her fiftieth birthday. The first event was rather more spectacular; twenty thousand workers had prepared the site where George V would be crowned King-Emperor, and where he would announce the transfer of the capital from Calcutta to Delhi. A million pounds were spent in building drains and polo grounds for 233 camps spread over twenty-five square miles. The king's camp alone covered eight-five acres and had green lawns and specially transported English roses.[48] It was the last pyrotechnic of Imperial splendour, the final roar of the Imperialist lion before World War I and Indian nationalism sapped his strength. No one at the Royal Durbar could have imagined that George V would be the last British monarch crowned in India. On December 22nd, Redney reached the half-century mark, and for her too the flames were sputtering. Her hair was almost white now, her jaw rigid, her mask firmly in place. Her public self was now unbending, very much in the austere mould, her nose as beak-like as her father's. Only with her intimates could her face relax into curves, her blue-grey eyes light up. Redney recalled, as she bent to blow out the candles on her birthday cake, what she had written at the age of twenty-six about the ideal fifty-year-old, whose

> subtle intelligence has played for half a century upon the human nature about her; she has all its divinations for her amusement . . . . If by this time she has not separated the false from the true in all the accessories of life — its ornaments, its amusements, its acquisitions, — and given a very fair guess at its real meaning and its noblest ends, she has not made full use of her opportunities. (Montreal *Star*, Jan. 3, 1888).

Life's "real meaning and its noblest ends" . . . elusive as smoke, thinned to small ironies.

As usual, Redney was in England in the spring of 1912, returning to India with her niece Nellie Masterman, then in her teens, whose mother May had died on January 6th, at the age of fifty-three. "I remember how great an interest she took", recalls Nellie of her Aunt Redney

> in choosing pretty frocks for me and making all the arrangements for the voyage out. In those days there was no such thing as air-conditioning in the cabins and fans were luxuries, so I was much impressed to see an electric fan in her cabin and to be told that it was a "compliment" from the shipping company or her publisher, I do not remember which.[49]

Nellie and Redney arrived in Bombay on Nellie's birthday; Evey met them there and all three went straight up to

Dormers. The only warmth and excitement left in Redney's marriage came from these roman-candle reunions—news to share, hugs all round—brief sputters of affection soon snuffed out by the old boredom.

Redney was relying more on outside social contacts than she used to, for stimulation. She usually gave a Sunday ten o'clock breakfast party for friends, where the political talk centered on the move of the capital from Calcutta to Delhi. "I do not think it would be going too far", writes Nellie of her aunt, "to say that she had a good deal to do with the outcome, especially as to the positioning of the main buildings". Redney made sure that she met the Chief Architect for New Delhi's splendours-to-be, Sir Edwin Lutyens, who had arrived in Simla in May with the other two members of the Delhi Planning Commission, and who, for the next twenty years while the capital took shape, would always be in India for the winter months. Lutyens was a small, balding man with his Irish mother's gift for fantasy and laughter. An "expression of mischievous benevolence" was, according to his friend Osbert Sitwell, his distinguishing mark, coupled with a boyish sense of fun rather like Evey's. He had married Lady Emily Lytton, daughter of a former Viceroy and grand-daughter of the novelist Bulwer Lytton. Lady Emily swam erratically in her own pool: she was a fanatic Theosophist and advocate of Indian Home Rule who spent little time at her husband's side,[50] which was perhaps just as well. For Redney, Lutyens was a useful link with James Louis Garvin, a close friend for whose country house at Beaconsfield Lutyens would later design a Romanesque chapel.

Redney caught an even bigger celebrity in her net in November, 1912, when E.M. Forster came to stay at Dormers for four days. Forster was then on his first visit to India with his Cambridge friends Bob Trevelyan and Lowes Dickinson. Redney had met Forster "for five minutes only" some years before at the home of mutual friends, the Theodore Morisons in Weybridge, where Forster also lived. Morison, also a friend of James Garvin's, had retired to Weybridge after being principal of the Muslim College at Aligarh—a kind of

Muslim Eton with a famous cricket team. It had been founded by Sir Syed Ahmed Khan whose grandson Syed Ross Masood, a tall, handsome Oxford graduate, had been adopted by Morison as his ward, and was passionately loved by E.M. Forster.[51]

When Redney learned that Forster was in India, she had written to him at Lahore, inviting him to come to Simla and stay for as long as he liked.[52] The publication of *Howard's End* in England two years before had brought Forster sudden literary fame, and a lionization from which he shrank. He was a slight man of thirty-two, with a long nose and moustache; with people he didn't know well he was quiet and retiring; gradually, however, he unfolded into wild, imaginative flights, witty school-boy fun. For Redney, he was a refreshing draught of spring water in Simla's cultural desert. Like her own, his had been a strange shadow-life, for he had lived in a dull circle of doting mother, aunts, tea-cups and clerics. He was an only child whose father had died when he was a year old; his mother had hedged him with velvet suits and ringlets, heading him for life-long homosexuality and guilt. Redney must have been interested to learn that for five months in 1905, at her Pomeranian *schloss*, Forster had tutored the children of Elizabeth, she of the German garden.[53]

Forster's letters and Indian diary give an intimate glimpse of Redney's Simla life. In a letter to his mother of November 21st, he describes the train trip there, arriving November 14th:

> We all left it [Lahore] by the night train—Dickinson and Trevelyan in the Delhi carriage and I in the Simla. I slept nicely, and got out at the junction for Simla early in the morning. There I got into the mountain railway, which takes 7 hours more—too long to admire scenery however splendid —and I fell asleep again till we stopped at a station for breakfast. Such a twisty, wroggly journey; some people got ill with it. The engine turns round and looks into the carriage in a most alarming way.

He continues in the same letter:

Simla is on a very thin ridge, so that you get views on both sides.... The Cotes sent theirs [their rickshaw] for me and an assistant-journalist, Digby by name, also met me. I did not like him at first, but he turned out nice.... Mr. Cotes himself was charming—the vigorous athletic type, but not the least alarming. He took me a delightful ride. Mrs. Cotes was clever and odd—nice to talk to alone, but at times the Social Manner descended like a pall. Her niece completed the household; they were busy packing up for Delhi, and in great excitement over the change of the capital, as are all. Their Simla house is quite English, with a hall, staircase of dark wood, etc; indeed all the time I was in Simla, I forgot I was in India: there is nothing there but government and scenery.[54]

"Imagine my lovely bedroom", Forster enthuses to his mother, "a blazing fire one end, and French windows opening to a terrace of roses the other beyond which I saw over 70 miles of hills to the main chain of the Himalayas". During his first night at Dormers he was kept awake by "monkeys dancing on the corrugated tin roof". "The season is over in Simla", he comments in a letter to his aunt, "and when the big wigs go, the monkeys come—a very pleasant arrangement".[55]

On November 16th, Forster went with Redney and Everard Digby to a Mohammedan wedding "on rationalist lines": "the first wedding without Purdah that has ever taken place in the district". The bridegroom and bride, without a veil, sat on a sofa in the garden, the priest in an armchair opposite. "A more higgledy piggledy undignified performance I have never seen" comments Forster. "As Mrs. Cotes said, it was like George Trevelyan's marriage, with a service tinkered up for the occasion by Mrs. Humphrey Ward".[56] In his diary, Forster records how this wedding imprinted India's irreconcilable contrasts on his mind:

It was depressing, almost heart rending, and the problem of India's future opened to me. For at one end of the garden burst a gramophone—I'd rather be busy with my little Lizzy—and at the other, on a terrace before the house, about 20 orthodox Muslims had gathered for the evening prayer. Facing the sun, which sets over Mecca here, they went through their flexions, bowing down till they kissed the earth in adoration to God, while the gramophone burred ahead, and by a diabolic chance, reached the end of its song as they ended the prayer".[57]

Redney impressed Forster with her Indian acquaintances, for next morning, the 17th, Mr Bishen Singh, a Sikh, came to breakfast, followed by the bridegroom's brother, to thank Redney for coming to the wedding. During the day, Forster took a walk around Simla with Nellie who made no bones about her racism: "I came out with no feeling against Indians, and now I can't bear them. The change came slowly, though I don't mind servants" she told Forster.[58] "I don't talk about politics", writes Forster to his aunt, "although at the Cotes, I have been living in them".[59]

On the 18th, Forster walked twelve miles up the Himalayan-Tibet road to Fagu, feeling the magnetic pull of the Himalayas. For him this was the highlight of his visit:

> Malcolm Darling had told me what to do, and the Cotes were very kind in helping me. I hired two coolies, at ten pence each, put my bedclothes and Baldeo's [his Indian servant] on their heads, and walked for four hours into the mountains . . . . The last four miles were the most impressive I've ever walked — the whole range of the Himalayas along the horizon and between them and me the queer crinkled outlines of the lower hills, coloured purple and dark brown. The Himalayas too were odd shapes . . . — and all were covered with snow which turned pale rose at sunset . . . . At sunset I reached the Dak Bungalow or Rest House — to which I had previously telephoned . . . . There was a broad verandah, where I sat till it grew too cold, watching the mountains in the moonlight. Dinner — very good — then bed, and all my clothes, and an eiderdown of Mrs. Cotes kept me warm.[60]

Next morning, Everard Digby joined Forster at the Dak Bungalow for breakfast, having risen at 6:30 and ridden up from Simla. They then walked back to Dormers, "disputing most of the way on the nature of the Universe — he is a scientist, or, rather, has the scientific mind — and reached Simla in time for lunch", Forster tells his mother.[61] To his diary, he confided: "My opinion of him [Digby] has altered greatly. Owing to his abuse of Shakespeare, I thought him an ass at first. I like Cotes too. Mrs. Cotes difficult, and I fancy unhappy."[62]

Redney revived briefly when, just after Forster's visit, she and Evey and Nellie moved to Delhi, since Evey needed to be close to the source of government news. Redney could, yet again, throw herself into interior-decorating. Everard Digby stayed in Calcutta, taking a flat at 1 Garstin Place. The ceremony inaugurating the new capital was slated for December. At the rehearsal the day before, Nellie rode the Commander-in-Chief's elephant in the processional route through old Delhi. Next day, a bomb landed in the Viceroy's howdah, killing one of the jamadars and wounding Lord Hardinge. The ceremony was immediately cancelled, and Redney "was among those who wondered if this incident would spark off more trouble, and the air was tense and electric".[63] Life in India was becoming more and more unbearable.

Three months later, in March, 1913, Evey and Redney had another short visit from Forster, accompanied by his friend the Maharajah of Dewas Senior, in Delhi for a conference, along with sixty-five courtiers. Forster describes the visit in a letter to his mother:

> On the second day the Raja paid some official calls, and I drove round with him but did not go in, remaining in the carriage with "Lady" the elderly pug, who goes everywhere. I can't make out why. We ended up at the Cotes', whose acquaintance, as friends of Malcolm's, he wished to make, and then, like a boy loose from school, he grew mad with joy that his duties were over, and bounced up and down among the cushions.[64]

Malcolm Darling, who had been at Cambridge with Forster and who later tutored the Rajah, was, like Lutyens, another ameliorating acquaintance for Redney in India. It was through Darling that Forster had first met the boyish, effervescent Rajah, whom Forster would later serve as secretary.

Redney spent most of 1913 not at Delhi, but at Dormers, where a romantic fantasy was gradually adding its rosy tinge to the snows at sunset, and the terrace of roses. It would be Evey's favourite novel. She called it *His Royal Happiness*, and it was published by Appleton's in New York at the end of

1914, by Hodder and Stoughton in London, early in 1915. It was also serialized in London's *Woman at Home* and America's *Ladies Home Journal* under the caption "The Lively Story of a Prince of England and the Loveliest Girl in the United States", where the April installment shared space with a Bliss Carman poem entitled "Now the Spring is Here Once More". Everything in *His Royal Happiness* suggests eternal springtime, and the *Ladies Home Journal* is exactly where it belongs. It is all too coy for words. Its hero, King Alfred of England, has a valet called Catkin, and a cat who wears a silver collar with "I am the King's Cat" picked out in small turquoises.

As with *An American Girl in London*, the seed for *His Royal Happiness*, in which England's king marries the daughter of the American President, came from Redney's early journalism:

> And now, to literally crown the vaulting ambition of our Republican cousins, Prince Albert Victor, it is gravely said, will marry an American; and if hereditary monarchy in Britain lasts until the contingency arrives, "an American girl will yet be queen of England" (*Week*, Sept. 23, 1886).

The book's dedication reads: "To the dear memory of M.C., India, 1899-1905". M.C., of course, is Mary Curzon, a good symbol for American-British alliances; she had been secretly engaged to Lord Curzon for two years before they could marry, during which time they saw each other for exactly two days. Redney's love-denied theme is even more extreme: Prince Alfred and Hilary Lanchester are secretly married in the States, then kept apart for five years, while Hilary moves in her mantle of silence "like a young abbess" (p. 230), sharing her secret with no one, proud of her sacrifice.

His Royal Happiness reveals Redney knee-deep in roses. At the White House ball where the Prince meets Hilary:

> A whirling fan sent a rose, loosed from its place in the decorations, through the air to her [Hilary's] feet. It was a very perfect red rose, and Prince Alfred picked it up where it lay between them, and presented it to her. He could do no less, and she, perhaps, was equally, obliged to lift it to her face (p. 73).

As they sit holding hands, in the book's final saccharine scene, on the eve of their public wedding in Westminster Abbey, there are "roses in the room, and a green twilight from the garden" (p. 328). Redney's romantic musings in *His Royal Happiness* may have germinated when she learned of the death, on February 17th, 1913, of the Rose-Petal King himself, her old friend Joaquin Miller, still alive in her memory. He had died, aged seventy-four, at The Hights, his home in Oakland, California, but not before he had "made of the place a green paradise of roses, acacia, and a hundred kinds of shrub`.[65]

If *His Royal Happiness* is the lowest form of formula fiction, it is nevertheless interesting as autobiography. Prince Alfred gets tuberculosis, and, like Redney, when she was ill with it in the summer of 1900, he loses his will to live. He is suffering from too much "pre-digested" life, from the stuffy formality of princely protocol. He needs something, according to his doctor, to "counteract the damned alkaloid of his life and training, that neutralises the very vital spring in him", just as Redney herself needed an antidote for the damned alkaloid of Anglo-Indian society. Alfred makes his symbolic break for freedom in the Adirondacks by sneaking off without his equerry, symbol of British restraint, to paddle a canoe, just as Redney used to slip away alone to paddle up Brantford's Grand River, on early mornings. Redney was back visiting in Brantford when war was declared on August 4th, 1914.[66] Her mother, now seventy-seven, in the black widow's weeds which she would wear for the rest of her life, was still full of energy, going to market every Saturday, working in her garden, routing a burglar one night from the coal-cellar with her cane when, as usual, she was reading late in bed, and heard a suspicious noise below.

Redney was still in Canada in December of 1914, adapting *His Royal Happiness* into a play to be given a Toronto production starring Annie Russell. Hector Charlesworth took a dim view of Redney's own performance at this time:

> The public knows nothing and the aspiring playwright is perhaps equally ignorant of what good stage directors and intelligent actors do to give life and interest to manuscripts that would otherwise be still born. The novelist, for instance,

who thinks he knows more than an experienced stage director as to how a play should be done is doomed to failure . . . . The inexperienced playwright who conceives the idea that his text is sacred is seeking disaster. I remember an instance in the case of a noted Canadian fiction writer, the late Sarah Jeannette Duncan. She had written a serial . . . based on the theme of an imaginary marriage of a British Heir Apparent to an American girl . . . . Annie Russell, a really gifted artist, secured the right to produce a dramatic version. Miss Duncan thought that with her long experience as a fiction wrtiter she was fully competent to write a play and stipulated that she should make her own dramatization. When the script was put into rehearsal it was found to be almost hopeless, bristling with lost opportunities to evoke dramatic interest and full of useless padding. But Miss Duncan insisted that it must remain unaltered, and though urged by experienced people like Miss Russell and the stage director, Eugene Presbrey, who knew immensely more about the theatre than herself, she refused all advice. The play was of course a 'flop' even when produced in friendly Canadian cities, and Miss Duncan thought she was an injured person. In reality the injury was to Annie Russell, who had expended a large sum of money on the production in anticipation of being permitted to put an interesting story into something like presentable form.[67]

The imperious Redney appears, in this instance, to be very set in authority indeed.

Redney now was too inflexible, too stubborn. When someone crossed her strong will, she dug in her heels. A *Globe* account of the tea given for her on Saturday, January 2nd by Marjory MacMurchy for members of the Toronto Women's Press Club makes this clear:

Mrs. Cotes was persuaded by little groups of interested ones to say something about "His Royal Happiness" who, she says, is going to be as princely on the stage this week as she made him in her novel. With the charming whimsicality which gives piquancy to her characters and situations, [she] almost admits that one reason for choosing Toronto for the Canadian premiere of her play was a very feminine one. Someone here had thrown cold water on the idea and what more could the natural woman desire by way of stimulus (*Globe*, Jan. 4, 1915).

Over the teacups, Redney persuaded Marjory to write the article entitled "Mrs. Everard Cotes" which would appear in the London *Bookman* in May, 1915, in which Marjory loyally calls her friend "incontestably first among Canadian novelists" and "in the first rank of women novelists in English-speaking countries".[68] The first Mrs John Willison (Marjory would be the second) also gave a tea for Redney and members of the Women's Press Club, on Thursday, January 7th ("Social Events", *Globe*, Jan. 4, 1915). *His Royal Happiness* had opened on Monday evening, January 4th at the Princess Theatre on King Street West, with seats priced at 35 and 50 cents, competing with a production of *The Mikado* at the Royal Alexandra. Redney donated the opening-night royalties to the Canadian Red Cross and enjoyed bowing from her box, with the Lieutenant Governor of Ontario, Mr Hendrie, and the Premier of the Province, Mr Hearst, in adjoining boxes. In spite of the fact that the supporting company was "one of the best of the season" and Annie Russell breathtakingly beautiful in a series of gowns which were "the latest word in the modiste's art" (*Globe*, Jan. 2, 1915), the *Globe*'s drama critic, E.R. Parkhurst panned the production, with most of his criticism aimed at the playwright. "The play is a dramatisation of the book by the same name, and, as frequently happens in such cases, the story has lost in the metamorphosis", he writes.

> With the material at her disposal, Miss Annie Russell did most excellent work. She might well complain that the play was too "talky" as some of the scenes seemed to drag, but in the third act, when pleading with her father for her love there was pathos in her emotion, and the lines, "Treaty or no treaty, there will always be roses in America for England" were rendered with exquisite feeling ("Music and Drama", *Globe*, Jan. 5, 1915).

The play ran for only one week, and Redney, disgruntled and disappointed — the Canadian critics had rejected her again — sailed for England shortly after, the first of several tense, war-time sea voyages. On this one, the Captain flew the Stars and Stripes to prevent the ship being torpedoed.[69] In March, taking Nellie with her, Redney returned to

Dormers. All passengers on the P and O had to wear life-jackets until they got to Port Said, and to sleep in their clothes, in case of sudden submarine attack. "People were resigned to indifferently lighted bridge in the saloon", complains Redney, who all her adult life was a keen and constant bridge-player.

The shadows of war stretched all the way to Simla, now "very sober and quiet so far as social functions are concerned" with tennis parties the "only relaxation" (Simla correspondent, *The Englishman*, June 15, 1915). "The female population devoted itself to war work of all descriptions and numberless fetes and festivals were organised in aid of war charities".[71] Redney did her part by writing a play called *The Convalescents* for the Simla Amateur Dramatic Club. It ran for four nights in mid-October, 1915, with 25% of the proceeds going to the St. John Ambulance Society.[72] "It is not every season that Simla witnesses a play written by a local resident", says the Simla correspondent for *The Englishman*, who pronounced it "the most interesting play of the season" with "half a dozen highly amusing situations, and plenty of those opportunities which a Simla audience really enjoys for hearty laughter".[73]

Emboldened by this success, Redney made plans to take *The Convalescents* to London's West End. In late fall, she left India for England and this time, given the exigencies of the war which made sea voyages difficult, it was for good. Nellie and Everard remained in India, where they would stay until 1919. Evey continued to run the Eastern News Agency and to recruit, as he had for the Boer War. Redney rented a London flat at 36 Buckingham Gate, an elegant building with triple colonnaded front, and distinguished tenants; in flat 26 lived His Honour Judge John Shortt and in flat 14 the Right Honourable Laurence Hardy, M.P.[74] Redney moved into flat 22, but her reprieve from India had come too late: her physical and creative energies were waning fast. On March 31st, her Simla play *The Convalescents*, now entitled *Beauchamp and Beecham*, opened at a special matinee at London's Lyric Theatre, the proceeds going to Irish Regiments and their Prisoners. Redney tried to enjoy her new role; she bowed from her box as the curtain fell and cries of

"Author" arose, was presented to Royalty afterwards. The play subsequently toured the country for two years where "it became so vulgarised and altered" that Redney tried, without success, to get it taken off the boards.[75]

Liking the public attention, the new source of income, Redney became an active playwright for the years remaining. A play called *Julyann* was staged at the Globe Theatre, London, on July 24, 1917, produced by W.G. Fay from Dublin's Abbey Theatre. One called *Billjim from Down Under* had a three-night run in Adelaide, Australia, produced by Robert Courtneidge's London Company. In addition to *His Royal Happiness*, Redney also adapted her last two novels, *Title Clear* and *The Gold Cure* for the stage. With a British playwright called Forbes Dawson, whose *Wearing of the Kilt* had had a London production in 1910, she dramatized *Sonny Sahib: An Indian Play for Children and Grown-Ups*.

Redney had absolutely no talent for drama. Plot and character development had always been her weak points. Her plays are full of unlikely coincidences, contrived situations, characters with only heavy dialect to distinguish them. These dramatic works, twelve of which have survived in manuscript, make a depressing coda to her career.[76] She was now very far indeed from the true fountainhead of her creativity.

On the other hand, the plays have some faint interest in a psychological context. First of all, the title pages of all play manuscripts bear the words "By Sara Jeannette Duncan", although all of them were the products of her married years. The unfinished version of *Molly-Mary, A Play in Four Acts*, has a heroine about to enter a convent. "I have no more life— I have no more happiness. Take me with you, Sister", pleads Molly-Mary at the end of Act One. "Keep me safe and teach me your peace".[77] *Beauchamp and Beecham* centres on two convalescent soldiers, the Honorable Robert Beauchamp, gentleman, and Robert Beecham, former linen draper's assistant. They decide to switch identities and impersonate each other. *Julyann* also deals with identity-swaps. Private Gallagher of the King's Own Fusiliers, serving in France, bets his friend and look-alike Private Dempsey that when he goes on leave he can successfully persuade Julyann, Dempsey's wife, that he is her husband. Fleeing the old self for a new one would also preoccupy Redney in her last two novels.

At the beginning of 1919, Everard sold the Eastern News Agency to Reuters and came home to England with Nellie. He and Redney had been apart for four years and remeshing their lives was not easy. They took a long lease on a Chelsea town house, at 17 Paulton's Square, just off the King's Road, a small square with the usual wrought-iron fence, locked gate and plane trees full of blue shadows. In September and October of 1919, for once travelling together, Evey and Redney came to Canada. As Reuters agent, Everard was part of the press entourage for Edward, Prince of Wales' Western tour. The Cotes were particularly pleased to have a chance to visit British Columbia's Prince Rupert, for in 1913, Redney's nationalist feelings had taken concrete form: she had purchased four lots in Prince Rupert, just then beginning to boom. The lots had been bought for $8000 from the Grand Trunk Pacific Development by Michael Scheady and Donald McLoud, who, in turn, sold them to the Cotes for $15,000.[77] While in Prince Rupert, Redney wrote two articles for *The Globe*, "The Dignity of Prince Rupert" by "S.J.D." (Oct. 4, 1919) and "The Melting-Pot Bubbles a Bit" (Oct. 13, 1919). Both of them are written by the hard-headed business woman, conscious of her stake in the town's development and trying to promote its mining, fishing and tourist trade.

On Monday, October 20th, Evey and Redney accompanied the Prince of Wales to Brantford. It was a fine autumn day, a busy one for the townsfolk, being election day as well, but they welcomed Prince Edward with the usual bands and bunting. Redney thought the Prince quite as debonair as her fictional one, his blond hair catching the sun as he chatted and laughed, but he had to shake hands with his left hand, his right suffering from the brisk Canadian handclasp.[78]

Back at Paulton's Square by November, the wild young Redney of the cow-catcher surfaced for the last time. In a party of forty, she took her first plane ride in a four-engine bomber at Cricklewood, a large airplane factory outside London; she describes it all in "A Record Trip" for two

Indian newspapers.[79] She managed to get one of the two coveted seats next the pilot. "You have a real feeling of enterprise if you sit beside the pilot", she enthused.

In 1920, Redney was relieved to have seven months in England on her own while Everard toured Australasia with the Prince of Wales as *Times* correspondent, gathering notes for a magazine article[80] and *Down Under With the Prince*, his book-length account of the trip. *Down Under With the Prince* is a repetitious account of the usual receptions and speeches—material which would defeat a better writer than Everard. The only lively scene, in which the Prince's railway car overturns in an Australian gulley, windows to the sky, describes how the Prince climbed out unperturbed, waving a cocktail shaker.[81]

In 1921 and the early part of '22, Redney was working on her last two novels. The first one, *Title Clear*, was published in June, 1922. Recalling her trip to Scotland in '94, Redney uses a little village near Pitlochry as setting. There is a great deal of heavy Scottish dialect, unlikely twists of plot, stereotyped characterization, treacly sentiment. Redney is again obsessed with identity switches: Campbell Fraser returns to his native Scotland after twenty-three years in America, pretending to be his twin brother William, because he has sullied his own "title clear" in moral terms. Campbell Junior, his American-born son, complains of the lack of a title clear in a geographic sense, declaring himself "a Highlander with the bad luck to be born away from home" (p. 125). A title clear . . . the phrase comes from the hymn which Redney repeats, her own personal dirge, throughout the book:

> If I could read my title clear
> To mansions in the skies,
> I'd bid farewell to every fear
> And wipe my weeping eyes.

There had been many wasted years before Redney, in the act of writing *The Imperialist*, had found her title clear to her homeland. "Act, act in the living present", advised her commonplace-book, but emotionally, as she aged, Redney could only respond long after the fact. The nun had been cloistered too long, the title clear come too late.

Redney was not writing because she had anything new to say; she was merely using the habit of years as drug and diversion. Her health was rapidly deteriorating; her chest had always been her weak point; now she had chronic bronchitis, asthma, the shadow-threat of another tubercular flare-up always hovering. She was continually short of breath, forced to spend hours in bed. She needed her roses.

The Gold Cure, published posthumously in 1924, is a pot-boiler. The world it portrays is a depressing post-war English one, for the war has "made the world a flatter place than ever the ancients thought it" (p. 13), a vulgar world where "the beauty of propriety" is in short supply, a world from which Redney's sensibility had long since retreated. In *The Gold Cure*, the main character again sheds the old self for a new one. The heroine of *The Gold Cure* is a rich American girl about to marry a stodgy stockbroker. "Life seemed a blank wall on every side and she, Betty van Allen, bricked up in it" (p. 52). "This getting married ... it's all right till you come to the day before. Then you sort of ask yourself what you're doing it for, anyway" (p. 37), says the beleaguered Betty. Betty bears a remarkable resemblance to the young Redney, for she has a close relationship with her father, is a "person of courage and resource" (p. 174) with plenty of self-confidence, zest for life and sense of adventure. Redney's solution to Betty's problems, however, is the same tired identity switch which is the older Redney's perennial solution. Betty runs for her life by disguising herself as her maid Norah and sailing away to England. She lands in another cage in London, however, for, without funds, she is forced to take a dull job as typist, and "the world seemed to have closed about her as unfeelingly as this miserable yellow fog" (p. 120). Ultimately, Betty wins the pot of gold at the end of the rainbow in the form of a titled Englishman, the Honourable Roderick Trenchard, who comes to avail himself of her typing skills.

A recurring theme preoccupied Redney's final years, and is a desperate exaggeration of her expatriate quest: one can escape the old self only by opting for a completely new one. This idea obsessed Redney in *The Pool in the Desert* ("An

Impossible Ideal"), *The Consort, Beauchamp and Beecham, Julyann, Title Clear, The Gold Cure*. Why did Redney turn to this theme in her last years? Was she looking for a way out of that public mask, all Social Manner and Stern Matriarch? Two of her English nieces thought her, in later life, "formidable" and "terrifying"; her wit could be sarcastic; she was "cool and reserved" and "in a way quite alarming".[82] Redney had always been part rebel, part reactionary, sometimes ahead of her time, as in her views on women's role, sometimes behind it, as in her views on social etiquette. She was an unjelled blend of brave new world and hidebound old one; in her later years, the latter triumphed. Already, in her fifties, Redney was as imperious as her mother was in her eighties. When motor cars became common in Brantford, Mrs Duncan would hold up her hand for them to stop when she wished to cross the road. One of Redney's Canadian nephews notes, however, that when Aunt Redney "came into the household, everyone else took a back seat", including her mother.[83]

"England is a dangerous country to live in; you run such risks of growing old", says a Canadian in *The Imperialist* of his English relatives who are far gone in "rigidity of body and mind" (p.116). Redney's own rigidity grew in her final years in England; she felt its tightening grip, and the urge to escape it. Her preoccupation with identity-changes may also have been the panicky response of a self slipping towards the void as she felt herself moving farther and farther away from true creativity. The desk at which she wrote in her later years is small, made of dark-stained wood, with beaded trim in the fashion of the day. Above are two narrow shelves, ridged to hold her precious bits of china. In the middle of the sloping top "S.J.C" is deeply incised, writ large in Redney's slanting scrawl. Did Redney snake a fingernail down the dips and curves of that "S.J.C", remembering earlier shining marks, wanting again that self's sure imprint? Earlier in her life, her solution to boredom and apathy had always been to move to a new setting and a new challenge. Now she was too old, too ill, and too tired to seek another country.

She was still, however, even in those final days, as she worked on *The Gold Cure*, doing what she could with the smaller setting, if not the larger. She was busy decorating her last house. She and Everard had decided to buy a house outside London, and in early spring of 1922 found one to their liking in Ashtead, Surrey, a quiet village of about 2,000 people, a short train ride from London. They christened the house "Barnett Wood Lodge", for it stood in Barnett Wood Lane, a narrow country road meandering from a nearby pond to the larger village of Leatherhead. The house, still standing, is red brick with a red-tile roof, a large bay window facing the road, a pretty garden behind. A large fir tree and a small magnolia on the lawn are surely Redney's planted symbols of Canada and New Orleans. At right angles to the house is Green Lane, but Green Lane leads to nothing but a large, empty field.

Nellie Masterman had now become Redney's companion, as Rhoda Cotes had been earlier, both of them welcome buffers for an apparently uncomfortable marriage. With Nellie helping, Redney and Everard moved into Barnett Wood Lodge in May of 1922, but its interior decoration was still far from finished. Redney had chosen green for the drawing-room's walls and carpet: a pale shade of green. She hung flowered chintz curtains at the windows, four beautiful prints in gold-and-blue, bought long ago in Japan, on the walls. Upstairs was a fine Georgian mahogany chest-on-chest, similar to those her father had imported for his store.

Everard was now going daily to London where he was parliamentary correspondent for the Boston-based *Christian Science Monitor*, a position he would hold for the next seventeen years. One June morning just after breakfast, Nellie heard Redney call her suddenly from the garden:

> I went in to the garden . . . she was standing on a flower-bed with a fork in her hands, and said "I feel awfully queer". I got her to bed with hot bottles, and then ran across to some kindly neighbours to ask who and where was a doctor; then I phoned my Uncle.[84]

So many gardens . . . but this was the final one, and, in her last active moments, fork in hand, Redney was helping its flowers to grow.

She was ill with pneumonia for five weeks. Nellie and Evey, distraught and as devoted as ever, sat by her bedside. Rhoda was sent for from Oxford. When Redney knew that the end was near, she took her husband's hand, and, with a gentle pressure, said: "Go on, Evey". Then she turned her head to Nellie, opened her blue-grey eyes wide, "so live and clear, as if she would impress something on my mind, and then closed them for ever".[85]

"If you are asked to an entertainment you do not reproach your host that it is so soon over", Redney had written:

> nor are you supposed to resent other people getting more extended invitations. The lights and the music please you, but at the end you never hesitate to step outside again into the dark. Perhaps we are all here quite as long as we are wanted. Life is very hospitable, but she cannot put on every card, "1 to 70 years" (*On the Other Side of the Latch*, p. 251).

Her own card had read "1 to 60 years"—not a long span, but Redney was ready to step outside. She had made her will on the sixth of May, 1921, bequeathing everything to Everard and making him her sole executor. The probate of the will reveals that her money, as well as her heart, had stayed in Canada. She had only 150 pounds in assets in Britain, with her cash savings in the Bank of Montreal on Threadneedle Street. Not including the Prince Rupert lots, her Canadian property totalled 2,970 pounds, including Canada War Bonds, Canadian Pacific Railway shares, Town of Port Arthur bonds. She also had substantial cash savings in Brantford's Bank of Montreal. The probate of her last will and testament neatly underlines Redney's belief in Canada's bright future.[86]

The after notes to Redney's death are fittingly ironic. The Toronto *Mail and Empire's* notice, for the very last time in print, misspelled her name. An oil portrait of her done in England was sent home to sister Ruby in Canada. Many years later, it was so badly restored that it is unrecognizable, for the brown skin tones are quite unlike Redney's freckled fairness. She was buried in a lead-lined coffin, so that it could eventually be sent home to Canada, but it never was. Everard remarried within a year; this time he made an extremely happy match.

At least, Redney, romantic that she was, would have liked her final picturesque setting. She lies in the church-yard of St Giles' Anglican church in Ashtead. The cemetery is on a hill, fronting St Giles' weathered grey stone and square Norman tower. The cemetery spreads out, rambles down green slopes, with the benediction of tall firs and blossoming fruit trees. Beside Redney's tombstone is an English holly bush, its prickles and barbs almost covering the stone, a simple, curved one, with swag-leaf decoration.

She had had many names. She was to come full circle; in her end was her beginning. The inscription on the stone reads:

> Sarah Janet
> Beloved Wife of
> Everard Cotes
>
> 22nd July 1922

Many names, many gardens. Gouged deeply into the grey granite, near its base, are the words:

> "This leaf was blown far".

Notes

I. Brantford

1. Marjory MacMurchy, "The Bookman Gallery. Mrs. Everard Cotes", *The Bookman* (May, 1915), p. 40.

2. For details of Charles Duncan's life, see "Do You Remember", Brantford *Expositor*, Oct. 8, 1957 and obituary, *Expositor*, Oct. 7, 1907.

3. Rae E. Goodwin, "The Early Journalism of Sara Jeannette Duncan, with a Chapter of Biography", University of Toronto M.A. thesis, 1964, p. 11.

4. Letter from Archibald Duncan to Professor R.E. Watters, Dec. 23, 1955, quoted by Goodwin.

5. *Ibid.*

6. *Ibid.*

7. The house at 96 West Street is still standing and looks very much as it did in the Duncans' time. It is now Thorpe's Funeral Home, and a memorial plaque marking the house as an historic site was erected on October 6, 1962, by the Brantford Historical Society.

8. For many of the details of house and garden I am indebted to Mr. Edward Blake Duncan.

9. "How an American Girl Became a Journalist", in Thomas E. Tausky, *Sara Jeannette Duncan. Selected Journalism*, p. 6. The origin of this article, which Prof. Tausky found in the Stirling Library at Yale University, is not known, but internal evidence suggests that it appeared in an English periodical and was written while SJD was in Washington (1885-6).

10. Florence Donaldson, "Mrs. Everard Cotes", *The Bookman* (June, 1898), p. 66.

11. "How an American Girl", p. 6.

12. *Ibid.,* p. 7.

13. Her commonplace book is a black-bound undated volume whose initial page reads "Dots and Dashes. Private Scribbles". This is not, as one might think, a quotation from Mrs. Gaskell's *Cranford,* and so may be SJD's own coinage.

14. Douglas Reville, *History of the County of Brant,* I, 229.

15. *Ibid.,* I, 237.

16. *Brantford Gazeteer and Directory for 1875-6.*

17. Goodwin, p. 11.

18. The Ladies College was operating from 1874 to 1900, situated on Brant Avenue, on E.B. Wood's former estate, the present site of

the Brantford Collegiate Institute. See C.M. Johnston, *Brant County: A History 1784-1945,* p. 85 and Reville, I, 236. When the college burned down in 1900, all records were lost, including those for SJD.

19. Told to me by Mrs. Florence Bingle of Brantford, whose mother was a classmate of SJD at the Ladies College.

20. Reville, I, 138.

21. Brant Historical Society, *A Glimpse of the Past,* p. 48 and Reville, I, 241-2.

22. Reville, I, 201-2.

23. See J.M.S. Careless, *Brown of the Globe,* particularly Vol. II.

24. See C.M. Johnston, pp. 110-12, and Reville, I, 312-13, 320.

25. Charles Duncan Jr. is quoted in an interview in which he lists cogent reasons for the formation of a Young Liberal Club, "if the next election is to result in a victory for the Grit party" (*Expositor,* Jan. 13, 1891).

26. *A Glimpse of the Past,* pp. 52-4 and Reville, II, 648.

27. In a letter to Dr. Archibald MacMechan of May 4, 1905, SJD acknowledges that Dr. Cochrane was her model for Dr. Drummond in *The Imperialist.*

28. See diary of Rev. William Cochrane, Jan. 1, 1870 to April 5, 1885, mss. #409, Province of Ontario Archives, also R.W. Grant, *The Life of Rev. William Cochrane* and Reville, II, 653-4 and 667-8.

29. See Marcus Van Steen, *Pauline Johnson: Her Life and Work,* Walter McRaye, *Pauline Johnson and Her Friends* and Jean Waldie, "The Iroquois Poetess: Pauline Johnson", *Ontario History,* XL (1948), 65-75.

30. For this anecdote, see J.W.L. Forster, *Under the Studio Light,* p. 87. For details of Ross' life, see Henry Morgan, *Canadian Men and Women of the Time,* 1912 edition, p. 886, Hector Charlesworth, *Candid Chronicles,* p. 183 and John Willison, *Reminiscences Political and Personal,* pp. 326-7.

31. Unless a teacher taught long enough to be pensionable, there are no complete Ontario lists of teachers for this time. In her *Bookman* article, M. MacMurchy states that SJD "taught the most junior class of all", p. 39. There is some evidence to suggest that SJD may have taught in Strathroy, Ontario, but, as a check by Rae E. Goodwin shows, the Strathroy *Western Dispatch* never mentions SJD in lists of teachers there 1880-84.

32. Carlotta Hacker, *The Indomitable Lady Doctors,* pp. 17-19, 23, 29, 49, 66, 68.

33. "How an American Girl", p. 8.

34. *Ibid.,* pp. 8-9.

35. Marcus Van Steen, "Brant Girl Quit Teaching Job to Gain Fame as a Novelist", *London Free Press,* Sept. 29, 1962.

36. Charlesworth, pp. 72-77.

37. "How an American Girl", pp. 9-10.

38. Reville, I, 140-143, 290.

39. "How an American Girl", pp. 10-11.

40. *Ibid.,* p. 11.

41. Willison, p. 66.

42. "How an American Girl", p. 11.

43. "Miss Sara Duncan left on Thursday, to spend a few weeks at the World's Fair and Cotton Exposition at New Orleans", *Expositor* Dec. 6, 1884.

II. New Orleans

1. "Montreal, June 19. Joaquin Miller, the poet of the Sierras, left this morning by boat for Toronto and Hamilton" (*Brantford Expositor,* June 19, 1880). "Joaquin Miller, the poet, is holidaying in Canada" (*Brantford Expositor,* June 24, 1880).

2. Eugene V. Smalley, "In and Out of the New Orleans Exposition", *Century Magazine,* XXX, no. 19 (1885), 188. For additional descriptions of the Exposition, see Eugene V. Smalley, "The New Orleans Exposition", *Century Magazine,* XXX, no. 1 (1885), 3-14 and Anon., "A Visit to the New Orleans Exposition" *Demorests's,* XXI, no. 5 (1885), 275-81.

3. *Globe* articles appeared Dec. 26, 1884, Jan. 2, 12, 20, 1885. *London Advertiser* articles appeared Dec. 19, 29, 1884, Jan. 1, 6, 12, Feb. 27, Mar. 5, Apr. 9, Apr. 17, May 12, 1885. *Memphis Daily Appeal* articles appeared Jan. 15, 20, Feb. 5, 13, 20, Mar. 4, 1885. These articles largely duplicate the Canadian copy. In addition there was one article printed in both the New Orleans *Times-Democrat* (Jan. 1885) and the *Washington Post* (Feb. 1, 1885) and reprinted in the *Brantford Expositor* (Feb. 13, 14, 1885).

4. M.M. Marberry, *Spendid Poseur. Joaquin Miller — American Poet,* p. 46.

5. Marberry, p. 56. For biographical details on Miller see also *Dictionary of American Biography,* ed. Dumas Malone, VI, 621-22.

6. *Ibid.,* p. 183.

7. For details of Miller's stay in New Orleans, see Arlin Turner, "Joaquin Miller in New Orleans", *Louisiana Historical Quarterly,* 22, no. 1 (Jan. 1939), 216-25.

8. George Sterling, "Joaquin Miller", *American Mercury,* 7 (1926), 224.

9. Marberry, p. 155. I am indebted to Marberry for biographical details of Miriam Leslie, nee Follin.

10. *Memorie and Rhyme,* p. 192.

11. *The Poetical Works of Joaquin Miller,* edited by Stuart P. Sherman, p. 420.

12. Sterling, p. 226.

13. Marberry, p. 284.

14. Sterling, p. 222.

15. *Ibid.,* p. 223

16. Quoted by Orcutt William Frost, *Joaquin Miller,* p. 77.

17. Marberry, p. 128.

18. *Memorie and Rhyme,* p. 46.

19. From *The Building of the City Beautiful,* quoted by Frost, p. 107.

20. *Memorie and Rhyme,* p. 39.

21. Sherman, p. 38.

22. *The Complete Writings of Charles Dudley Warner,* Vol. VIII: *Studies in the South and West with Comments on Canada,* p. 49.

23. Frost, p. 34.

24. Marjory MacMurchy, "The Bookman Gallery: Mrs. Everard Cotes", *The Bookman* (May, 1915), p. 39.

25. Sterling, p. 229.

26. "Her Picture" in Sherman, p. 434.

27. *Memorie and Rhyme,* p. 89.

28. *Joaquin Miller's Poems,* III, 21-22.

29. "The Voice of the Dove" in Sherman, p. 405.

30. "Garth on the Gulf. New Orleans, Jan. 29" appeared in the *Washington Post,* Feb. 1, 1885 (partially reprinted in *Sara Jeannette Duncan: Selected Journalism,* edited T.E. Tausky, pp. 13-16). The same article appeared in the New Orleans *Times-Democrat* at the end of January and was copied by the *Brantford Expositor,* Feb. 13 and 14, 1885.

31.   Magnolia Blossoms

> The broad magnolia's blooms are white;
> Her blooms are large, as if the moon
> Had lost her way, some lazy night,
> And lodged here till the afternoon.
>
> Oh, vast white blossoms breathing love!
> White bosom of my lady dead,
> In your white heaven overhead
> I look, and learn to look above. (Sherman, p. 384).

32. Arlin Turner in "Joaquin Miller in New Orleans" states that Miller stayed "until about the end of January" (p. 219) and Marberry that he left "early in 1885" (p. 186) but Miller, as we know from SJD's accounts, figured prominently in Mardi Gras celebrations Feb. 16-23.

33. "How an American Girl Became a Journalist", Tausky, p. 12.

34. "How I Came to be a Writer of Books", *Lippincott's Monthly Magazine,* 38 (July, 1886), 109-10.

35. Sterling, p. 224.

36. In the "Personal" column of April 7, 1885, the *Expositor* reports: "Miss Sara Duncan returned home on Saturday, after having spent the greater part of the winter in the Sunny south".

37. "How an American Girl Became a Journalist", p. 12.

III. Washington, Toronto, Montreal, Ottawa

1. Rae E. Goodwin, "The Early Journalism of Sara Jeannette Duncan", pp. 30-31.

2. Chalmers Roberts, *The Washington Post: The First 100 Years,* pp. 38-39. I am indebted to Roberts for most of my information on the *Post.*

3. *Ibid.,* pp. 6-7.

4. *Ibid.,* p. 16.

5. *Ibid.,* p. 27.

6. "At the age of twenty [she was actually twenty-three], Miss Duncan went to Washington and occupied the unusual position, for one so young, of being on an editorial footing on the staff of a daily paper. Her work consisted of book reviews, papers on special subjects, and occasional leading articles" (F. Donaldson, *The Bookman* (June, 1898), p. 66.)

7. "How an American Girl Became a Journalist", pp. 12-13.

8. Rae E. Goodwin in "The Early Journalism of Sara Jeannette Duncan" does a fine job of listing all work in the *Post* likely to be SJD's. Goodwin believes that some *Post* book reviews from June to October, 1885, before SJD went to Washington, are her work. My own feeling is that the evidence for this is inconclusive.

9. "Garth Grafton spent Thanksgiving Day in the City" (*Brantford Expositor,* Nov. 19, 1885). Since Lord Dufferin's 1877 decree, the Canadian Thanksgiving holiday fell in November, not in October as at present.

10. Erastus Wiman, *Chances of Success: Episodes and Observations in the Life of a Busy Man,* p. 11.

11. Roberts, p. 35.

12. Constance M. Green, *Washington. Capital City 1879-1950,* p. 78.

13. "Diogenes on Bric-a-Brac", *The Canada Monthly* (June, 1880), p. 637.

14. Roberts, pp. 20, 36-37.

15. From Rev S. Reynolds Hole, *A Little Tour of America* (1895), quoted by Green, p. 77.

16. Roberts, p. 25.

17. Hector Charlesworth, *Candid Chronicles*, p. 296.

18. M.M. Marberry, *Splendid Poseur*, pp. 177-79.

19. Van Wyck Brooks, *The Confident Years 1885-1915*, p. 165.

20. M. MacMurchy, *The Bookman* (May, 1915), p. 39.

21. Edwin H. Cady, *The Road to Realism. The Early Years of William Dean Howells 1837-1885*, p. 1.

22. Brooks, p. 110.

23. *Ibid.*, p. 109.

24. See Marian Fowler, *The Embroidered Tent: Five Gentlewomen in Early Canada*, pp. 74-75.

25. For SJD's account of this holiday, see *The Week*, Nov. 25, 1886.

26. Jarvis Street had been named for Sam Jarvis, a wildly impulsive young man who had killed John Ridout in an 1817 duel, led the gang of fourteen youths who smashed William Lyon MacKenzie's printing press in 1826. In 1845, Sam subdivided his 100-acre property and laid out Jarvis Street from Bloor Street south to Lake Ontario. See Austin Seton Thompson, *Jarvis Street: A Story of Triumph and Tragedy.*

27. See Desmond Morton, *Mayor Howland: The Citizen's Candidate.*

28. *Studies in the South and West with Comments on Canada*, p. 509.

29. Katherine Hale, *Toronto. Romance of a Great City*, pp. 155-56.

30. F. Donaldson, p. 66. Goldwin Smith and SJD seem to have corresponded after she left Canada in 1890, although there are no extant letters in public collections. She refers in an editorial in *The Indian Daily News* to "a private letter received in Calcutta from Goldwin Smith" (Nov. 25, 1896).

31. Goldwin Smith, *Reminiscences*, pp. 450-51.

32. See SJD, *Week*, Oct. 21, 1886 and Douglas Reville, *History of the County of Brant*, I, 56-59.

33. "Miss Duncan, Brantford, Ont. [wore] pale green silk *en traine*, ostrich tips and pearls", listed in Anon., "Carnival Ball. The Costumes Worn by the Ladies at the Windsor Last Night" (*Star*, Feb. 12, 1887).

34. Anon., "Carnival Ball at Windsor Hotel", *Star*, Feb. 12, 1887.

35. Charlesworth, p. 89.

36. Rose, *Cyclopaedia of Canadian Biography*, p. 340.

37. *Chances of Success*, p. 319.

38. *Ibid.*, p. 43. For biographical details, see also Elgin Myers, "A Canadian in New York": *The Canadian Magazine* (August, 1893), pp. 435-43.

39. Myers, p. 439.

40. Advertisement in Lovell's *Montreal Directory 1889-89.*

41. Anon., "The *Star*. Its Origin and History", *Star*, Feb. 23, 1889, p. 1.

42. "Diogenes on Bric-a-Brac", *The Canada Monthly* (June, 1880), p 638.

43. A.Y. Jackson, *A Painter's Country*, p. 102.

44. William Brymner to Achille Fréchette, March 5, 1888. Howells/Fréchette Collection, Herrick Memorial Library, Alfred University, New York.

45. James Doyle, *Annie Howells and Achille Fréchette*, pp. 35, 37, 66 and 87-89.

46. [in the list of Press Gallery members] "Miss Brodlique who represented the London *Advertiser* last session, has arrived and will take her seat in the gallery today. Miss Duncan, known as 'Garth Grafton' in literary circles is attached to the Montreal *Star* representation; the Gallery will be unusually strong in numbers this session. It will be a difficult matter to provide seating accommodation for all the scribes" ("Notes of the Day", *Ottawa Citizen*, Feb. 24, 1888).

47. John Willison, *Reminiscences. Political and Personal*, p. 129.

48. *Ibid.*, p. 119.

49. "It is a regrettable fact that her [Canada's] prophets are not all Tuppers or Cartwrights or Lauriers or Chapleaus. And so there is no denying the fact that we have been bored, bored deeply, exhaustively, laboriously, and not always grammatically" (*Week*, April 19, 1888).

50. Willison, p. 125.

51. Lord Frederic Hamilton, *The Days Before Yesterday*, p. 255.

52. *Ibid.*, pp. 247-48, 256-57 and Hon. James David Edgar, *Canada and Its Capital*, p. 119.

53. "Miss Sara J. Duncan, who has been a contributor to the Toronto WEEK and the Montreal STAR since the opening of the late session of Parliament, leaves for Montreal this morning, and after spending a few days there, will return to her home at Brantford" ("Personal", *Ottawa Citizen*, June 14, 1888).

54. "Miss Sara Jeannette Duncan, well known in Canada as 'Garth Grafton', was entertained at the Woods of Arden, Staten Island, yesterday by Mr. Erastus Wiman, who invited a party of journalists to meet his distinguished fellow-countrywoman. The

party included editors of the New York *Times, Mail,* and *Express, World* and *Harper's Weekly* ("Personal", Montreal *Star,* Sept. 3, 1888). See also SJD's account, *Star,* Sept. 13, 1888. Ford, Miller, Nye and Curtis all lived on Staten Island.

IV. World Travels.

1. *A Social Departure: How Orthodocia and I Went Round the World By Ourselves,* pp. 44-45. Subsequent references occur in brackets following the quotation, using the abbreviation *SD.*

2. See entry for Lansing Lewis in Charles G.D. Roberts and Arthur L. Tunnell, *The Canadian Who Was Who,* pp. 303-05.

3. There is strong internal evidence in *Star* articles for believing that Redney was already in England at the time of writing. "I am beginning to have a haunting knowledge of London's places of refreshment, from High Holborn restaurants ... to modest chop-houses in the Strand" she wrote (*Star,* Sept. 25, 1889). "I have actually met since leaving India more than one gentleman of intelligence and culture who had spent the best part of a quarter of a century there and had never seen the Taj, or Calcutta, or Ceylon", she wrote later (*Star,* Feb. 15, 1890). Then too, there are five *Star* articles from "Louis Lloyd" written from Paris between May and September, 1889, describing current art shows and other events. In the *Star* on August 31, 1889, and October 16, 1889, appear articles from "Louis Lloyd" in Paris and right beside them articles by "Garth Grafton" purportedly written from Kandy and Calcutta, both of which mention "Louis" as still being with her, and one of which mentions being en route to Calcutta "the end of February". *The Week* for June 13, 1890, notes that "Garth Grafton is rapidly winning a reputation in England, where she has been for many months past engaged in literary work" (p. 445). All this evidence together suggests that Redney reached England in May, 1889.

4. Roberts and Tunnell, pp. 303-05.

5. Hector Charlesworth, *More Candid Chronicles,* p. 24.

6. Archibald MacMurchy, *Handbook of Canadian Literature,* p. 122 and G. Mercer Adam, *Prominent Men of Canada,* pp. 78-81.

7. Warner, *Studies in the South and West with Comments on Canada,* p. 52.

8. For biographical details on Warner, see James White, *The National Cyclopaedia of American Biography,* Vol. II, 116-17.

9. See Warner's *As We Were Saying,* were one essay supports women's rights to higher education, suffrage, and even to marriage proposal.

10. *Ibid.,* p. 61.

11. *My Summer in a Garden*, pp. 166-67.

12. *Studies in the South and West*, p. 485.

13. *Ibid.*, p. 485.

14. *Ibid.*, pp. 480-1.

15. For an excellent description of Government House see G.W. Steevens, *In India*, pp. 78-79.

16. *A Catalogue of the Moths of India*, by Col. C. Swinhoe and E.C. Cotes appeared in 1889, sometime after May, which is when EC wrote the preface.

17. See Black, *Who Was Who 1941-50*, entry for Everard Cotes., p. 255. For most of the biographical information, I am indebted to Dr. John Everard Cotes and Dr. Mary Phoebe Cotes.

18. Steevens, p. 267. Steevens was in India in the 1890's; the introduction to his book is dated 1899.

19. In *A Social Departure*, Orthodocia's young man Jack proposes to her in the Taj Mahal garden, but Dr. John Cotes assures me that it was in fact Everard who proposed to SJD. The latter painted a watercolour of the Taj to mark the event.

20. McClure Mss. IV, Lilly Library, Indiana University.

21. See Peter Lyon, *Success Story: The Life and Times of S.S. McClure.*

22. All quotations from Chatto and Windus correspondence come from hand-written letterbooks held at the library of the University of Reading, Berkshire, England.

23. Frederick Willis, *A Book of London Yesterdays*, p. 237.

24. For details of the March 14 Drawing-Room, see "The Court", *The Illustrated London News*, March 22, 1890. Over one hundred persons were presented at this drawing-room.

25. Thomas E. Tausky, *Sara Jeannette Duncan: Novelist of Empire*, p. 54.

26. M. MacMurchy, *Bookman* (May, 1915), p. 40.

27. A. MacMechan, *Headwaters of Canadian Literature*, p. 137.

28. This letter is pasted in the front of Lord Lansdowne's copy of *A Social Departure*, now in the Baldwin Room, Metropolitan Toronto Library.

V. India

1. *The Simple Adventures of a Memsahib*, p. 205. Subsequent references occur in brackets following the quotation, using the abbreviation *Memsahib.*

2. "COTES-DUNCAN. On the 6th of December, at St. Thomas's Church, Calcutta, by the Rev. S.B. Taylor, M.A., Chaplain, Everard Charles Cotes, of the India Museum, Calcutta, to Sara

Jeannette, eldest daughter of Charles Duncan, Esq. of Brantford, Ontario, Canada (*The Englishman,* Dec. 8, 1890, p. 1). The same announcement also appeared in *The Englishman's Overland Mail,* Dec. 10, 1890, p. 20 and in the *Brantford Expositor,* Jan. 13, 1891, p. 2.

3. See *The Englishman's Overland Mail,* Dec. 10, 1890, p. 11.

4. See *Memsahib,* pp. 72-73. In an interview with G.B. Burgin, SJD affirmed that the descriptions of the house, garden and neighbours in *Memsahib* were indeed her own ("A Chat with Sara Jeannette Duncan", *The Idler,,* [Aug. 1895], p. 117.)

5. Nigel Nicolson, *Mary Curzon,* p. 115.

6. Charles Allen, ed. *Plain Tales from the Raj,* p. 101.

7. Lieutenant-General Sir Robert Baden Powell, *Indian Memories,* p. 199.

8. See Allen, pp. 113-14 and Dennis Kincaid, *British Social Life in India 1608-1937,* pp. 274-75, 278-79.

9. Florence Donaldson, *The Bookman* (June, 1898), p. 67.

10. *The Days Before Yesterday,* p. 295.

11. For details of Calcutta see G.W. Steevens, *In India,* Sir Harry Cotton, *Calcutta Old and New* and Kathleen Blechynden, *Calcutta, Past and Present.*

12. When the Dalai Lama visited the Museum in 1910, he wanted most of all to see the lion and the tiger fighting, whose fame had reached Lhassa (Anon., *The Indian Museum 1814-1914,* p. 86).

13. *Ibid.,* p. 123.

14. *Silkworms in India,* 1890. Indian Museum Notes, Vol. 1, no. 3. EC's other pamphlets include *The Experimental Introduction of Insecticides into India,* 1888, Notes on Economic Entomology no. 2, *A Preliminary Account of the Wheat and Rice Weevil in India,* 1888, *The Locusts of Bengal, Madras, Assam and Bombay,* 1889, and *The Wild Silk Insects of India,* 1891.

15. For establishing the place of residence for SJD and acquaintances, *Thacker's Indian Directory,* published annually and listing all Anglo-Indian residents' addresses and occupations was invaluable.

16. Steevens, p. 101 and William Golant, *The Long Afternoon. British India 1601-1947,* p. 47.

17. "A Tale of Two Cities" from *Departmental Ditties,* p. 164.

18. *Something of Myself,* p. 64.

19. Chatto sent twice yearly royalty cheques. The July, 1892 cheque for *A Social Departure* and *An American Girl* was £51, the January, 1894 one, for SJD's first three books, was £86.9.9 and the January, 1895 one was £68.4.2.

20. "Mr. A.E. Davidson, lately an assistant in the employ of Messrs. Hart Bros., Calcutta, was found dead in his room yesterday

morning. Death was due to heat apoplexy" (*Indian Daily News*, May 23, 1896.)

21. Several early critics noted SJD's resemblance to Jane Austen. An anonymous one in the *Montreal Standard* noted that she "possesses a light, bright, incisive style and a maliceful feminine wit that puts her in the same class with Jane Austen" (Henry Morgan, *Canadian Men and Women of the Time*, 1912 ed., p. 263). A reference in *A Social Departure* to a telegram "which probably concerns some forgotten washing-bill" (p. 352) and a reference to children being little "olive branches" (*Week*, Nov. 25, 1886), shows that SJD was very familiar with *Northanger Abbey* and *Pride and Prejudice*, respectively.

22. Peter Lyon, *Success Story: The Life and Times of S.S. McClure*, pp. 46-47.

23. It was serialized in *The Youth's Companion* July 12, 19, 26, and August 2, 9, 16, 1894. The four articles were "An American Girl in East India" (Sept. 7 and 14, 1893), "Servant Folk in India" (May 22, 1902), "What Masudi Saw" (April 9, 1903), "The Elephant and His Job" (Dec. 1, 1904).

24. Letter from Chatto and Windus to SJD, March 4, 1893.

25. Reprinted in Barrie Davies, ed., *Archibald Lampman, Selected Prose*, pp. 71-72.

26. *The Canadian Magazine*, (May, 1893), p. 191.

27. Letter from Chatto and Windus to SJD, July 6, 1894.

28. Contract dated May 10, 1894, and letter from Chatto to SJD, May 15, 1894.

29. Letter from Chatto to SJD, Nov. 14, 1894.

30. "Early in 1894, Mr. and Mrs. Everard Cotes left India with the intention of not returning, as the former had decided to sever his connection with Government service, for the more congenial pursuit of journalism" (Florence Donaldson, p. 67).

31. Henry Morgan, *Canadian Men and Women of the Time* (1912 ed.) and private information obtained from Miss Gwyneth Lewis, Lily's niece.

32. Letter from SJD to Howells, Houghton Library, Harvard, n.d.

33. Letters from SJD to Jerome, May 11, 1894 and May 16, 1894, Humanities Research Center, The University of Texas at Austin.

34. See Marcus Van Steen, *Pauline Johnson, Her Life and Work*, pp. 18, 22, and Walter McRaye, *Pauline Johnson and Her Friends*, pp. 43, 61 and D. Reville, *History of the County of Brant*, II, 633-34.

35. *Down Under with the Prince*, p. 40.

36. SJD's London addresses were usually listed in *Boyle's Fashionable Court and Country Guide and Town Visiting Directory.* Boyle's was published twice a year, in January and May, listing "the names and places of abode in town and country of the nobility and gentry."

37. "I find that Bret Harte, H. Rider Haggard, Wilkie Collins & a number of the most famous authors in England do all their business through a gentleman named Mr. Watt. I called on him, found him a most agreeable man". Letter from S.S. McClure to his wife, March 7, 1887, quoted by Peter Lyon, p. 78.

38. For biographical details of A.P. Watt, see Black *Who Was Who 1897-1915*, p. 748 and Nuel Pharr Davis, *The Life of Wilkie Collins.*

39. *The Idler* (Aug. 1895), p. 115.

40. *Ibid.,* p. 117.

41. "Yesterday's mail brought out five new volumes of Messrs. Macmillan and Co's Colonial Library Series, including *His Honor* [*sic*] *and a Lady* by Mrs. Cotes ("By the Way", *Indian Daily News,* May 14, 1896).

42. In *Sara Jeannette Duncan. Selected Journalism,* Prof. Tausky identifies editorials of May 16, June 15, June 27, July 24, August 29, 1896 as SJD's work.

43. "News Notes", *Bookman* (Sept. 1896), p. 158.

44. "Readers of Mrs. Everard Cotes' (Sara-Jeanette Duncan's) 'American Girl in London' will be interested to learn that she has now completed the MS of a sequel to that interesting book, entitled 'An American Girl Abroad' which will first see the light in the columns of *The Queen,* where the first chapter will appear in April next" (*Indian Daily News,* March 25, 1897).

45. E. Buck, *Simla Past and Present,* p. 171. For details of Simla, see also *Thacker's Guide to Simla,* 1899.

46. *Ibid.,* p. 20.

47. See Major P.H. Denyer, *The Centenarian. History of Simla Amateur Theatricals During the Past 100 Years.*

48. Rae E. Goodwin, "The Early Journalism of Sara Jeannette Duncan", p. 317.

49. Private information from Dr. John Cotes.

50. M.E.R. [Mrs. Sandford Ross], "Sara Jeannette Duncan. Personal Glimpses", *Canadian Literature* 27 (Winter, 1966), p. 18.

51. *Literary Biography,* pp. 35-36.

52. Letter from Henry James to SJD, Jan. 26, 1900 from Lamb House, Rye, in Percy Lubbock, ed., *The Letters of Henry James,* II, 347

53. From Forster's manuscript novel "Arctic Summer", quoted by P. Furbank, *E.M. Forster: A Life*, I, 207.

54. George Woodcock, *Faces of India*, p. 9.

55. E.M. Forster, *A Passage to India*, p. 156.

56. "Mrs. Everard Cotes", *The Bookman* (June, 1898), p. 67.

57. Douglas Reville, *History of the County of Brant*, I, 129 and I, 211.

58. Willison papers, Public Archives of Canada.

59. *Ibid.*

60. For biographical details of Mary Curzon, see Nicolson.

61. *Ibid.*, p. 124.

62. *Ibid.*, p. 159.

63. Private information from Dr. John Cotes and Mrs. Alison Payne. A thorough search of all Indian and Baptismal Registers in the India Office Library, London, and of birth announcements in *The Englishman*, *The Indian Daily News*, and *The Englishman's Overland Mail* yielded no mention of the birth. A check was also made, equally fruitless, of birth registries for England, in case the baby had been born in England rather than India.

64. Buck, p. 126.

65. Lady Wilson, *Letters from India*, p. 322. Lady Wilson lived at Holcombe after the Cotes sold it. Her husband, since 1903, had been Secretary to the Government of India, in the Department of Revenue and Agriculture.

66. This observation is based on the recollections of Mrs. Alison Payne and Mr. Edward Blake Duncan who knew EC as children, and of Dr. John Cotes and Dr. Mary Cotes.

67. *My Summer in a Garden*, p. 20.

VI. Final Years

1. Public Archives of Canada, Willison Papers, MG 30, D 29, vol. 10, file 78.

2. Nigel Nicolson, *Mary Curzon*, p. 146.

3. M.E.R., "Sara Jeannette Duncan: Personal Glimpses, *Canadian Literature* 27 (Winter, 1966), p. 16.

4. *Sara Jeannette Duncan. Novelist of Empire*, pp. 156-57.

5. *Ibid.*, p. 162.

6. PAC, Willison papers. Willison would resign as *Globe* editor in November, 1902.

7. *Sara Jeannette Duncan. Novelist of Empire*, pp. 161-62.

8. See for example, Alfred G. Bailey, "The Historical Setting of Sara Duncan's *The Imperialist*" and Joseph M. Zezulka, "The

Imperialist: Imperialism, provincialism and point of view", both in John Moss, ed. *The Canadian Novel: Beginnings.*

9. *Sara Jeannette Duncan: Novelist of Empire,* p. 166.

10. Introduction to *The Imperialist,* New Canadian Library edition, p. ix.

11. One of the best accounts of the Durbar is to be found in John Oliver Hobbes' (pseudonym for Pearl Craigie) *Imperial India.* She was one of those who came out with the party from England.

12. PAC, Willison papers.

13. *Ibid.*

14. Hathaway Collection, Harriet Irving Library, University of New Brunswick.

15. PAC, Willison papers.

16. Wiman obituary, *New York Times,* Feb. 10, 1904, p. 7.

17. James Johnson was a newspaperman who had worked for the *Ottawa Citizen* when SJD was in Ottawa.

18. "Present Situation in the Persian Gulf" appeared in the *Contemporary Review* [New York] (April, 1904), 85: 480-86.

19. PAC, Willison papers.

20. See Louise Reynolds, *Agnes. The Biography of Lady Macdonald.*

21. Anon., *Canadian Magazine* (April, 1904), 22: 593. For the most part, I have refrained from quoting reviews of SJD's work because the matter has been given full and judicious treatment by Professor Tausky in *Sara Jeannette Duncan. Novelist of Empire,* Appendix II, pp. 265-72.

22. Letter pasted onto flyleaf of Lord Landsowne's copy of *The Imperialist,* now in the Metropolitan Toronto Library.

23. Dr. Drummond died in 1900.

24. University Archives, Dalhousie University Library, Archibald MacMechan papers.

25. *Headwaters of Canadian Literature,* p. 138.

26. See *Bookman* (August, 1906), p. 163.

27. See P.H. Denyer, *The Centenarian. History of Simla Amateur Theatricals During the Past 100 Years,* pp. 3-4, 16 and E. Buck, *Simla Past and Present,* pp. 139-43.

28. By "S.J.D.", *Outlook,* March 17, 1906, p. 375.

29. H.E.A. Cotton, *Calcutta Old and New,* p. 284.

30. January, 1906, p. 147.

31. Letter of March 12, 1906 from JG to SJD. Garvin papers, Humanities Research Centre, The University of Texas at Austin.

32. See Katharine Garvin, *J.L. Garvin. A Memoir.*

33. Nicolson, p. 165.

34. December, 1908, p. 155.

35. PAC, Willison papers, letter of April 4, 1907, from SJD to JW.

36. "A new novel which Mrs. Everard Cotes has written under the title "Cinderella in Canada" will be published this spring. In Canada, curiously enough, the title is to be changed to "A Canadian Girl in London", "News Notes," *Bookman* [London], March, 1908, p. 222. *Cousin Cinderella* was published by Methuen in London, Macmillan in New York.

37. Obituary, *Brantford Expositor*, Oct. 7, 1907, p. 1.

38. Garvin papers, Humanities Research Centre, The University of Texas at Austin. Since SJD never added the year when she dated her letters, the problem of dating them is formidable. By a process of deductive reasoning, I have dated this one 1908.

39. William Golant, *The Long Afternoon*, p. 89.

40. Thomas E. Tausky, *Sara Jeannette Duncan. Novelist of Empire,* p. 247.

41. Percy Landon was special correspondent for *The Times,* active in the Far East; in 1908 he was in Persia, India and Nepal. Lovat Fraser, editor of *The Times of India* for several years, was on the editorial staff of *The Times* from 1907-22.

42. Garvin papers, Humanities Research Centre, The University of Texas at Austin.

43. *Ibid.*

44. *Ibid.*

45. *Ibid.*

46. C.E. Buckland, *Dictionary of Indian Biography,* pp. 119, 127-28.

47. *Sara Jeannette Duncan. Novelist of Empire,* p. 175.

48. Golant, pp. 32-33.

49. M.E.R., "Sara Jeannette Duncan: Personal Glimpses". Subsequent quotations are also from this article.

50. See Christopher Hussey, "The Personality of Sir Edwin Lutyens", *RIBA Journal* (April, 1969), pp. 141-54 and Lady Emily Lutyens, *Candles in the Sun.*

51. P.N. Furbank, *E.M. Forster: A Life,* I, 142-43.

52. Letter from Forster to Mrs. Maimie Aylward, Nov. 14, 1912. Forster papers, King's College Library, Cambridge.

53. For biographical details see P.N. Furbank.

54. Forster papers.

55. Letter from Forster to Laura Mary Forster, Nov. 18, 1912, Forster papers.

56. Letter from Forster to his mother, Nov. 21, 1912. Forster papers.

57. Forster's Indian Diary, 1912-13. Entry for Nov. 16, 1912. Forster papers.

58. Forster's Indian Diary 1912-13. Entry for Nov. 17, 1912.

59. Letter from Forster to Laura Mary Forster, Nov. 18, 1912. Forster papers.

60. Letter from Forster to his mother, Nov. 21, 1912. Forster papers.

61. *Ibid.*

62. Indian Diary 1912-13. Entry for Nov. 18, 1912. Forster papers.

63. M.E.R., "Sara Jeannette Duncan: Personal Glimpses", p. 18.

64. Letter of March 10, 1913. Forster papers.

65. George Sterling, "Joaquin Miller", *American Mercury* (1926), 7:225.

66. "Mrs. Everard Cotes (Sara Jeannette Duncan) of Simla, India belongs to Brantford by birth and is our foremost woman novelist . . . . She has written about a score of novels, all of which are characterized by delightful humour and a subtle beauty of descriptive style. Mrs. Cotes is at present visiting her old home in Brantford" (*Saturday Night,* Aug. 1, 1914, p. 1).

67. *More Candid Chronicles,* pp. 335-36.

68. p. 40.

69. M.E.R., "Sara Jeannette Duncan: Personal Glimpses", p. 18.

70. "A Record Trip", *Civil & Military Gazette* [Lahore], Jan. 10, 1919, p. 9.

71. H. Beresford Harrop, *Thacker's New Guide to Simla,* p. 21.

72. Denyer, p. 26.

73. "New Play Produced in Simla: A Comedy in Khaki", *The Englishman,* Oct. 22, 1915, p. 4.

74. See *Boyle's Court Guide,* May edition, 1915 and 1916.

75. M.E.R., "Sara Jeannette Duncan: Personal Glimpses". Mrs. Ross calls the play *Brown with an E* but since she states that the play to which she refers had been produced at Simla in 1915, it must have been *Beauchamp and Beecham.*

76. Thanks to the generosity of Mrs. Phoebe Cotes, the D.B. Weldon Library, University of Western Ontario, London, Ontario, has a collection of twelve mss. plays, including all those mentioned above except *His Royal Happiness.*

77. I am grateful to Dr. Mary Cotes for this information.

78. See Douglas Reville, *History of the County of Brant,* I, 198 ff.

79. "A Record Trip" by Mrs. Everard Cotes appeared in *The Statesman* [Calcutta] Jan. 12, 1919, as well as in the *Civil & Military Gazette* [Lahore] Jan. 10, 1919.

80. See "Australasian Tour of the Prince of Wales", *Nineteenth Century and After* [London], (December, 1920), 88: 967-78.

81. *Down Under with the Prince,* pp. 150-53.

82. These are the impressions of Mrs. Sandford Ross and Mrs. Alison Payne.

83. The nephew was John P. Duncan, son of SJD's brother Gordon, quoted in Marcus Van Steen, "Brant Girl Quit Teaching Job to Gain Fame as a Novelist", *London Free Press,* Sept. 29, 1962.

84. M.E.R., "Sara Jeannette Duncan: Personal Glimpses", p. 19.

85. *Ibid.*

86. I am grateful to Lee and Pemberton, Solicitors, for the opportunity to read the will and probate.

Bibliography

The following editions of Sara Jeannette Duncan's work have been used:

A Social Departure. London: Chatto and Windus [1890] 2nd. edition, 1891.

An American Girl in London. London: Chatto and Windus, 1891.

Two Girls on a Barge (Issued under the pseudonym V. Cecil Cotes). London: Chatto and Windus, 1891.

The Simple Adventures of a Memsahib. London: Thomas Nelson and Sons [1893] n.d.

A Daughter of To-Day. London: Chatto and Windus [1894] 2nd edition, 1895.

Vernon's Aunt. London: Chatto and Windus, 1894.

The Story of Sonny Sahib. New York: D. Appleton and Company, 1895.

His Honour, and a Lady. Toronto: G.M. Rose and Sons, 1896.

A Voyage of Consolation. London: Methuen and Company, 1898.

The Path of a Star. London: Methuen and Company, 1899.

On the Other Side of the Latch. London: Methuen and Company, 1901.

Those Delightful Americans. [1902] London: Everett, 1912.

The Pool in the Desert. New York: D. Appleton and Company, 1903.

The Imperialist. [1904] Toronto: McClelland & Stewart, 1961.

Set in Authority. London: Constable and Company, 1906.

Two in a Flat (Issued under the pseudonym Jane Wintergreen). London: Hodder and Stoughton, 1908.

Cousin Cinderella. New York: Macmillan Company, 1908.

The Burnt Offering. [1909] New York: John Lane, 1910.

The Consort. 3rd edition, London: Stanley Paul & Company, 1912.

His Royal Happiness. Toronto: Hodder and Stoughton, 1914.

Title Clear. London: Hutchinson & Company, 1922.

The Gold Cure. London: Hutchinson & Company, 1924.

The following is a selection of the works consulted, and includes all those cited in the footnotes, with the exception of biographical dictionaries.

I. *Periodical Articles:*

Anon. "A Visit to the New Orleans Exposition". *Demorest's Monthly Magazine* (March, 1885), XXI, 275-281.

Anon. "Our Women Writers". *Canadian Magazine* (October, 1905), 25: 583-85.

Anon. "The Mem-Sahib's Point of View". *Cornhill Magazine* (May, 1920), XLVIII, 590-99.

Bailey, Alfred G. "The Historical Setting of Sara Duncan's *The Imperialist*", *Journal of Canadian Fiction*, II, No. 3, 205-10.

Burgin, G.B. "A Chat with Sara Jeannette Duncan", *Idler* (August, 1895), VIII, 113-18.

Burness, Jean F. "Sara J. Duncan—A Neglected Canadian Author", *Ontario Library Review* (August, 1961), 45: 205-06.

Charlesworth, Hector W. "The Canadian Girl", *Canadian Magazine of Politics, Science, Art and Literature* (May, 1893), 186-193.

Cotes, Everard. "Present Situation in the Persian Gulf", *Contemporary Review* (April, 1904) 85: 480-86.

Cotes, Everard. "Mesopotamia, Tragedy of an Impossible System", *Nineteenth Century and After* (August, 1917) 82: 276-82.

Cotes, Everard. "Australasian tour of the Prince of Wales", *Nineteenth Century and After* (December, 1920), 88: 967-78.

Donaldson, Florence. "Mrs. Everard Cotes", *Bookman* (June, 1898), 14: 65-67.

Duncan, Sara Jeannette. "Diogenes on Bric-a-Brac", *The Canada Monthly* (June, 1880), VI, 636-38.

Duncan, Sara Jeannette. "By Stage to Montmorenci", *Outing* (May, 1884), IV, 129-31.

Duncan, Sara Jeannette. "On Two Wheels to Lorette", *Outing* (March, 1885), V, 439-41.

Duncan, Sara Jeannette. "Eurasia", *The Popular Science Monthly* (November, 1892), 42: 1-9.

Duncan, Sara Jeannette. "The Mission to the Harem", *To-Day*, (Sept. 29, 1894), p. 233.

Duncan, Sara Jeannette. "In Burma with the Viceroy", *Scribner's Magazine* (July, 1902), 32: 58-72.

Duncan, Sara Jeannette. "Little Windows of a Dynasty", *Harper's Monthly Magazine* (December, 1902) 106: 115-21.

Duncan, Sara Jeannette. "Home Life of Lady Curzon", *Harper's Bazar* (March, 1903), 37: 222-24.

Duncan, Sara Jeannette. "In All Parts of London", *The Outlook*, (March 17, 1906), pp. 375-76.

Duncan, Sara Jeanette. "The Melting-Pot Bubbles a Bit", *Globe* (Oct. 13, 1919), p. 5.

Duncan, Sara Jeannette. "Dignity of Prince Rupert", *Globe* (October 4, 1919), p. 14.

Duncan, Sara Jeannette. "A Record Trip", *Civil & Military Gazette* (January 10, 1919), p. 9.

Gerson, Carole. "Duncan's Web", *Canadian Literature* (Winter, 1975), 63:73-80.

Hussey, Christopher. "The Personality of Sir Edwin Lutyens", *RIBA Journal* (April, 1969), 76: 141-54.

MacMurchy, Marjorie. "Mrs. Everard Cotes", *Bookman* (May, 1915), 48: 39-40.

Miller, Joaquin. "How I Came to be a Writer of Books", *Lippincott's Monthly Magazine,* (July, 1886), 38: 106-110.

Myers, Elgin. "A Canadian in New York", *The Canadian Magazine of Politics, Science, Art and Literature* (August, 1893), I, 435-43.

Nagarajan, S. "The Anglo-Indian Novels of Sara Jeannette Duncan", *Journal of Canadian Fiction* (1975), III, no. 4, 74-84.

Noble, R.W. *"A Passage to India.* The Genesis of E.M. Forster's Novel", *Encounter* (February, 1980), pp. 51-61.

Pennanen, G. "Goldwin Smith, Wharton Baker and Erastus Wiman", *Journal of Canadian Studies* (1979), 14: 50-62.

[Ross, Mrs. Sandford] M.E.R. "Sara Jeannette Duncan—Personal Glimpses", *Canadian Literature* (Winter, 1966), 27: 15-19.

Shrive, Norman. "What Happened to Pauline?", *Canadian Literature* (1962), 13: 25-38.

Smalley, Eugene V. "The New Orleans Exposition", *Century Magazine (1885),* XXX, no. 1, 3-14.

Smalley, Eugene V. "In and Out of the New Orleans Exposition", *The Century Magazine* (1885), XXX, no. 19, 185-199.

Sterling, George. "Joaquin Miller", *American Mercury* (1926), 7: 220-29.

Tausky, Thomas E. "The American Girls of William Dean Howells and Sara Jeannette Duncan", *Journal of Canadian Fiction* (1975), 13: 146-58.

Thomas, Clara. "Canadian Social Mythologies in Duncan's *The Imperialist"*, *Journal of Canadian Studies* (Spring, 1977), 12, no. 2, 38-49.

Turner, Arlin. "Joaquin Miller in New Orleans", *Louisiana Historical Quarterly* (January, 1939), 22, no. 1, 216-225.

Van Steen, Marcus. "Brant Girl Quit Teaching Job to Gain Fame as a Novelist", *London Free Press* (September 29, 1962).

Waldie, Jean. "The Iroquois Poetess: Pauline Johnson", *Ontario History* (1948) XL, 65-75.

II. *Books:*

Anon. *Bengal Past and Present:* The Journal of the Calcutta Historical Society. Calcutta, 1907-1918.

Anon. *The Indian Museum 1814-1914.* Calcutta, 1914.

Anon. *Boyle's Fashionable Court and Country Guide and Town Visiting Directory*. London, Annual volumes, 1890 to 1922.

Anon. *Thacker's Guide to Simla*. Simla, 1899.

Anon. *A History of Canadian Journalism in the Several Portions of the Dominion with a Sketch of the Canadian Press Association, 1859-1908*. Edited by a committee of the Association. Toronto, 1908.

Anon. *1890. Illustrated Montreal. The Metropolis of Canada*. Montreal, 1890.

Allen, Charles, editor. *Plain Tales from the Raj*. Images of British India in the Twentieth Century. London, 1976.

Amis, Kingsley. *Rudyard Kipling and His World*. London, 1975.

Baden-Powell, Lieutenant-General Sir Robert. *Indian Memories*. London, 1915.

Barker, Dudley. *Prominent Edwardians*. London, 1969.

Blechynden, Kathleen. *Calcutta, Past and Present*. London, 1905.

Brooks, Van Wyck. *The Confident Years, 1885-1915*. New York, 1952.

Buck, E. *Simla Past and Present*. Calcutta, 1904.

Cady, Edwin H. *The Realist at War. The Mature Years of William Dean Howells 1885-1920*. Syracuse, 1958.

Careless, J.M.S. *Brown of the Globe*. Vol. II: Statesman of Confederation 1860-1880. Toronto, 1963.

Charlesworth, Hector. *Candid Chronicles*. Toronto, 1925.

Charlesworth, Hector. *More Candid Chronicles*. Toronto, 1928.

Charlesworth, Hector. *The Canadian Scene*. Toronto, 1927.

Charlesworth, Hector. *I'm Telling You*. Being the Further Candid Chronicles. Toronto, 1937.

Clark, Robert, et al. *A Glimpse of the Past: A Centennial History of Brantford and Brant County*. Brantford, 1966.

Corfield, Wilmot. *Calcutta. Faces and Places in Pre-Camera Days*. Calcutta, 1910.

Cotes, Everard and Colonel C. Swinhoe. *A Catalogue of the Moths of India*. Calcutta, 1889.

Cotes, Everard. *Signs and Portents in the Far East*. London, 1907.

Cotes, Everard. *Down Under with the Prince*. London, 1921.

Cotton, H.E.A. *Calcutta Old and New*. Calcutta, 1907.

Cowan, John. *Canada's Governors-General*. Toronto, 1965.

Darling, Sir Malcolm. *Apprentice to Power: India 1904-1908*. London, 1966.

Davies, Barrie, editor. *Archibald Lampman: Selected Prose*. Ottawa, 1975.

Davis, Nuel Pharr. *The Life of Wilkie Collins*. Urbana, 1956.

Denyer, Major P.H. *The Centenarian. History of the Simla Amateur Theatricals During the Past 100 Years*. Simla, 1937.

Diver, Maud. *The Englishwoman in India.* London, 1909.

Doyle, James. *Annie Howells and Achille Frechette.* Toronto, 1979.

Edel, Leon. *Literary Biography.* Bloomington, 1973.

Edgar, James David. *Canada and Its Capital.* Toronto, 1898.

Eggleston, Wilfrid. *The Queen's Choice. A Story of Canada's Capital.* Ottawa, 1961.

Ferguson, Ted. *Kit Coleman. Queen of Hearts.* Toronto, 1978.

Forster, E.M. *A Passage to India.* London, 1947.

Forster, J.W.L. *Under the Studio Light.* Toronto, 1928.

Fowler, Marian. *The Embroidered Tent: Five Gentlewomen in Early Canada.* Toronto, 1982.

Fraser, Lovat. *India Under Curzon and After.* London, 1912.

Frost, Orcutt William. *Joaquin Miller.* New York, 1967.

Furbank, P.N. *E.M. Forster: A Life.* Vol. I: The Growth of the Novelist (1879-1914). London, 1977.

Garvin, Katharine. *J.L. Garvin, A Memoir.* London, 1948.

Golant, William. *The Long Afternoon.* British India 1601-1947. London, 1975.

Goodwin, Rae E. "The Early Journalism of Sara Jeannette Duncan, with a Chapter of Biography", Unpublished M.A. Thesis, University of Toronto, 1964.

Grant, R.W. *The Life of the Rev. William Cochrane.* Toronto, 1899.

Green, Constance McLaughlin. *Washington, Capital City, 1879-1950.* Princeton, 1970.

Hacker, Carlotta. *The Indomitable Lady Doctors.* Toronto, 1974.

Haig, Robert. *Ottawa: City of the Big Ears.* Ottawa, 1969.

Hale, Katherine. *Toronto: The Romance of a Great City.* Toronto, 1956.

Hamilton, Lord Frederic. *The Days Before Yesterday.* London, n.d.

Harrop, H. Beresford. *Thacker's New Guide to Simla.* Simla, 1925.

Haultain, Arnold, editor. *A Selection from Goldwin Smith's Correspondence.* London, 1913.

Hobbes, John Oliver [Pearl Craigie]. *Imperial India.* Letters from the East. London, 1903.

Howells, Mildred, editor. *Life in Letters of William Dean Howells.* New York, 1968.

Howells, William Dean. *Literary Friends and Acquaintance: A Personal Retrospect of American Authorship.* New York, 1900.

Johnston, C.M. *Brant County: A History 1784-1945.* Toronto, 1967.

Kincaid, Dennis. *British Social Life in India 1608-1937.* 2nd ed. London, 1973.

Kipling, Rudyard. *Departmental Ditties and Other Verses.* London, 1898.

Kipling, Rudyard. *Something of Myself.* London, 1937.

Lubbock, Percy, editor. *The Letters of Henry James.* New York, 1920.

Lutyens, Lady Emily. *Candles in the Sun.* London, 1957.

Lyon, Peter. *Success Story: The Life and Times of S.S. McClure.* New York, 1963.

MacMechan, Archibald. *The Headwaters of Canadian Literature.* Toronto, 1968.

MacMurchy, Archibald. *Handbook of Canadian Literature.* Toronto, 1906.

McRaye, Walter. *Pauline Johnson and Her Friends.* Toronto, 1947.

Marberry, M.M. *Splendid Poseur. Joaquin Miller—American Poet.* New York, 1953.

Miller, Joaquin. *Memorie and Rhyme.* New York, 1884.

Miller, Joaquin. *The Destruction of Gotham.* New York, 1886.

Miller, Joaquin. *The Building of the City Beautiful.* Chicago, 1893.

Morton, Desmond. *Mayor Howland: The Citzens' Candidate.* Toronto, 1973.

Moss, John, ed. *The Canadian Novel: Beginnings.* Toronto, 1980.

Nicolson, Nigel. *Mary Curzon.* London, 1977.

Oaten, Edward Farley. *A Sketch of Anglo-Indian Literature.* London, 1908.

Parratt, John, editor. *Montreal Pictured and Described.* Montreal, 1889.

Reynolds, Louise. *Agnes. The Biography of Lady Macdonald.* Toronto, 1979.

Reville, Douglas. *History of the County of Brant.* Brantford, 1920.

Roberts, Chalmers McGeagh. *The Washington Post: The First 100 Years.* Boston, 1977.

Sherman, Stuart P., editor. *The Poetical Works of Joaquin Miller.* New York, 1923.

Singh, Bhupal. *A Survey of Anglo-Indian Fiction.* London, 1975.

Sitwell, Constance. *Flowers and Elephants.* New York, n.d.

Smith, Goldwin. *Reminiscences.* Edited by Arnold Haultain. Macmillan, 1910.

Steevens, G.W. *In India.* London, n.d.

Tausky, Thomas E., editor. *Sara Jeannette Duncan. Selected Journalism.* Ottawa, 1978.

Tausky, Thomas E. *Sara Jeannette Duncan. Novelist of Empire.* Port Credit, 1980.

Thompson, Austin Seton. *Jarvis Street.* Toronto, 1980.

Van Steen, Marcus. *Pauline Johnson: Her Life and Work.* Toronto, 1965.

Waldie, Jean. *Centennial Sketches of Brant County.* Paris, 1952.

Wallace, Elizabeth. *Goldwin Smith: Victorian Liberal.* Toronto, 1957.

Warner, Charles Dudley. *Studies in the South and West with Comments on Canada.* Vol. VIII of *The Complete Writings of Charles Dudley Warner.* Hartford, 1904.

Warner, Charles Dudley. *As We Were Saying.* New York, 1892.

Warner, Charles Dudley. *My Summer in a Garden.* Boston, 1896.

Weaver, Sir Lawrence. *Houses and Gardens of Sir Edwin Lutyens.* London, 1913.

West, Bruce. *Toronto.* Toronto, 1979.

Willis, Frederick. *A Book of London Yesterdays.* London, 1960.

Willison, John. *Reminiscences. Political and Personal.* Toronto, 1919.

Wilson, Edmund. *Patriotic Gore.* Studies in the Literature of the American Civil War. New York, 1962.

Wiman, Erastus. *Chances of Success.* Episodes and Observations in the Life of a Busy Man. New York, 1893.

Woodcock, George. *Faces of India.* London, 1964.

Woodruff, Philip. *The Men Who Ruled India.* Vol. II: *The Guardians.* London, 1954.

Selected Index

MARIAN FOWLER, winner of the Canadian Biography Award and author of the widely acclaimed *The Embroidered Tent: Five Gentlewomen in Early Canada* now gives us a rich and fascinating critical biography in the grand tradition.

REDNEY tells the story of Sara Jeannette Duncan, author of *The Imperialist* and a popular Canadian writer at the turn of the century. Redney began as a beautiful young journalist, a restless romantic and a world traveller. Her writing career took her from her home in Brantford, Ontario, first to New Orleans—where she had a romantic fling with the "Byron of the Rockies," the flamboyant Joaquin Miller—and then to adventures in Washington, Toronto, Montreal, and as far afield as Tokyo and London.

Redney married and settled in India amid the sunset splendours of the Raj. Feeling trapped, she began to write her many novels and at last summoned up the Canada of her childhood in her masterpiece, *The Imperialist*. Marian Fowler, who has taught at York University and has published widely on 19th Century writing, here explores the psychology and talent of a remarkable woman and evokes for us the scenes and manners of a vanished, colourful past.